University of London Historical Studies

XXXV

BISMARCK AT THE CROSSROADS

This volume is published with the help of
grants from the late Miss Isobel Thornley's
Bequest to the University of London
and from the Twenty-Seven Foundation

BISMARCK AT THE CROSSROADS

The Reorientation of German Foreign Policy after the Congress of Berlin 1878-1880

by

BRUCE WALLER

UNIVERSITY OF LONDON

THE ATHLONE PRESS

1974

Published by
THE ATHLONE PRESS
UNIVERSITY OF LONDON
at 4 Gower Street London WC1

Distributed by Tiptree Book Services Ltd
Tiptree, Essex

U.S.A. and Canada
Humanities Press Inc
New York

© Bruce Waller 1974

ISBN 0 485 13135 8

Printed in Great Britain by
WESTERN PRINTING SERVICES LTD
BRISTOL

PREFACE

The appearance of this study gives me the opportunity to acknowledge the obligations I have incurred during the thirteen years devoted to its preparation. First of all I would like to thank the many libraries which have given me access to their collections, especially the British Museum, the libraries of the Universities of London and Bonn, and, above all, the library of University College, Swansea. I would also like to express my gratitude to the efficient staffs of several archives: the Foreign Office library; the Public Record Office; the political archives of the German Foreign Office, Bonn; the Federal Archives, Koblenz; the German Central Archives, Potsdam; the archives of the French Foreign Ministry, Paris; and the State Archives, Vienna. Prince Otto von Bismarck and Lord Salisbury kindly allowed me to examine their grandfather's and great-grandfather's papers respectively. Mr Plessow in Friedrichsruh and Dr Mason in Christ Church, Oxford offered much friendly assistance. Dr R. Griffiths shared with me the burden of proof reading. The research and publication of this book were facilitated by generous grants from University College, Swansea, the Isobel Thornley Bequest and the Twenty-Seven Foundation. Part of chapter 2 appeared as an article, 'Bismarck and Gorchakov in 1879: the two chancellors' war', in a collection of essays, *Studies in International History*, edited by K. Bourne and D. C. Watt and published by Longmans in 1967. Finally, I have a special and personal debt to acknowledge to four people. For several months I was privileged to enjoy the hospitality and friendship of Professor Helferich in Bonn. Professor Glanmor Williams has given guidance and moral support for many years. Professor Alun Davies has helped me at every stage of the work. But, most of all, I would like to thank Professor W. N. Medlicott. Without him this book could never have been written.

B. W.

CONTENTS

ABBREVIATIONS

BA	Bundesarchiv, Koblenz
DDF	*Documents Diplomatiques français (1871–1914)*
DZA	Deutsches Zentralarchiv, Potsdam
FA	Friedrichsruh Archiv
FFM	French Foreign Ministry
FO	Foreign Office
GFO	German Foreign Office
GP	*Die grosse Politik der europäischen Kabinette 1871–1914*
GW	*Gesammelte Werke Bismarcks*
HZ	*Historische Zeitschrift*
JMH	*Journal of Modern History*
PRO	Public Record Office
SP	Salisbury Papers
Windelband	*Bismarck und die europäischen Grossmächte 1879–1885*
WS	Wiener Staatsarchiv

Introduction

It is difficult to speak of precise dates which clearly divide one era in history from another. Each era flows into the next and any attempt at exact definition is to a certain extent arbitrary. But, with this reservation in mind, the period 1878–9 can be considered one of the important points in nineteenth-century European history, marking the end of *laissez-faire* liberalism and the beginning of a new conservative trend. The break with the past at this time was perhaps clearest in Germany.

There, on the domestic scene, a generation of liberal reforms had removed many evils, but new problems were being created for which the Liberals, Bismarck's main political supporters, had no answer.[1] After 1873 the developing industrial machine was in a slump and there was a clamour for protection. German agriculture was in a deplorable state. American and Russian competition had virtually monopolized the export markets and forced prices down year after year. Agriculture, too, was believed to need protection for survival. A new poverty-stricken industrial working-class had arisen and—especially since the onset of the depression—was coming under the guidance of radical leaders. The Liberals realized the danger, but they were willing neither to fight it nor to ameliorate by state interference the conditions behind it; because of this they were beginning to lose their hold on the public. The struggle with the Catholic Church had been carried too far and was only partly successful. Important elements of the German nation had thus been driven into opposition to the state, and the Liberals knew of no solution.

It is true that on another level liberal aspirations had been amply fulfilled. The national state had been created. There were still Germans living outside the imperial frontiers, but it would not have been wise to attempt to incorporate them.

[1] For some of the wider issues see Rosenberg.

Otherwise, however, the Liberals' programme had been only partly realized. They had hoped to form the German empire into a centralized state with a strong government under parliamentary control. Towards the end of the seventies they had had to agree to a compromise—the strengthening of the central government, but without corresponding parliamentary control —which, in effect, was a defeat. The government was consequently less dependent than ever on parliament and sought support wherever it could be found. This last point was the main theme in Bismarck's struggle with the Liberals in the years 1878–9, for the anti-Liberal reform measures he proposed tended to increase the strength and independence of the central government.

Bismarck was never really a Liberal at heart. As long as the Liberals supported him he was willing to grant them a certain amount of latitude. In the first decade after the war with Austria Delbrück[2] introduced one liberal reform after another. Bismarck did not approve of everything, but in the beginning abstained from interference. Later he became more critical, and in 1876 Delbrück, sensing approaching doom, resigned. Capitalizing on the growing disenchantment with liberalism, Bismarck set his hand to the task of strengthening the imperial government to combat particularism, and, primarily, to extend his own position of power. Changes in personnel were made and the imperial administration was reorganized. But more was necessary. In the seventies the empire depended financially on the several member states of the federation. As Bismarck saw it, greater power could be attained only by a thoroughgoing reform making the empire financially independent of the states—but also free from the control of the *Reichstag*. Indirect taxation, not subject to yearly approval by parliament, was the logical solution. The industrial slump, but particularly the long standing agricultural crisis, suggested tariffs both to provide an additional source of income beyond parliamentary control and to shelter the industrial and agricultural producers suffering from foreign competition. Tariffs

[2] RUDOLF VON DELBRÜCK (1817–1903). Department director in Prussian ministry of trade, 1859–67; president of *Bundeskanzleramt* and *Reichskanzleramt*, 1867–76; member of parliament, 1879–81.

were also a useful instrument of foreign policy. Without them a state could not easily prevent others from discrimination. This was certainly one of the more compelling reasons for Bismarck's advocacy of a tariff. At first he probably intended to use it solely to obtain trade concessions, but economic pressure was used later for political ends.

This plan could not be implemented without parliamentary backing. Since the Liberals in control of parliament were unwilling to accept wholeheartedly a plan so inimical to their fundamental principles, the chancellor had to seek support elsewhere, that is, from the Conservatives and clericals. The need for aid and the corresponding necessity for concessions to these groups lessened Bismarck's reluctance to drop parts of the Liberal programme which had never really appealed to him and did not seem to work very well. He succeeded in obtaining this support. His desire to increase the strength and independence of the central government thus led to a more or less complete break with the Liberals. However, he did not go to the other extreme of dependence on the Conservative and clerical parties. In the 1880s he remained independent of any particular party, accepting support from one side or the other according to circumstances. Administrative reforms, changes in personnel, new taxes, the tariff, the law against the social democrats and the changed attitude towards the *Kulturkampf* brought with them a new spirit which in turn affected foreign policy.

In this period the relations of the great powers were also undergoing fundamental change. The crisis in the east, which began in June 1875 and culminated in the Russo-Turkish war of 1877, ended a period of imperialistic quiescence and national *recueillement*. For a generation national feeling had been absorbed either by the creation of national states or in their internal development. With the eastern crisis nationalism was carried to other areas, and was given a new turn in those countries where it was already firmly established. There it was directed henceforth towards the subjugation of alien peoples rather than towards the development of the national state. The frustration and the search for more security caused by the Great Depression gave this aggressive feeling added impetus. The Congress of

Berlin (June–July 1878) and accompanying events did much to further this trend. Apart from Germany, Italy alone had gained neither territory nor promise of it, but she, too, quickly joined the quest for possessions. In this new period of imperialism following the Congress Germany initially played a minor role. Her only tangible gain was the Austrian promise no longer to insist on a plebiscite in North Slesvig. But the attitude of the chancellor was changing. Previously, he had offered little protection to German businessmen abroad—and with good reason because, on the whole, there was ample opportunity in eastern Europe. But with the gradual closing of the Russian market they had to look elsewhere.[3]

After the Congress he became more aware of their plight and began earnestly defending their interests. An attempt to rescue German capital invested in the Rumanian railways was the first determined effort in this direction. At the same time he began to press the claims of German business in the South Seas, and, although this cannot be regarded as the beginning of an effort to establish an overseas empire, it helped create a frame of mind which later made that possible and even desirable. Protection for German business at home suggested protection for business abroad.[4]

The *Kulturkampf*, German anti-clericalism in the seventies, had been fought with a vengeance and was very popular amongst Liberals. Bismarck attempted to guide it against his real or imagined enemies. By the end of the decade he had obtained most of what he had sought. Particularists and ultra-conservatives had lost ground, but the Catholics had probably gained, and Bismarck was faced with some unforeseen difficulties which caused him to revise his approach. This changed attitude towards the *Kulturkampf*, made possible by his abandonment of the Liberals and necessary by his need for at least some support from the clericals, coincided approximately with the adoption by the French of their own *Kulturkampf*. The firm establishment of the republican spirit in France after 1877 lessened the likelihood of an opposing Catholic coalition. Bismarck's alliance in October 1879 with Austria-Hungary, the most Catholic power in Europe, which was also in the process of divesting

[3] See Kehr, pp. 167f.   [4] Cf., for instance, Böhme, pp. 538f.

itself of Liberalism and turning towards a more conservative policy, was surely facilitated by his rejection of the *Kulturkampf*, but the decision to conclude the alliance—or later to strengthen it—was probably neither an essential motive for, nor the result of, the abandonment of the *Kulturkampf*.

The law against the social democrats and the implied partial rejection of the liberal principle of equal treatment by the law fostered a new spirit in Germany which made close cooperation with the western powers more difficult. Bismarck never did have any desire to sacrifice good relations with the other empires for a western orientation, but the crusade he conducted against the republicans and social democrats made an eventual changeover less likely, even after the death of Emperor William I.[5]

If in the early seventies Bismarck had been more or less satisfied with the power at his disposal both in internal and external affairs, towards the end of this decade his mind was clearly occupied by the necessity of extending his power. First he set about consolidating his domestic position; then he concentrated on increasing his strength in the international sphere. The tactics used on his domestic ally, the national liberals, as well as on his ally Russia in order to obtain recognition of his leadership were really quite similar. The position, but not the pretentions, of the two had been weakened by the depression and the eastern crisis respectively. Initially he attempted to induce acceptance of his ideas. Both resisted and Bismarck adopted increasingly severe measures in order to force his plans on them; he showed them that if they submitted to his leadership, they could become friends again. Both the national liberals and Russia waited for a final show of force before submitting. But they waited too long and found that in the future they would have to share the chancellor's friendship with others; and Bismarck won a Pyrrhic victory. It is indeed extraordinary, but understandable, that he should have cooperated with, and then estranged, both at the same time. The common denominator between the domestic changeover from Liberalism to a new kind of Conservatism and Bismarck's

5 WILLIAM I (1797–1888). Regent, 1858, then King of Prussia, 1861; German Emperor from 1871.

renunciation of the policy of the free hand in the diplomatic sphere appears to be his endeavour to increase and secure his own position of power both at home and abroad. In so doing, he identified the public welfare with his own.

In view of the significance of the period 1878–9 not only for German, but for European, history the justification of a detailed examination of these years would appear self-evident. As far as Bismarck's domestic reform programme is concerned the need for such a study was soon recognized. Most surveys of the second empire go into the subject in some detail and Ludwig Maenner offers perhaps the best monographic contribution to its illumination.[6] Nevertheless, despite the attention which Bismarck's efforts at reform have received, there still exists quite a difference of opinion as to his ultimate motives for the change from Liberalism to Conservatism. And these differences can be ascribed only in part to a lack of sufficient material. Interesting detail is uncovered in Helmut Böhme's thorough and broadly based recent study. Its approach is original and its conclusions suggestive, but it does not really convince. In an attempt to substantiate some of the theses of Kehr and Hallgarten whose works are focused on the Wilhelmine period, he has sought to show, if not the 'primacy of domestic policy', then at least the interrelationship of foreign and domestic policy, especially in economic affairs. Scholars will agree with Böhme that the various pieces of the puzzle must somehow fit together, but his vast detail does not help much.[7]

Historians of Bismarck's foreign policy for this period are just as much at odds. At the Congress of Berlin Bismarck seemed to have climbed a new pinnacle of prestige and power. Already acclaimed by his countrymen, he received at the Congress, or so it seemed, the due recognition of Europe for his accomplishment in the service of peace. His policy of freedom from binding commitments and apparently wise moderation was crowned with ostensible success. And just before the Congress, in March and April, he had with seemingly irrefutable eloquence turned down an alliance offer by Andrássy.[8] How odd that he should

---

[6] L. Maenner, *Deutschlands Wirtschaft und Liberalismus in der Krise von 1879.*
[7] See below, p. 104, 196ff; H. Böhme, *Deutschlands Weg Zur Grossmacht.*
[8] See correspondence in GFO, IAAl 41.

argue with equal conviction in favour of an alliance with
Austria eighteen months later, and then in the course of the
eighties contract an iridescent array of commitments which
horrified his successors!

We know that for two months after the Congress Bismarck
continued to think in terms of the Three Emperors' League, in
existence since 1873, although the mutual suspicion of Austria
and Russia had grown too great to suffer even such a loose
association; but when it disintegrated in the autumn of 1878
Bismarck did not seem to care. He had arrived at the crossroads and was apparently going to take a new path. One year
later he had an alliance with Austria and was working for a
more formal triple agreement with Vienna and Petersburg.
What had happened in the twelve months preceding the
October treaty with Austria must have been of crucial importance. If Bismarck's foreign policy is examined with traditional
reverence, we are at a loss for a solution. Either Bismarck
sympathized with Austria or was troubled by Russia. From
the beginning of 1879 it looks very much as if he was trying
to provoke Russia so as to have an excuse for an alliance
with Austria. In fact, in the first nine months of 1879 relations
between Berlin and Vienna grew steadily closer; by April
1879 he was obviously thinking about an alliance. And yet
there was no clear break with Russia and the signs of affection
for the Habsburg monarchy are not altogether convincing.
One wonders also why a link with Vienna should have to
take such a strong anti-Russian form; this had not been the
case with the German Confederation. He must have been very
troubled by Russia, but here, too, the disputes with that
country were largely trivial. Both sides complained of general
unfriendliness and ingratitude. The Russians were angry about
the new German tariff, security measures against an outbreak
of the plague on the lower Volga and lack of support in the
commissions supervising the execution of the Berlin Treaty
in the Balkans. The Germans complained of a Russian military
build-up, but the threat from a country that was exhausted
after the war in 1877 with Turkey did not justify the leap in
the dark which was the dual alliance.

We are confronted with a puzzle which might perhaps be

solved if we put aside for a moment Bismarck's axiomatic
astuteness and study the facts which have so far been explored
much less thoroughly than is the case with his domestic policy.
For our knowledge of Bismarck's foreign policy in the years
1878–80 we are largely indebted to the official German document publication, the *Grosse Politik*. Understandably, the
documentation is fairly complete for the negotiations leading
up to the Congress of Berlin. Although exaggerated, Bismarck's role in these negotiations seems sufficiently clear. But
for the twelve month period following the Congress there is
almost nothing. The documentation then becomes rather full
for the actual negotiations for the alliance with Austria in
October 1879, but dwindles again for the following eighteen
months. Thus, the high points of Bismarck's diplomatic
activity—the pre-Congress period and the negotiations for the
Austro-German alliance—are amply documented, but some
of the warts have been lovingly overlooked, and as Medlicott
has pointed out, the important period between the Congress
and the alliance remains neglected.[9] This was a period of
continued Russo-German friction which began to subside during the negotiations for the alliance, but there was no fundamental improvement in relations until the discussions for the
Dreikaiserbund were earnestly taken up in February 1880. This
study covers the period of Russo-German tension when Bismarck was at the crossroads.

Besides the few documents printed in the *Grosse Politik* there
is little printed source material available. Documents have
been published on the question of the nullification of part of
article v of the Treaty of Prague, but this is only a minor
question.[10] The forty-eight documents published by Müller[11]
are a real contribution. The materials which Goldschmidt
prints also deserve mentioning.[12] Others have published single
documents or bits of documents, but still the picture remained
fragmentary. Of the memoir literature only Schweinitz has

---

[9] Medlicott, *Congress*, p. vii, *Bismarck, Gladstone*, p. 13; cf. Winckler's criticism
in *HZ*, 186 (1958), pp. 137–40.

[10] *Bismarck und die nordschleswigsche Frage*, eds. W. Platzhoff, K. Rheindorff,
J. Tiedje. *L'Europe, Le Danemark et le Slesvig du Nord*, eds. Friis & Bagge.

[11] M. Müller, *Die Bedeutung des Berliner Kongresses für die deutsch-russischen Beziehungen*.   [12] H. Goldschmidt, 'Mitarbeiter Bismarcks'.

made a noteworthy contribution, in both interpretation and the material he presents.[13] Radowitz could have told us much, but his memoirs are particularly disappointing, although interesting for the Congress itself and the actual negotiations for the Austrian alliance.[14] Hohenlohe[15] and the rest give but fragments. Bismarck's memoirs are notoriously unreliable. In the *Gesammelte Werke*, which tactfully avoid some points, there are a few interesting conversations—most of them reprints from the published memoirs. Otherwise the emphasis is on domestic policy. The published source material from foreign archives and the memoirs and biographies of contemporary statesmen are valuable for the foreign policy of the particular country, but except where they reproduce conversations with Bismarck and reliable documents, this is merely second-hand material as far as German foreign policy is concerned.

A number of historians[16] have seen parts of the documents in the German archives, but only one, Windelband,[17] appears to have made much use of the correspondence. Bismarck's private papers were also available to him. In his excellent, but brief, treatment of the period in question, he makes a number of new points. To the best of my knowledge the present study is the first attempt to use extensively the material recently made available through the microfilming of the German foreign office archives for the period of Bismarck's foreign policy immediately following the Congress of Berlin.

My aim has been to examine the background of the Austro-German alliance of October 1879 and the subsequent Russo-German *rapprochement*. Hitherto historians have had to base their accounts or interpretations of Bismarck's foreign policy to a great extent on his own more general policy statements. But these statements are often of a contradictory nature, and they do not always correspond exactly to their practical application. So it was thought that from a detailed study a more clear and exacting, although certainly more complex,

---

[13] *Denkwürdigkeiten des Botschafters General von Schweinitz*, ed. W. von Schweinitz.
[14] *Aufzeichnungen und Erinnerungen aus dem Leben des Botschafters Joseph Maria von Radowitz*, ed. H. Holborn.
[15] *Denkwürdigkeiten des Fürsten Chlodwig zu Hohenlohe-Schillingsfürst*, ed. F. Curtius.
[16] Goldschmidt, Meisl, Müller, Rothfels, Schünemann, Schüssler, Wertheimer.
[17] W. Windelband, *Bismarck und die europäischen Grossmächte 1879–1885*.

image of Bismarck's foreign policy would emerge which would portray him not only in the role of the supreme theorist he was, but also in that of one thoroughly involved in the frustrating daily struggle for power and material interests.[18]

For the contemporary German sources use has been made of both the films and the original despatches, now in the foreign office archives of the Federal Republic of Germany, Bonn. The films are generally satisfactory, but a glance at the catalogue[19] will show that some files have not been completely photographed. A more important limitation is the inaccessibility of some sources. British, Austrian and French official and unofficial material is available in some detail. The publication of documents from the Italian archives, now under way, may clear up some points. Russian documents are still all but inaccessible. Official German material located in the files of other ministries is not all generally open to the public and might add a few minor points. As far as private papers are concerned, the memoirs of most of the key figures have been published in one form or another. It is not very likely that important evidence still waits to be discovered.

Aside from this, one difficulty in the interpretation of Bismarck's political activity remains. Although notoriously frank, he had no real confidants. Most of his evidence consists of *ad hominem* argumentation. Even his minutes on despatches and instructions to his foreign office—obviously not meant for the gallery—were designed to supply effective arguments for official policy. His closest collaborators were often puzzled about his ulterior motives. He was almost always sincere to a certain degree, but it is difficult to sift the extraneous matter from the essential, or to decide what was left unsaid on purpose. In addition, Bismarck was constantly rethinking foreign policy and while his instructions often appeared as pronouncements of absolute truth, he did not hesitate to change them. Some of these difficulties may be overcome if evidence originating with Bismarck is not taken out of context.

. . .

[18] Medlicott, *Bismarck, Gladstone*, p. 13.
[19] F. G. Stambrook, *A Catalogue of Files and Microfilms of the German Foreign Ministry Archives, 1867–1920.*

In some ways a study concentrating on the foreign policy of a single man is open to criticism. Bismarck was not always in complete control of foreign policy. At the beginning and end of his term of office especially, much of public opinion was critical and he had powerful rivals—kings, ministers, officials and other highly placed personages. But after the empire was created and mighty rivals stood checked or enthralled, the aura of peacemaker enveloped him and he was free as yet from the lengthening shadows which darken the career of aging statesmen; he was never more independent of inhibiting forces than during and shortly after the Congress of Berlin.

A study of these years therefore should and does reveal the chancellor's character shimmering through events. What emerges? The chancellor of iron or granite? The master chess player? The God of peace? Hardly. Relatively untrammelled at home, Bismarck, in reality, lacked the steady hand which seemed to steer the German ship so surely through difficult shoals. The amount of work he accomplished is impressive, but its quality betrays a man unaccustomed to routine. Overindulgence at the writing and dining tables was the rule rather than the exception. It is a tribute to his intellect and good health that he could continue so long with such excruciating habits. But they took their inevitable toll. Immoderation was at the root of many of his physical ailments and political embarrassments. It is no wonder that a man, often at the point of exhaustion and suffering from indigestion, should, in spite of his vast intellectual and intuitive powers, on occasion see bitter enmity and coalitions with far reaching ramifications where there was only rivalry. These figments of his imagination licensed vindictiveness which could not be sufficiently checked. Many historians regard this period as the high point of his career, yet he was neither without problems nor in absolute control.

William I was an uncomplicated soldier with a great store of unsophisticated common sense. Above all he was loyal, loyal to the traditions of his house and to his duty as he saw it. Bismarck's superb memoranda did not really make much impression since he could not easily be persuaded. If he was to be prodded into making a new departure, a conflict of loyalties had to be created. This necessity helps explain some of Bismarck's tactical moves in the last third of 1879. The intensity of the struggle between chancellor and Emperor over the dual alliance, as well as the uncertainty of the outcome, should not be overlooked. It was, of course, possible for Bismarck to outmanœuvre William, but in the last analysis the Emperor regarded his dilemma as that of deciding between Bismarck and his nephew, Tsar Alexander II. It is instructive to note his reluctance to decide for Bismarck. The chancellor wisely did not force him to do so but presented his case as merely a different road to the same goal—friendship with Russia.

Bismarck's ostensible success in reforging the link with Russia, thus reconciling William, more or less, to his paradoxical diplomacy, accounts for the subsequent decline in imperial interference throughout William's reign. In the period covered by this study the Emperor also exerted pressure in a number of other less important issues. Although this was nearly always embarrassing, Bismarck could generally go ahead as planned without making more than a minor concession.

In the latter half of 1878 the heir apparent, later Emperor Frederick III, deputized for the Kaiser who was recovering from wounds inflicted by an assassin. The brevity of his term of office, which provided but the shadow of a regent's power, left him with little influence. His coolness towards Russia added to Bismarck's consternation in the autumn of 1878 but was welcome a year later when he, as well as the Empress, helped to talk William into the alliance with Austria.

If imperial influence was waning after the conclusion of the alliance with Austria, the influence of the foreign office staff began to rise, but only slowly. The memory of the Arnim affair was still fresh and for some time no one in the foreign office or the diplomatic service dared show much initiative.

The secretary of state, B. E. von Bülow,[20] was about as close as anyone to Bismarck's ideal associate. Able, hardworking, and above all reliable, he identified himself with Bismarck's policy and at his best was an extremely gifted secretary.

[20] B. E. VON BÜLOW (1815–79). Envoy of Mecklenburg-Strelitz in Berlin, 1868–73; state secretary, 1873–20 October 1879.

Radowitz[21] was very different—a relatively young man who was envoy to Greece but served much of his time in the late seventies in the foreign office dealing with the eastern crisis. Dr C. Busch,[22] the expert on Balkan affairs, took care of most of the detailed work, while Radowitz as Bülow's deputy had the more responsible assignments. After Bülow's death in October 1879 he was for a while pretty nearly in charge of the foreign office. But then his star began to fade because of his own weaknesses, bad luck and the activity of rivals. Rado-witz was an admirer of Bismarck and willingly supported his general policy, but he aspired to more than Bülow. Quick, imaginative and brash, he was a little more reluctant than Bülow to request instructions. It was this reluctance which was the real cause of his downfall and not any independent policy which he may, conceivably, have wished to follow. When Bismarck was away from Berlin he did not hear from Radowitz often enough and became suspicious. This was not entirely Radowitz's fault since he was unlucky enough to be in charge when Bismarck was tired and not inclined to follow business closely—such as immediately after the Congress and the conclusion of the Austrian alliance.

Holstein[23] was one of Radowitz's rivals and obviously had a hand in his downfall. He was the other promising young man in the foreign office but until Radowitz's fall his position was vastly inferior except in one crucial respect; he was often Bismarck's personal secretary in Varzin and Friedrichsruh. He had the opportunity of playing on the chancellor's suspicions through daily conversation and was able to exercise a certain amount of influence in personnel matters. He played an active part in getting his friends Hohenlohe and Hatzfeldt into the

[21] J. M. VON RADOWITZ (1839–1912). Consul-general in Bucharest, 1870–1; chargé in Constantinople, 1871–2; counsellor in foreign office, 1872–4; envoy in Athens, 1874–82; ambassador in Constantinople, 1882–92; ambassador in Madrid, 1892–1908.

[22] DR C. BUSCH (1834–95). Dragoman in Constantinople, 1861–72; consul in Petersburg, 1872–4; counsellor in foreign office, 1874–9; consul-general in Buda-pest, 1879–80; temporary director of political department in foreign office, 1880–1; under secretary of state, 1881–5; envoy to Bucharest, 1885–8, Stockholm, 1888–92, Bern, 1892–5.

[23] F. VON HOLSTEIN (1837–1909). Second secretary in Paris embassy, 1871–6; counsellor in foreign office 1876–1906; director of political department, 1906.

foreign office. But at this time his political importance was practically nil. He was still a virtually unquestioning admirer of Bismarck's policies and had very little responsible work to do. His hey-day was yet to come.

Bucher,[24] the former radical lawyer, was apparently in the midst of things, but had lost most of his influence and was soon to lose virtually all that remained. He was not one to encourage sympathy for England, the Vatican or social democracy which were his concern in the foreign office, and some of this must have rubbed off on Bismarck, but his views were of little importance in day to day affairs. Completely loyal to the chancellor, he was perhaps most useful as an intermediary with the press.

All in all, Bismarck could have been quite satisfied with the foreign office staff: its significance was minimal. It even made very little use of the customary methods of influencing a minister by withholding or colouring information. Whenever Bismarck was not in close touch with affairs it was generally his own fault.

Because of the nature of their duties, ambassadors in the last century had greater influence than at present on foreign policy. How they reported or carried out their orders was often of more than incidental importance. But this kind of influence defies accurate assessment. It is also only natural for ambassadors to make suggestions about tactics and even general policy, but this was rarely done in Germany during this period.

Prince Reuss, ambassador in Vienna, was a loyal and able, if not very imaginative follower of Bismarck. Conservative by birth and education, he was Russophile, if anything, while in Petersburg, but developed appreciation for Austrian views during his long stay in Vienna. Although socially the highest ranking of Bismarck's great ambassadors, he was the most obscure and probably the least influential.[25]

Count Münster in London was more than usually interested in court gossip. One of the very few conservative Hanoverian supporters of Bismarck, he was born in London, knew the royal

[24] A. L. BUCHER (1817–1892). Counsellor in foreign office, 1864–86.
[25] HENRY VII PRINCE REUSS (1825–1906). Envoy and ambassador in Petersburg, 1867–76; Constantinople, 1877–8; Vienna 1 August, 1878–94. See Pfitzer.

family intimately and was in many ways more English than German. Münster was richly endowed with common sense and self-confidence. He had some inclination but little opportunity to put his pro-English and anti-Russian ideas to the test: he had little standing or influence in Berlin.[26]

Prince Hohenlohe,[27] a Catholic Bavarian, was another rare bird in imperial service. Perhaps a little more liberal in outlook than Münster, cautious, conciliatory and dignified, he was a steadying influence in Paris. His duty, as he saw it, was not to advance a new policy, but to blunt the antagonism between France and Germany. In the mid-seventies without him things might have run less smoothly, but by the time of the Congress relations between the two rival powers had improved so much that there was little more for him to do.

Count Hatzfeldt in Constantinople was, Bismarck is reported to have said, the best horse in his diplomatic stable; on the other hand, the chancellor also referred to him as a peacock. He was a little of both. Gifted with political insight, Hatzfeldt was an able and ambitious man—but no worker. In the late eighties he and Holstein conducted their own private policy in competition with Bismarck's. At this stage, however, Hatzfeldt, who had pro-English sympathies, was closely reined. When in the autumn of 1878 he tried to develop his role as mediator, Bismarck rebuked him sharply for showing *trop de zèle*. Thereafter Hatzfeldt promised to behave and did so as long as he remained in Constantinople.[28]

The only ambassador of any real independence of mind in the period following the Congress was Schweinitz in Petersburg. His origins were modest, but his was surely the most difficult and important post. Schweinitz, a stiff but humane Prussian

---

[26] GEORGE HERBERT COUNT (FROM 1899 PRINCE) MÜNSTER (1820–1902). Member of Reichstag, 1867–73; ambassador in London, 1873–85; Paris, 1885–1900. See Nostitz.

[27] CHLODWIG PRINCE ZU HOHENLOHE-SCHILLINGSFÜRST (1819–1901). Ambassador in Paris, 1874–85; temporary director of foreign office, 30 April–September 1880; viceroy in Alsace-Lorraine, 1885–94; chancellor, 1894–1900.

[28] PAUL COUNT VON HATZFELDT-WILDENBURG (1831–1901). Counsellor in foreign office, 1868–74; envoy in Marid, 1874–8; ambassador in Constantinople, 1878–81; state secretary, 1881–5; ambassador in London, 1885–1901. See Krausnick, 'Botschafter Graf Hatzfeldt'; *The Hatzfeldt Letters*, p. vi; St. Vallier to Waddington, 27 February 1879, private, FFM, Allemagne M & D 166 bis.

general, was the best informed and most influential foreign representative in Russia. Although not enamoured of Gorchakov, he was on intimate terms with the Tsar—and trusted his word implicitly—partly because of his position as intermediary between uncle and nephew, but also because of his discretion and undisguised pro-Russian sympathies. He thought some of Bismarck's ideas unrealistic because of their disregard for ancient Prussian traditions and the concept of conservative solidarity. Like Hohenlohe, Schweinitz thought it his duty to conciliate. He was much less disturbed by the situation in Russia than Bismarck apparently was. He disliked the alliance with Austria and argued that Russian ill-feeling would pass and that, anyhow, Russia was in no position to be really dangerous; he proposed therefore a policy of *bons procédés* in order to preserve the stock of goodwill which Prussia had accumulated over the decades. Schweinitz failed, of course, to persuade Bismarck and he failed to prevent the gradual deterioration in Russo-German relations, but in the crucial period before the negotiations for the renewal of the Three Emperors' League his steadiness was a major obstacle for Bismarck. How much of Bismarck's manœuvring was aimed at surmounting it is an open question. One wonders, too, whether the starry-eyed conservative did not see some things more clearly than his chief.[29]

Clearly, at this point in his career Bismarck did not have to reckon with much countervailing activity amongst his own officials. Within five years, however, things were different.

Fearful of the deviousness of others, Bismarck, typically, was reluctant to rely exclusively on official channels. In his banker, Bleichroeder,[30] he found an able adviser and assistant for economic affairs. In this sphere his influence was perceptible, but in political affairs his role was more modest, that of a mouthpiece and reporter. Bleichroeder furnished a steady flow of miscellaneous information and passed on many of Bismarck's comments to foreign diplomats. For Bismarck this 'paradiplomacy' provided a check on his subordinates; it also

[29] H. L. VON SCHWEINITZ (1822–1901). Envoy and ambassador in Vienna, 1869–76; ambassador in Petersburg, 1876–92. See Sumner, pp. 34–5; Helms.

[30] G. VON BLEICHROEDER (1822–93). British consul-general in Berlin, 1872–93.

allowed him to put across his views privately and without compromising the government.

Public opinion, too, at this time was putty in his hands for his policy during and after the Congress was broadly in line with the sentiment of the age. There was some resistance to a few minor aspects of his foreign policy, but public opinion needed little moulding to give solid support for the *rapprochement* with Austria and at this stage Bismarck had the knack of presenting his actions in such a way as to gain popular approval. Few have professed greater disdain for the press, but few have studied it more closely or influenced it more consistently, because he knew from experience just how helpful an ally or dangerous an enemy the press and public opinion could be. This does not mean that he explained his ultimate goals and tried to persuade public opinion—far from it; he simply used whatever arguments he thought would be effective to achieve a fitting reaction to the shifting international scene. For once, Liberals, clericals and socialists—for different reasons—stood shoulder to shoulder. Many Conservatives also supported the seemingly pro-Austrian swing in Bismarck's foreign policy— not so much at this stage for the obvious economic reasons which were later to push many into the front ranks of the anti-Russian party, but simply because many of them had traditionally elected for Austria when forced to choose. Catholics and South Germans were more pro-Austrian, the progressives and socialists more anti-Russian in orientation.[31]

The subsequent improvement in relations with Russia would have been less popular, but it was not advertised. Public opinion did have an indirect effect on the general line of Bismarck's policy inasmuch as the very popularity of an understanding with Austria was a strong, but for Bismarck marginal, argument in its favour. More important, perhaps, was the influence it had on Russian public opinion. Widespread German dislike of Russia and sporadic press campaigns against that country were an important factor in the estrangement of the two nations.

Bismarck's freedom of choice in foreign affairs was un-doubtedly influenced to some extent by economic factors although they did not dictate any one policy. Protective

[31] See Hatzfeld; Carroll, chapter iv; *Gedanken und Erinnerungen*, II, 12, iii.

legislation seemed a logical solution to the depression. Of the great powers Russia would probably suffer the most from effective measures to protect the German economy, and a sour reaction in Petersburg was likely. This meant in turn that if Bismarck wanted good relations, some show of counterbalancing gestures of friendship would have to be made. But this was a minor irritant which could have been easily overcome given sufficient goodwill on his part. Austria's economic interests were also injured by the tariff, but political relations improved.

Bismarck's attempt to rescue the German capital invested in the Rumanian railway system had perhaps more important immediate consequences: it complicated German relations with most of the powers. To obtain cooperation, he had to make concessions to one power and then another. In the end they were all puzzled and suspicious.

All in all, the economic factor immediately after the Congress was not a great barrier to Bismarck's diplomacy, but in the eighties the inherent logic of a policy of protection steadily narrowed the terrain on which he could manœuvre.

If Bismarck immediately after the Congress was more free of encumbrance than at any other time, a study of this period should be well suited to reveal the man and his foreign policy in what was for him and Germany a decisive hour. The first two chapters deal with Bismarck's foreign policy to the end of 1878. Chapter one shows him at first listlessly following his accustomed policy of solidarity with the other two empires; during the autumn his pace slackened and the Three Emperors' League collapsed. He was at the crossroads. Chapter two shows Bismarck from a very different angle, charging against a small opponent (Rumania) and an important one (the Russian chancellor). Chapters three to seven show that his will to battle against these opponents for political, economic and personal reasons very largely determined the future direction of his foreign policy. In chapters eight, nine and ten we see that the road to the dual alliance and the revival of the Three Emperors' League followed the rocky contours mainly of the dispute with Russia, but also of the squabble with Rumania.

CHAPTER I

Bismarck and the End of the First *Dreikaiserbund*

I

By the beginning of 1875 Bismarck had apparently succeeded in consolidating the gains of three wars: victory, peace and security were obtained. And German ascendency in Europe had been achieved. England was aloof, France feeble and isolated, Austria ostensibly reconciled with Russia and both associated with Germany and linked to Italy. But, hardly achieved, the proud edifice began to crumble. The 'war-in-sight' crisis and rumblings in the Balkans brought Britain back into European politics, qualified French isolation, threatened Austro-Russian cooperation, and jeopardized their friendship with Germany. Throughout 1876–7 and the first half of 1878 Bismarck sought by means of intermittent displays of ingenuity to rebuild the old or lay the foundation of a new structure. The simplest and most effective policy still appeared to be the perpetuation of French isolation through domination of Austria and Russia who should be on tolerably friendly terms with one another. But the 'war-in-sight' crisis showed him the necessity, and the Balkan crisis the possibility, of keeping Britain busy on the fringes of Europe in ways which would induce her to court rather than rival Germany. The balance to be achieved was a fine one and Bismarck knew only too well that any of a number of factors could easily upset it. That is why he repeatedly considered the possibility of a fundamental reorientation, but his main concern was to shift those weights he controlled nervously from one to the other side of the scales and back again. In fact, much of his tortuous diplomacy was quite unnecessary. If he had more calmly watched the balance, his end could probably have been more easily attained. War or reconciliation between Austria and Russia was not so likely as Bismarck thought at different times during the crisis. His attempts to prevent both puzzled Austrians and Russians alike. The British and Italians, too, were made suspicious through approaches which were not followed up.

The Balkan crisis beginning in 1875 led two years later to a war between Russia and Turkey. In March 1878 the Treaty of San Stefano ended hostilities, but led to a threat of European war. Between San Stefano and the Congress of Berlin (13 June–13 July) the eastern crisis was at its peak, but for Bismarck it had the distinct advantage of clarifying the relations of the other powers with one another. Since he had no reason to want war and there was little chance of intimate relations rapidly developing between either Austria or England and Russia, Bismarck's course was to work for the preservation of peace by a sincere but idiosyncratic attempt to reach a practicable compromise between the antagonists. In this way he could regain the ascendency he had temporarily reached early in 1875. The complete isolation of France was probably unobtainable, but in working for peace Bismarck could try to assure a settlement of the Eastern Question which would so preoccupy the other powers as to make effective support for France unlikely.

From this point of view Bismarck's activity at the Congress of Berlin can probably best be described in his own terms as that of an 'honest broker who really wants to do business'.[1] His role was important, but it depended on his clients' desire to do business; and it might be doubted whether the Congress would have failed without him. In his own way he strove to prevent a rupture between the powers and probably hoped that they would gratefully look to him for future guidance. In effect, his diplomacy at the Congress served Russia and Austria the most, and Britain the least. Turkey and the lesser powers were either ignored or bullied; but they were negligible quantities to him. In a sense Bismarck's activity was in accordance with the spirit of the *Dreikaiserbund*; still, he did not stress

[1] See, Medlicott, *Congress*, pp. 36–136 and Müller, chapter ii. Böhme does not substantiate his belief that Bismarck had 'opted' for Austria in the autumn of 1876 and in the first half of 1878 was on the Austrian side, pp. 439, 495–9.

exclusive cooperation with his imperial neighbours. He wanted good relations with all the great powers. This attitude enabled him to play the role of 'honest broker', but it also hindered the functioning of the badly weakened Three Emperors' League.

Five days after the last session of the Congress, on 18 July, Bismarck left for his usual summer cure in Kissingen and Gastein where he remained until mid-September. Bülow, next in command, took leave on the 23rd and returned six weeks later. In the meantime Radowitz, the promising young envoy in Athens, was in charge of the foreign office.

Severely tried by the events of the last few months, Bismarck anticipated little difficulty, for the time being at least.[2] Although he had no illusions about the permanence of the Berlin settlement, he looked forward to a long overdue rest. His correspondence during these weeks is scanty and he was probably occupied more with problems of domestic policy than with the vexations of the near eastern crisis. It was here that serious talks on the relaxation of the *Kulturkampf* were begun the papal nuncio in Munich, Masella. Virtually no progress was made in Kissingen or next summer in Gastein when Bismarck spoke with Cardinal Jacobini, but at least a start towards subsequent improvement in the religious atmosphere of Germany was made.

As for foreign affairs, directives from the chancellor were concerned almost wholly with pressing the Porte for an early and strict execution of the Treaty. This was his main concern and it is from this point of view that German foreign policy up to the first week in September can best be understood. During this period he was still thinking in terms of the Three Emperors' League and realized that a closer *entente* could have brought about a more favourable solution to the near eastern difficulties.[3] But, expecting little trouble, he desired to return to a more passive role, and his support, especially for Russia, was somewhat vague, if willing enough. Nevertheless, the recent encounter with Gorchakov[4] and

---

[2] Windelband, p. 51; *GW*, XIV, ii, no. 1587; VIII, no. 211.

[3] –to Radowitz, Kissingen, 17 August, GFO, IAAl 63.

[4] PRINCE A. M. GORCHAKOV (1798–1883). Envoy in Stuttgart, 1841; also Russian representative to *Bundestag* in Frankfurt, 1850; envoy in Vienna, 1854; foreign minister, 1856; chancellor, 1867.

Shuvalov,[5] as well as events in Russia before and after the Congress, cast a shadow upon Russo-German relations.

When the two Russian statesmen returned to Petersburg from Berlin a struggle for power ensued which was both a personal contest and one of two varying conceptions of foreign policy. Shuvalov, who was reputedly conciliatory, pro-German, and thoroughly in favour of the *Dreikaiserbund*, had the sympathy of Bismarck and, apparently, Andrássy.[6] Gorchakov, who wished to follow an independent line, was disliked by Bismarck; but he was in the stronger, because more established, position. Gorchakov was away on leave from August to December; when he returned he quickly emerged the victor. During the time of Gorchakov's absence Bismarck was intent on obtaining his replacement by Shuvalov. Without a doubt it was a difficult game to play and, as it turned out, Bismarck was the loser. His backing of the *Dreikaiserbund* was lukewarm, and at decisive moments he failed effectively to second Shuvalov's efforts to resuscitate this understanding. Instead of official support for Shuvalov, which Bismarck probably feared would have achieved the opposite of his intended purpose, he chose to have Gorchakov and his policy attacked in the press and otherwise defamed, but this did little to help Shuvalov, and much to poison Russo-German relations.

There was an element of fate in the subsequent deterioration of relations with Russia. The decline in Russian prestige and power brought about by German unification and documented by the Treaty of Berlin was bound to be resented in the long run. Understandably, this resentment was aggravated by lack of German aid in some directions. Yet, ironically, the fact that the relative decline would have been greater had it not been for German support in other crucial matters was more a cause of disaffection than gratitude.

Injured, but mounting, nationalism in Russia was also nurtured by the effects of the Great Depression, which brought in its trail German capital and increasing quantities of German

---

[5] COUNT P. A. SHUVALOV (1827–89). Chief of the third section, 1866; ambassador in London, 1874–9.

[6] JULIUS COUNT ANDRÁSSY, SR. (1823–90). Hungarian prime minister, 1867–1871; Austro-Hungarian foreign minister, 1871–9.

imports at falling prices and then, finally, a German tariff which hindered Russian exports. Previous Prussian intellectual ascendency had been willingly accepted because the Russians had been dominant in most other respects. But the seventies not only upset the political *status quo*, they also threatened Russia with what could possibly be economic subjugation. Resentment was natural. Only a self-effacing German policy could have halted this trend, but that surely would not have corresponded with the actual power relationships of the period. Nor would it have solved the problem of achieving the correct balance of good German relations with Austria and England as well. Any marked improvement in friendship with Russia would have to be purchased with a deterioration in relations with her rivals.

If German relations with Russia had been clear and were to become murky, the reverse applied to Austria. Since the Hungarian, Andrássy, had replaced Beust[7] as foreign minister in 1871 the Austro-German storm clouds had dispersed. In certain, particularly military, circles the past had not been forgotten, but the realization of weakness and the disappointments of the Balkan crisis induced most, apart from the Slavs, to favour closer cooperation with Germany.

Nevertheless, in the months following the Congress German relations with Austria were complicated. In the first six weeks the German government supported Austria and Russia separately against the Turks, without attempting to use an *entente* between the three empires. In this period Shuvalov made overtures to Austria for a revival of the *Dreikaiserbund*, but these were received rather coolly.[8] Andrássy was prepared to cooperate with Russia occasionally in his own interest, but his mistrust was unremitting. Then, as Austria gravitated towards England, Bismarck apparently showed increased interest in the Three Emperors' League, but he did not want to estrange England, nor could he free himself from fear of a close Austro-Russian understanding which would leave Germany

---

[7] FREDERICK FERDINAND COUNT VON BEUST (1809–86). Austrian foreign minister, 1866–71; ambassador in London, 1871–8; in Paris, 1878–82.

[8] Berchem to Bismarck, Petersburg, 7 August, no. 250 most confid., GFO, IABi 53; Andrássy to Langenau, Vienna, 29 July, tel. 47; Langenau to Andrássy, Petersburg, 1 & 9 August, private & confid., WS, PA X 71.

standing in the cold. Andrássy's parliamentary position made it inexpedient to associate himself with anything that smacked of *Dreikaiserbund*; but he strongly desired Bismarck's support and treated him with courtesy.

Anglo-German relations were not yet troubled by the trade and naval rivalry. Prussia and Britain were traditional friends on religious and dynastic grounds. The logic of foreign policy had also repeatedly dictated cooperation. As far as domestic politics were concerned, the harmony was less than complete, but at the time this caused little trouble. Derby had been consistently suspicious of Bismarck, much more so than Disraeli, although his chief did eventually share some of his mistrust. Salisbury, who replaced Derby[9] as foreign secretary on 28 March 1878, was no more willing to trust Bismarck, but he was prepared to work with him.

To the chancellor, Derby was merely a cat tossed into water and struggling to keep from drowning; he thought that the English lord had never understood a word of high politics and was glad to see him out of office. When Bismarck first met Salisbury towards the end of 1876, he had been favourably impressed, but at this stage the chancellor did not hold him in very high esteem. If he had fallen in Bismarck's eyes, the prime minister had risen. Of course, remarks never ceased about the great political novelist who was only too willing to use literary devices in diplomacy,[10] but Bismarck was apparently pleased with Disraeli, not so much by his flamboyant role at the Congress as by his business-like approach off stage and the seizure of Cyprus. This was another sign of British involvement in European politics and a step towards the partition of the Turkish empire which Bismarck seemed to want. Nevertheless, England was a passive factor in Bismarck's foreign policy till the first week in September. She was thought to be in accord

---

[9] EDWARD HENRY STANLEY, 15TH EARL OF DERBY (1826–93). Foreign secretary, 1874–March 1878. ROBERT CECIL, MARQUIS OF SALISBURY (1830–1903). Secretary for India, 1874–8; foreign secretary, March 1878–April 1880; prime minister and foreign secretary, 1885; prime minister, 1886–92, 1895–1902; foreign secretary, 1887–92, 1895–1900.

[10] St. Vallier to Waddington, 25 March 1878, no. 30 confid., FFM, Allemagne 22; 29 March and 20 April 1878, private, FFM, Allemagne M & D 166; passage omitted from *DDF*, ii, no. 477, in FFM, Allemagne 31.

with the other powers in opposing the Porte. Then, while embarrassing Germany, England demonstrated that she would not allow Turkey to be bullied too severely. In October and November tension in the Near East reached a peak and Bismarck, pressed to join one side or the other, tried to remain neutral. The value of English friendship lay not only in her possible role as an alternative ally to Russia, but also in her rather close relations with Austria which might as a result be less inclined to come to terms with Russia or France at German expense.

The certainty of French enmity remained the guiding light of Bismarck's foreign policy. But since the victory of the republicans in the French assembly and the installation of Waddington as foreign minister in December 1877 a new policy of *bons procédés* was introduced by both governments in secondary matters. Most of the credit for this goes to Waddington[11] and the new French ambassador in Berlin, St. Vallier,[12] an able, conciliatory, but also scheming diplomat who immediately became a favourite with Bismarck and sent instructions to Paris almost as often as he received them. St. Vallier was the most pretentious, but also the ablest member of the diplomatic corps in Berlin.

Bismarck was convinced that the republicans would be less adventurous than Bonapartists or royalists because less united on the home front. As long as the radicals were not at the centre of power he also felt that a moderate republic with its inherent trend to the left would not easily find allies in monarchical Europe; but the closer the radicals got, the more he worried. Waddington, staid and thoroughly bourgeois, was in fact unwilling to gamble with the uncertain advantages of Russian friendship as an alternative to the sure, but meagre, returns of a policy of less acrimonious relations with Germany. He was also reluctant to sacrifice the fairly good relations with his ancestral home—England. Bismarck appreciated this more conciliatory line and gave what diplomatic support

[11] W. H. WADDINGTON (1826–94). Foreign minister, December 1877–December 1879; prime minister, February–December 1879; ambassador in London, 1883–93.
[12] CHARLES-RAYMOND COUNT ST. VALLIER (1833–86). Chef du cabinet, 1866; envoy in Stuttgart, 1868; various special missions to the German forces, 1871–3; ambassador in Berlin, December 1877–December 1881. See Daudet.

he could, but he was repeatedly troubled by the thought that Waddington's reserve resulted more from weakness than conviction. It seemed wise, therefore, to guide French interests to areas far from the Vosges where friction with Britain, Russia or Italy would be likely.

Italian governments had been friendly with Germany throughout the seventies, and especially since the outbreak of war between Russia and Turkey. They were mainly interested in preventing Austrian expansion in the Balkans, or, failing that, in obtaining territorial compensation (preferably at Austrian expense). Before the Dufaure-Waddington government came to power in France they also wanted a common front against that country. In the bluntest of terms Bismarck had refused to give help against Austria, but suggested compensation elsewhere (Albania or Tunis). After the *coup d'état* of 16 May 1877 in France he was, if anything, more concerned than Italy with the threat from the west. In June 1877 he suggested an Italian alliance. Obviously, he wanted reassurance of Italian amity. In addition, he hoped that such a dramatic move would be betrayed to the French. It was in fact part of a vigorous campaign of intimidation waged against the French government.[13] As soon as he had obtained this object, he seemed almost totally to lack consideration for Italy. There was little change till Italy was prepared to come to terms with Austria in 1881–2. German-Italian relations in the period covered by this study were perhaps worse that at any other point in Bismarck's term of office.

II

In the six weeks following the Congress the Turks alone put up determined opposition to the execution of the Treaty of Berlin. They were, it seemed, at odds with all the great powers. Even before the ratification of the Treaty on 3 August the German foreign office had put pressure on the Porte on three separate occasions—concerning the evacuation of Batum, the completion of a convention with Austria on Bosnia, and the ratification

---

[13] Correspondence in GFO, IABc 79 and IABe 61; see also Palamenghi-Crispi, pp. 27ff.

of the Treaty itself. After the exchange of ratifications there was a period of relative inactivity as far as Berlin was concerned which lasted until the despatch of a circular to the powers on 2 September suggesting joint action against the Porte. This time was occupied by some confused correspondence on the setting up of the international commissions stipulated in the Treaty.

Bismarck correctly foresaw some Turkish resistance to the exchange of ratifications and approved of the strong line Radowitz took with the Turkish representative, arguing that if obstruction continued, collective remonstrances could be considered. At the Congress he had stood for no nonsense from the Turks; he continued this policy, most likely believing that everyone was convinced of the need to hold Turkey to the strict execution of the Treaty. At this point he did not err. Radowitz's firmness found general approval. Finally, after a delay of more than three weeks the Turkish documents were also exchanged.[14]

The Turks might not have been treated quite so brusquely if their procrastination in the Batum and Bosnian questions had not already come to light. The Congress had promised the Russians Batum, and Shumla and Varna were also to be evacuated, but all these places were still held by the Turks. Bismarck had not been in Kissingen a week when the Russian government asked for assistance in obtaining Batum. Since Germany was already backing the surrender of the other two fortresses, cautious support was immediately given, and on 5 August Berlin heard that the Sultan had ordered the immediate surrender of Varna and promised an identical order for Batum.[15] During the next two weeks the Turks seemed willing to proceed with the evacuation of the fortified places and no further attempt was made to exert pressure; towards the end of August, however, resistance was renewed. This was the immediate cause of the German circular on 2 September.

German support of Russia in the Batum question was not decisive, although together with Russian pressure it sufficed

---

[14] See the correspondence in GFO, IABq 130.
[15] See the correspondence in GFO, IABq 128; *GP*, no. 424.

to extract a promise from the Sultan. Austrian aid was probably even less emphatic. There is no indication that the three empires attempted to act jointly in this, or for that matter in the Bosnia-Herzegovina, question. Although Gorchakov, Shuvalov, and Langenau, the Austrian ambassador to Russia,[16] had preliminary talks at the end of July, these did not advance beyond the stage of vague affirmations of the desire to cooperate.[17] Gorchakov felt certain he could expect assistance from Austria; and Langenau, doing some wishful thinking, thought an understanding had been reached, but knew nothing of the details himself. Nevertheless, he realized that the Russian government was not disposed to make any public display of friendship. Gorchakov distrusted Andrássy, and Russia made no signs of demobilization on the Austrian frontier.[18] On the other hand, a basis for cooperation existed in the common opposition to the Porte, and, if active German assistance had been given, a closer understanding might have been achieved.

In contrast to the somewhat grudging support granted Russia for the surrender of Batum, that given Austria in the Bosnian question was generous.

In the Habsburg monarchy Slavs and military men welcomed the addition of territory; the Germans were less keen. Andrássy, like most Hungarians, was naturally troubled by the thought of more Slavs within the empire, but his hand was not as steady in resistance as it might have been, he had to make allowance for the views of others, and he did not want the Russians alone to win laurels, land, and increased influence. So at the Congress he contrived to have Europe assign Austria the task of occupying and, by implication, civilizing the area. By and large Austria's acquisition of Bosnia troubled Bismarck's countrymen because they feared that the new territory

---

[16] BARON F. LANGENAU (1818–81). General; envoy in Hanover, Oldenburg, and Brunswick, 1850–1; in Sweden and Norway, 1851–9; in the Netherlands, 1859–71; envoy in Petersburg, 1871–4; ambassador, 1874–80.

[17] Langenau to Andrássy, Petersburg, 1 & 9 August, private and confid. letters; Andrássy to Langenau, Vienna, 8 August, tel. no. 50, WS, PA X 71.

[18] Berchem to Bismarck, Petersburg, 30 July 1878, no. 227, GFO, IABq 130; 7 August, no. 250 most confid., GFO, IABi 53.

would be more a source of weakness than strength,[19] but the chancellor was interested in dividing the Balkans into Russian and Austrian spheres of influence (which would not exclude annexations), and this was a step towards the realization of that plan. In April help had already been promised; then on 25 July Bismarck's son, Herbert, wrote to Radowitz from Kissingen:

My father has read in the papers that Austria is still negotiating with the Porte over the occupation of Bosnia. If the Austrians should meet with difficulties in the execution of the Congress stipulations—which must not be compromised by Turkish dishonesty—he wishes to give all possible support for the preservation of the peace. Our embassy in Constantinople should be instructed to make remonstrances in this sense and to mention that we will be the determined friends of Austria in the further development of the Bosnian question. We must also give a similar assurance in Vienna, adding that we will be prepared to grant generous diplomatic support, if Andrássy should require it.[20]

The Austrians immediately requested aid, explaining that public opinion in Hungary desired voluntary Turkish consent to the entry of Austrian troops into Bosnia; but since the Porte was still stalling and the anarchic conditions in Bosnia made further delay impossible, Andrássy was determined, even without consent, to march in on the 29th.

German diplomatic assistance was given in Constantinople and in the middle of August Bismarck offered Austria further vigorous support,[21] but no more steps were taken that month. Continued reports of passive resistance in Bosnia as well as the stubborn Turkish refusal to conclude a convention with Austria on the occupation probably served as an additional spur to the German initiative on 2 September.

The support given Russia on Batum and Austria in the Bosnian question showed a preference for Austria which—it

[19] Carroll, p. 152.

[20] COUNT HERBERT VON BISMARCK-SCHÖNHAUSEN (1849–1904). *Assessor*, 1874–80 (employed as private secretary to his father); envoy in The Hague, 1884; undersecretary of state in the foreign office, 1885; state secretary, 1886–90. H. Bismarck to Radowitz, Kissingen, 25 July, GFO, IABq 125 iv; *GP*, nos. 434–5, 438–9.

[21] Reuss to GFO, Vienna, 12 August, tel. 166, GFO, IABq 131.

will presently be seen—was more apparent than real.[22] The support given to Russia was not wholehearted and no attempt was made to mobilize the *Dreikaiserbund*, although Vienna and Petersburg had exchanged assurances in this direction. Bismarck, far from Berlin and inadequately informed, was trying to keep in the background. This emerges clearly from the confused negotiations on the setting up of the international commissions; but the proceedings of the Rhodope commission show equally as clearly that Austria had no preferred position in Bismarck's eyes at that time.

Early in August the negotiations started for the establishment of the international commissions required by the Treaty. The latent differences between the powers did not yet appear because they were in a cooperative mood and had no precise understanding of the various Treaty stipulations concerning the commissions. Although the Russian cabinet was as confused as the others, it tried to get things moving and received loyal but perfunctory support from Germany. The Russians, however, expected more and on two occasions drew the attention of Berlin to the importance of the Eastern Rumelia organization commission. Obviously, they wanted the German delegate to that commission to be specially selected and instructed, but Radowitz gave special consideration only in the selection of the delegate to the *ad hoc* commission for Bulgaria who was to be *persona grata* for Russia. The delegate for the Eastern Rumelia organization commission[23] seems to have been selected on the basis of his experience and knowledge of near eastern affairs. Their initial instructions contained nothing of a political character and it is doubtful whether they received anything more than a few hasty words of advice before leaving Berlin.[24] The choice of the other delegates was left to the minister of war who presumably selected them on the basis of their

---

[22] Cf., however, the oral instructions Bismarck gave Hatzfeldt (probably in August) to insist on the execution of the Treaty, especially where Austrian interests were involved. Raschdau, p. 262, was probably correct in believing that this surely did not imply a lack of consideration for Russia. Hatzfeldt to Bülow, Buyukdere, 4 October 1878, private, GFO, Türkei 108.

[23] See articles vi and xviii of the Treaty of Berlin.

[24] See the correspondence in GFO, IABq 133.

military record. Berlin undoubtedly intended to play an in-
conspicuous role in the commissions whose task was thought
to be mainly technical, although the proceedings of the Rhodope
commission might very well have served as a forewarning of the
difficulties of remaining reserved when the other powers
disagreed.

The matters discussed so far have tended to show the unity
of the great powers. In contrast to this the proceedings of the
Rhodope commission illustrate the fundamental, if then latent,
differences between the powers which in the following months
were to revive the eastern crisis. The history of the Rhodope
commission, spanning the period between the end of the Congress and the German note of 2 September, demonstrates perhaps more clearly the limitations of the *Dreikaiserbund* than its
successful functioning.[25] The Russian cabinet was unyielding,
ill-informed, and incapable of controlling its agents in the
Balkans. Berlin, although wishing to cooperate, was determined
to maintain its reserve. Austria had common interests with
Russia, but also with England.

In the last weeks of the war Moslem refugees had fled to the
Rhodope mountains where they had continued to resist the
combined military efforts of the Russian army and Bulgarian
militia to force observance of the San Stefano Peace. The
Congress had agreed to send an international commission to
verify on the spot the gravity of the situation and seek a remedy.
Although in conception the commission was calculated to
embarrass the Russians, the German cabinet troubled itself
little over eventualities. The selection and instruction of a
delegate were left to the *chargé* in Constantinople. He chose
one of the junior members of the consulate, Ludwig Müller,
later Raschdau,[26] probably in order to document Germany's
lack of interest in the affair and because of the strenuous nature

[25] Medlicott, *Congress*, pp. 157f, emphasizes the cooperation of the three empires.
English statesmen were also convinced of their cooperation. The following account
of the commission is based mainly on Raschdau, pp. 223–53; and Müller, pp. 74–7,
who prints most of the important documents from file, GFO, IABq 132.

[26] Ludwig Müller, born in Radoschau, Silesia, changed his name to Raschdau
on 4 August 1881. In 1877 he was appointed assistant in the consulate at Constantinople, and in July 1879 vice-consul in Alexandria. Radowitz, i, 235.

of the assignment as well as Müller's knowledge of Turkish. His initial instructions to cooperate with his Russian and Austrian colleagues were quite vague; and when Müller asked what should be done if Austria and Russia did not themselves agree, his answer was reputedly a mere smile. In fact, discord arose at once. The fugitives heaped abuse on the Russians, blaming them for their misery. The Russian delegate defended his countrymen and threatened to retire from the commission. With the exception of Müller, all the others opposed him. Although the German delegate tended to share the opinion of the majority, the very unanimity of the testimony against the Russian army made him suspicious. This, together with the belief that the withdrawal of the Russian would wreck the commission, persuaded Müller to side with him. That the commission was able to complete its work at all was due, to a great extent, to Müller's skilful mediation.

Müller telegraphed on 28 July that the delegates were gathering tendentious material against the Russian army instead of following their humanitarian purpose. But on 30 July Berlin heard that Austria was prepared to cooperate with the two other empires, and Gorchakov threatened to withdraw his delegate if the commission were to become blatantly anti-Russian. So Müller was told to adhere strictly to the task of the commission and cooperate as much as possible with his Russian and Austrian colleagues. United action by the three empires against the other powers seemed imminent; but owing to the difficulty of communication with the delegates, the previous constellation continued and when the commission returned to Constantinople it was irrevocably split.

Müller's conduct pleased Berlin and Petersburg. The Austrian delegate, who had sided with the western powers, was chastened by his government, but the damage had already been done and all Austria could do to make amends was to refuse to endorse the final report of the commission. So although the three eastern cabinets wanted to cooperate with one another, it proved difficult. A much more active means of cooperation would have to be found, and for this none seemed inclined.

Germany alone had given real aid to Russia but this put her into opposition to England, the leader of the anti-Russian majority. The somewhat unwitting support of Russia's position in the Rhodope commission showed the furthest extent of Bismarck's assistance for her and the *Dreikaiserbund*. Given Russia's unbending attitude, increasing English willingness to back Turkey, and Austria's desire to remain on good terms with England, a functioning of the Three Emperors' League would have required some German persuading in Vienna and Petersburg, and could have been purchased only at the cost of English annoyance. The following months show that Bismarck was unwilling to pay this price.

III

Towards the end of August tension mounted between Russia and Turkey over the fortress question. The German *chargé* in Constantinople reported that the Turkish authorities in Batum sought every possible excuse to postpone the evacuation. He added that the Russians believed an ultimatum would be necessary. Hearing this news Bismarck felt that 'if the Porte should continue to withhold fulfilment of the Berlin agreements, a collective or at least a simultaneous *démarche* in Constantinople should be suggested to the powers'.[27] Although this step was not actually inspired by Russia or Austria, Bismarck's firm belief in the culpability of the Turk doubtless strengthened his desire to support Russia's apparently just claims. Since Austria had similar experiences with the Porte, she was also meant to benefit from the *démarche*. Still, the proposed step did not aim at preserving the Three Emperors' League. Bismarck thought that all the powers were irritated by the Porte, so he did not want to limit common action to the three empires.

Since the German foreign office heard fresh complaints about Turkish double dealing, Radowitz took the step Bismarck had contemplated. He drafted a circular on 2 September which stressed the procrastination of the Porte, mentioning the points where it had failed to fulfil its obligations:

1. The fortresses of Varna, Shumla and Batum had not been surrendered.

[27] Müller, no. 11. For the rest of the chapter no reference will be made to the routine correspondence which is mainly in GFO, IABq 133.

2. The Porte had permitted its local authorities to encourage the resistance of the Moslem population to the occupation of Bosnia-Herzegovina.

3. The Porte had simply rejected the rectification of the Greek frontier.

4. It had no intention of fulfilling its obligation to transfer territory to Montenegro.

Renewed agitation in various parts of the Balkan peninsula had resulted from the attitude of the Turkish government. Further agitation would threaten the work of the Congress which the powers were bound to uphold. Berlin hoped that united remonstrances would demonstrate to the Porte the necessity of loyal and complete fulfilment of its obligations. The representatives of the powers should identically, or at least simultaneously, express the expectation that the Porte cease to obstruct the execution of the Treaty and give clear and exact instructions to those agents which were obliged to aid in the reformation of local conditions.

Radowitz probably expected no resistance to his suggested move; he considered it of such minor importance that he neglected to inform Bismarck, who then asked whether anything had 'been done as a result of my suggestion for collective remonstrances in Constantinople?'[28] Thus Bismarck inspired, although he did not actually draft the note.

Andrássy enthusiastically welcomed the German initiative, and in the following days he became the sole advocate of the proposal. On the 6th the sulky consent of the Russians was announced. 'We will not refuse to participate in a *démarche* concerning the execution of the stipulations of the Treaty of Berlin, although we must take the opportunity to mention the unfavourable reception the other powers gave our analogous suggestion at the Congress.'

So Vienna and Petersburg accepted readily enough, but England refused and France and Italy, although sympathizing with the German proposal, followed the lead of London. Salisbury argued that a collective or simultaneous note was premature and too strong; the German complaints were not very well founded; if at all, objections could be made to each separate point and not in the suggested general way. He felt

<hr>

[28] Bismarck to GFO, Gastein, 4 September, tel. 29, GFO, IABq 133.

that in Constantinople there was the will but not the power to execute quickly all the Treaty stipulations.

Bismarck was surprised that Salisbury should find the measure 'too strong' and decided to wait: 'as long as England holds back, the demonstrations of the other powers in Constantinople would probably not be sufficiently effective'. Henceforth Bismarck became cautious and made no attempt to persuade London to adopt the proposal; he professed to understand the British position although he was clearly vexed. In a semi-official newspaper article Bismarck washed his hands of the whole affair.[29] One of the main objectives of the collective remonstrance had been to force the Turks to surrender Batum and this they suddenly did. This news is supposed to have delighted the Tsar and a more peaceful disposition spread quickly throughout Russia; the imperial government lost what little interest it had previously had in the proposed collective step. On the other hand, Russian resistance to certain aspects of the Treaty rapidly developed, and conflict with England followed. The squabbles in the Rhodope commission were only the prelude.

The next few days were occupied by Andrássy's vain advocacy of the German proposal and Shuvalov's at least partially successful quest for Austrian support. Shuvalov, Russian ambassador in London, arrived in Vienna unexpectedly on 9 September ostensibly to visit his sick brother; but he found time for conversations with Andrássy. He said that Andrássy's projected Bosnian convention with the Porte[30] contained nothing harmful to Russian interests and he even advised the annexation of Bosnia, saying that it would be in the interest of Austria as well as Russia to deprive the panslavs of any hope of using that territory for selfish purposes. Andrássy argued against immediate annexation, but said finally that in six months he hoped to achieve it. Continuing in this genial vein, he spoke of the Turks' failure to conform with the Treaty and said that, should Montenegro and Serbia have to force execution

[29] Bülow to Bismarck, 8 September, tel.; 11 September, no. 7, GFO, IABq 133; Dering to Salisbury, Berlin, 21 September, no. 541, FO 64/908; St. Vallier to Waddington, 30 October, FFM, Allemagne M & D 166.

[30] See above, p. 29.

of the frontier stipulations, he would, if necessary, give them every aid.

Shuvalov expressed his hope that this declaration would please the Tsar and promised to continue working for the amicable relations between the three empires which Russia so badly needed. [31]

Although Shuvalov insisted he had no official commission, he was surely authorized to take soundings. The Tsar wanted support for his demands on the Porte, and he was especially interested in hastening the Turkish surrender of the village of Podgorica (now Titograd) to Montenegro as stipulated by the Treaty. All he could offer in exchange was support on Bosnia, and Shuvalov seems to have made a favourable impression. Equally, Andrássy's conciliatory attitude encouraged the Russians to ask the powers to demand the immediate surrender of Podgorica. Bismarck probably felt that rapid consent would be reckoned in Livadia, the Tsar's residence, as a triumph for his friend Shuvalov. So the German ambassador in Constantinople was telegraphed to cooperate with his Austrian colleague and urge the surrender.

Andrássy was willing, he said, to press the Porte for prompt execution of the Treaty. But he still preferred the German proposal of 2 September, and would not cooperate until he had realized the futility of further pursuing it. So Bismarck had to inform Vienna of his doubts whether further pressure on Salisbury would have the desired psychological effect.

We have reason to believe that Salisbury tends to see far reaching political plans of hidden animosity against Turkey in *démarches* that are uncomfortable to or unwanted by the Porte. Considering this attitude, insistence would perhaps harm more than it would help. In addition . . . the situation has changed since the conception of our initiative for a collective *démarche*, and Salisbury's remark that he was not against the principle of such a step, but only felt it inopportune allows the matter to be taken up again in time. For the

---

[31] Reuss to Bismarck, Vienna, 12 September, no. 249 most confid., GFO, IABq 131. One month earlier Shuvalov had encouraged the extension of the Austrian occupation to Salonika. Langenau to Andrássy, Petersburg, 9 August, private and confid., WS, PA X 71. Tatishchev, ii, 533, emphasizes Andrássy's conciliatory mood. Andrássy told Elliot he had taken a stronger line. Elliot to Salisbury, Vienna, 13 & 18 September, nos. 653 confid. and 666 confid., FO 7/934.

present Prince Bismarck is against any further initiative in the mentioned direction; on the other hand, he would gladly support and recommend special Austrian wishes at the Porte. Naturally he does not consider the Porte sincere.[32]

Actually, it was not Salisbury who stood in the way of concerted pressure on the Porte. He was suspicious of Bismarck and had opposed the chancellor's initial proposal, but became rather worried that continued reserve would drive Austria into the arms of Russia. It was Disraeli who opposed Bismarck's initiative. The prime minister was 'not at all disposed to follow in his wake'; the leading role he regarded as his own. In retrospect, Salisbury's views appear to have been more statesmanlike, although he too exaggerated Bismarck's desire to take the lead and Andrássy's willingness to follow.[33] He realized, however, that if this were the case further resistance to Austrian wishes would drive the three empires closer together. British resistance to joint pressure on the Porte had in fact created a basis for the revival of the *Dreikaiserbund*; but Bismarck did not show sufficient interest, the Tsar was independent, and Austria became too suspicious of Russian policy.

During the discussions on the Podgorica *démarche* Andrássy sought backing for the convention on the occupation of Bosnia. On 18 September Berlin was asked to press the Porte to conclude the convention. In July and August Bismarck had offered generous assistance.[34] He reaffirmed goodwill, but conveyed doubt, arguing that success would bring no advantage to Austria.[35]

What were the reasons for this change of attitude? Bismarck was surely irritated by Andrássy's repeated efforts to prod him into more activity. Seeing no point in the convention tomfoolery, he probably also wanted Andrássy to follow Shuvalov's advice and annex the area. This could very well have strengthened the common aims of Austria and Russia, at least for the moment, and thus also the Three Emperors' League. And

[32] Bülow to Reuss, 21 September, no. 577, GFO, IABq 133.
[33] Buckle, vi, 372–6; Cecil, ii, 336f; *DDF*, ii, no. 343 and note; Salisbury to Elliot, 19 September, private, SP, A/23.
[34] See above, p. 29.
[35] Bülow to Reuss, 19 September, tel. 201, GFO, IABq 131.

Bismarck would have come a step nearer his ideal of a division of the Balkans into Russian and Austrian spheres which would create a certain community of interest, but also perpetuate tension between them.

Whatever the reasons may have been, further reports of serious Turkish opposition to the Austrians caused him to think again and on the 21st Vienna was told that Bismarck had only wanted to express his personal doubts on the Bosnian *démarche*; he would gladly give support if Andrássy still wanted it. He did, and corresponding instructions were at once sent to Constantinople. [36] But no attempt was made to associate Russia with this move.

After a month's time no progress on the convention had been made, but by then both Austria and Turkey were preoccupied with the vagaries of Russian diplomacy and consequently desired to avoid friction with one another. In addition, Austria had by then completed the occupation which she had hoped to facilitate by means of the convention. Further discussion lapsed.

The failure of the German initiative on 2 September had created an uncomfortable situation from which Bismarck was anxious to retire. The suggested Russian *démarche* enabled him to shift attention from himself. His subsequent actions aided cooperation between the three eastern powers. But, initially, this was surely not an end in itself because no consistent attempt was made to establish a working agreement. He consented to the Russian proposal probably thinking that Austria would naturally follow. When he learned that Austria was still hesitant and holding on to his previous suggestion for a collective *démarche*, he killed Andrássy's hopes. At the same time he timidly helped to bring about collective action by the three eastern powers, and told Andrássy he would separately further Austrian demands on the Porte.

The cooperation of Russia, Austria, and Germany on Podgorica proved that there was some life left in the *Dreikaiser-bund*. In the following days Bismarck was occupied with vague thoughts of reviving the League; a further attempt to bring about a collective *démarche* of the three empires was made. He

[36] Bülow to Reuss, 21 September, tel. 203, GFO, IABq 131.

also tried to stimulate Russia's interest in an understanding with Austria; if there was a possibility of his two neighbours coming to terms Bismarck wanted to assist so as to avoid isolation. His initiative, however, was half-hearted and abortive. When he realized this he quickly withdrew, not without some relief. The Podgorica *démarche* was the last occasion for many months on which the three empires were able to act in unison.

IV

In October most of the commissions called for by the Treaty began work and the underlying differences between the powers at once reappeared in the ensuing squabbles over details. Austria and England drew rapidly together. In the latter half of September Bismarck had apparently become interested in reviving the *Dreikaiserbund*; he made a few weak efforts in October, but then quickly retreated. By this time differences between Austria and Russia were too great, and Bismarck—not altogether displeased—attempted to maintain his reserve. Thus Germany remained the only uncertain factor in the international situation till after the beginning of the new year when she also slowly drifted away from Russia. The complexity of the situation was increased by repeated requests for support which since the Congress had come to Bismarck mainly, but not only, from Russia; this undermined a policy of reserve and his irritation mounted.

At the beginning of October, however, Germany still sided unhesitatingly with Russia in cases where the English interpretation of the Treaty was doubtful. But reports began to come into Berlin indicating serious differences between Britain and Russia and Bismarck subsequently urged on Hatzfeldt more caution and greater consideration for England. At the same time he was supporting a Russian *démarche* concerning the deplorable state of the Christian population in the evacuated areas. His precautionary warnings to Hatzfeldt were aimed not so much against Russia as simply at avoiding the impression of giving excessive backing in a critical situation, and so forfeiting English goodwill.

.   .   .

On 11 October several despatches arrived from Hatzfeldt, ambassador in Constantinople, signalizing serious tension between Russia and England. He stated that the Russians were in a confident mood and the execution of the Treaty was seriously threatened if no compromise with England could be reached. To make matters worse, he reported that the German commissioners, especially Colonel Scherff, the delegate to the Bulgarian delimitation commission, had not remained impartial owing partly to the seriousness of the situation and partly to the ambiguity of their instructions. Scherff had been told in Berlin to work quickly.[37] Dilemmas in which strict adherence to instructions involved a vote against the Russian view had evidently been unforeseen; in such cases a reserved attitude would have been appropriate.

Bismarck wanted to avoid involvement; he also feared that, if Hatzfeldt were to try to mediate between Russia and England —a role he found congenial—Germany would be blamed by the power which felt it had lost the most in the bargain. Accordingly, he tightened the reins on Hatzfeldt who was told on the 12th and 14th that Bismarck approved of cooperation with Russia and Austria when they were united, but only as long as no conflict with the others resulted. More explicitly, Hatzfeldt was informed that Berlin had an urgent interest, based on experience, in preventing Russian diplomacy from habitually expecting German support. He was therefore to maintain the greatest possible reserve towards Russian requests and forward them to Berlin. It was difficult to gauge the future of Austro-Russian relations, but there was a real possibility of a *rapprochement* on the Eastern Question. Hatzfeldt was advised to watch this but forbidden to mediate or work for such an understanding.[38]

The reference to Russian demands could be interpreted as a

---

[37] Scherff was not very fond of the Russians anyhow. See Moltke to Bismarck, Berlin, 26 January 1877, no. 155, GFO, IABi 57 secretissima. Hatzfeldt's despatches are in files GFO, IABq 108, 133, 133 secreta, 133 i and 133 iv. Müller, no. 13.

[38] Müller, pp. 79–81. On the 11th Bülow had also written to Reuss that a *rapprochement* seemed to be in the air, which Germany would gladly support. Reuss was asked to make observations on this point. Bülow to Reuss, 11 October, most confid., GFO, IABq 133 secreta.

cooling in Bismarck's attitude.[39] But the German commissioners were obliged henceforth to maintain the strictest neutrality. They were instructed not to be guided by the theoretically or technically best solution, but by the idea of maintaining good relations with all the powers—a rather unclear directive, especially for military men. Nevertheless, their reserve would aid Russia, which otherwise was often in a minority of one. Bismarck was unwilling to hasten the solution of the remaining problems if he had to force one of the powers to give ground. But he wanted neither to stimulate trouble, nor to preserve the existing state of tension. At this point he was willing to clamp down on Turkey as long as he thought none of the great powers would resist.

On the morning of the same day that the instructions mentioned above were sent to Hatzfeldt, the 14th, Bismarck spoke with his old acquaintance and Shuvalov's close friend, Greig,[40] who was passing through Berlin on his way to Paris.[41] The chancellor said that Russia had accomplished much with the war and ought to be satisfied; he did not know what plans existed, but as long as she occupied Turkish territory an understanding with Austria should be reached; the Viennese court was amenable and Andrássy, hitherto restrained by his Hungarian compatriots, would welcome the opportunity to free himself of them; such an understanding would paralyse England and put Russia at ease in the East; if no adventures were planned, everything could be arranged; but time was of the essence. He promised moral and diplomatic support to facilitate this *rapprochement*.

It is difficult to reconcile this conversation with the instructions sent to Hatzfeldt on the same day. Bismarck may have wrongly assumed that Austria and Russia were inclined to come to terms. If so, he would have preferred to take part so that they could reach no understanding without his knowledge or to the detriment of Germany. On the other hand, his enthusiastic offers of moral and diplomatic support cannot be

[39] Müller argues this, but adds that Bismarck still valued good relations with Russia, pp. 64f, 71.

[40] S. A. GREIG (1827–87). Russian minister of finance, July 1878–November 1880.

[41] C. and B. Jelavich, 'Bismarck's Proposal for the Revival of the *Dreikaiserbund*', print Greig's report of this conversation.

taken seriously. Bismarck was a greater lover of academic discussion than is generally assumed and, as Greig's report of the conversation shows, he was in an excited state. This together with a desire to magnify his own cooperativeness explains some of the contradictions.

Meanwhile, on 9 October Oubril[42] had spoken of the flight *en masse* of the Christian population with the Russian troops, whose withdrawal had therefore been suspended; he had asked Berlin to join Russia in demanding from the Porte urgent and energetic measures to restore order. Bülow agreed to make oral representations and suggest a written collective *démarche* to Vienna; he said that it was inopportune to request the participation of all the cabinets in this *démarche* since Bismarck's earlier suggestion had been coolly received.

Andrássy readily agreed to help the Tsar. This was so unexpected and unwelcome in Berlin that Bismarck insinuated that the Russian initiative was based not so much on the Berlin Treaty as on that of San Stefano.[43] He clearly found the prospect of Austro-Russian intimacy as disconcerting as the increasing Anglo-Russian tension. The mention of San Stefano was entirely unnecessary because the breach between Russia and Austria was widening. Andrássy rejected the plan for a collective note; he stressed the need to be careful with public opinion in Hungary, saying that he must avoid participation in any *démarche* fostered solely by the three eastern powers; he argued that remonstrations by all the powers would be more effective. A confidential letter from Reuss was even more explicit. He thought Andrássy had no special desire for an understanding on common interests in the East; although all questions touching Russian interests were courteously handled, Andrássy tended to identify himself with the English point of view, believing that England could be more useful than Russia. British reports fully confirmed this; the ambassador in Vienna wrote on 2 October that he had never seen Andrássy

---

[42] P. OUBRIL (OUBRI) (1820–96). Russian envoy and ambassador in Berlin, 1863–79; Vienna 1880–82.

[43] Bülow to Reuss, 16 October, no. 631, GFO, IABq 133; Elliot to Salisbury, Vienna, 12 October, no. 729, FO 7/935.

show more distrust of Russia or less inclination to follow her lead.[44]

Thus Bismarck's initiative for a formal *démarche* by the three empires collapsed. Andrássy would not cooperate because of suspicion of Russia and a growing tendency to lean on England. Domestic difficulties also caused him many headaches. There was a ministerial crisis in both Budapest and Vienna and it seemed as if almost everyone in the empire opposed his handling of the Bosnian occupation. There were even suggestions that he could be forced to resign.

In an attempt to smooth over the failure, Bülow cautiously explained that Germany had only wanted to show Austria and Russia a possible solution to their difficulties; Berlin would now wait for the proposals of the other powers. He strangely argued in favour of dropping the matter since Petersburg and Vienna were apparently seeking an understanding.[45] The truth was that neither earnestly sought a real understanding. Bismarck had made his gesture and was glad it had failed.

V

In the meantime events in the Balkans—differences in the commissions, the fugitive question, and attacks by armed bands—had produced a serious crisis. Although Germany was only indirectly involved, the crisis was not without influence on her foreign policy. On the one side the Crown Prince and the British urged a stronger line against the Russians, and on the other Petersburg pressed for a revival of the *Dreikaiserbund*.

At the beginning of November the British ambassador officially regretted that Berlin saw fit to grant Russia extensive support in the commissions; the French took a similar line. A few days earlier, on 29 October, the Crown Prince, who was deputizing for the Emperor, had written that the 'slavic committee' was openly named as the sponsor of the turmoil in

---

[44] Reuss to Bismarck, Vienna, 13 October, no. 289, GFO, IABq 133; Reuss to Bülow, 14 October, most confid., GFO, IABq 133 secreta; see correspondence in FO 7/935.

[45] Bülow to Reuss, 19 October, no. 643 most confid., GFO, IABq 133.

Bulgaria and asked if the signatories and guardians of the Berlin Treaty were not bound to express their earnest disapproval of such a breach of the peace.[46] So on 2 November the chancellor requested Bülow to prepare for the Crown Prince an extract from his dictations of the previous two years, stressing the danger of coalitions. The content was briefly that because of her own weak geographical location Germany had no interest in a lasting peace in the Near East; she was hated by her neighbours who would probably unite against her as soon as they had their hands free; a change of government in Austria could with astonishing rapidity bring Germanophobes and ultramontane elements to the helm and in their wake a *rapprochement* with France; therefore Germany must stay on good terms with the Tsar. She had, however, by rejecting every unjustified Russian demand, also been able to remain on a good footing with England and Austria, and it would be a triumph of German statecraft if the eastern sore could be kept open to frustrate the unity of the great powers and assure her own peace. Obviously, the purpose of these illuminating arguments was to convince the Crown Prince of the necessity of good relations with Russia. He was, of course, assured that all unnecessary claims on German support would be rejected.[47]

As the eastern puzzle had grown more perplexing since the summer, Bismarck's position had become more difficult. Immediately after the Congress he had felt that the Turks alone hindered the peaceful outcome of the crisis. So, desiring to win recognition as an angel of peace, he had taken a firm line with the Porte. But soon this was impossible without offending a great power. The idea of keeping the eastern sore open had then suggested itself as a means of resisting pressure to take a stand against Russia. This was, of course, no new departure: the same policy had been clearly formulated in the Kissingen dictation in June 1877[48] and followed more or less consistently since late 1876. In the first eight or nine months of 1878, however, Bismarck had in fact been afraid that the sore might

[46] Frederick William to GFO, 29 October, most confid., GFO, IABq 133 secreta; Russell to Salisbury, 3 & 23 November, private, SP, A/9.

[47] Müller, no. 18; Bülow to Frederick William, 6 November, GFO, IABq 133 secreta.

[48] *GP*, no. 294.

develop into a serious infection. He had hoped to reduce it and take the credit for applying the antidote. His reference to keeping the eastern sore open was also therefore an expression of resignation to a state of affairs which hemmed him in on all sides but could, conceivably, offer Germany a measure of security. Such an approach, however, made it increasingly difficult to support Russia. Once these ideas were put to paper they became a programme for the future—the 1878 thaw had passed. Bismarck's apparent interest in a revival of the *Dreikaiserbund* in the last part of September and at the beginning of October could not survive odd fears of an Austro-Russian *rapprochement*, or the realization that Austrian and English interests coincided and that they conflicted with those of Russia.

Meanwhile, on 4 November, Oubril read to Bülow a letter in which Giers[49] complained of the obstacles thrown in the path of Russia since the Congress. He asserted that Russian and Austrian interests no longer clashed and would profit from cooperation; since Russia wanted nothing besides the execution of the Treaty, Bismarck's initiative for a revival of good relations and the collective action of the *Dreikaiserbund* was welcome; the three empires together could guarantee adherence to the Treaty. Could not the German ambassador in Vienna be instructed to talk along these lines? Giers mentioned also that although the other members of the various commissions had gone astray, the German delegates had conducted themselves without exception in a proper and praiseworthy fashion.[50] Bülow answered that a triple understanding was always welcome, but the moment appeared ill-chosen as far as Andrássy was concerned; under more propitious circumstances German influence would be used in the desired way.[51]

Bismarck had been in the embarrassing position of being asked to support and to chastise Russia at the same time; he had refused to do either. The German chancellor was not, however, necessarily the victim of circumstance, since the

---

[49] N. K. GIERS (1820–95). Director of Asiatic department and assistant foreign minister, 1875; foreign minister, 1882–95.

[50] Müller, p. 83.

[51] Bülow to Schweinitz, 6 November, no. 650, GFO, IABq 133.

dilemma was partly his own creation. What made the situation
even more painful for him was that Giers's letter heralded the
arrival of Shuvalov in Vienna and the early return of Gorchakov who had been on leave since 10 August.

While Shuvalov was journeying from Livadia to Vienna the
eastern crisis reached a peak. Having suspended the evacuation
of her troops from the Balkans, Russia met the resistance of
Turkey, England, and Austria. War threatened. Bismarck had
become very uneasy and irritable. He had always been bothered
by requests for support and was determined more than ever to
play a passive role. Then, in addition to pressure from the
Crown Prince, Britain, and Russia, Turkey sought advice on
the question of the definitive treaty[52] with Russia, and Waddington pushed an interpretation of the question which was
unfavourable to Russia. This was the immediate background
for new instructions sent to Constantinople on 12 November.[53]
Hatzfeldt was still displaying more activity as a mediator than
suited Bismarck, so he was told to maintain the strictest reserve.
He was informed that for some years the great powers had
tried to extort German aid in questions that did not concern
her. And when Germany had resisted she was accused of dere-
liction of duty or lack of consideration. Any such imposition
must be rejected. Hatzfeldt was lectured: if one of the powers
wanted war, Berlin would deplore but not hinder it; German
relations with other powers could not be jeopardized for the
sake of peace; neutrality would be maintained when and
wherever necessary; pressure must not be exerted on a minority
or a single power; if they could not cooperate, it was not for
Germany to force them.

One can speculate about the motives behind this set of
instructions. The most probable explanation is that Bismarck,
harassed from all sides, overstated his case. Tension he wanted,
but it is unlikely that he was unperturbed by the prospect of
war. At any rate a policy of reserve was emphasized with
important results. Hatzfeldt's mediation, mostly favourable to
Russia, was restrained while the delegates in the commissions,

---

[52] See below, p. 48.

[53] Bülow to Hatzfeldt, 10 November, no. 428, GFO, IABq 133; 12 November,
no. 432, GFO, IABq 133 secreta.

inexperienced in diplomacy and far from Constantinople, acted in such a way as to emphasize Russia's isolation.

Meanwhile, Shuvalov arrived in Vienna on 10 November and then travelled to Budapest where he talked with Andrássy on the 12th and 13th. He told Reuss that Tsar Alexander wanted the revival of an understanding between the three empires and, following Bismarck's advice, had ordered him (Shuvalov) to seek agreement with Austria in Balkan matters on the basis of strict adherence to the Berlin Peace because Russia's own interest required the early evacuation of Turkey. In return Alexander hoped that Austria would allow for the difficulties which so far had hindered evacuation.[54]

Bismarck cautiously instructed Reuss to support any understanding which could be reached, but to wait until Austria requested this. 'At the moment we want to avoid the appearance of having been won by Shuvalov to help guide Austria towards Russia.' In addition, Reuss was asked to tell Shuvalov that Bismarck welcomed an agreement on this basis and would help with the necessary caution. 'The chances of an understanding seem better the more voluntary it is.'[55] But Bismarck was no longer interested in furthering Austro-Russian reconciliation. He felt that the failure of Shuvalov's mission would not be necessarily harmful because, from the Russian point of view, Bismarck's seeming support could still contrast favourably with the opposition of all the other powers. However, Bismarck had given Greig a rather unqualified promise of support. As it was the feeling at the Russian court that the Germans had been more liberal with promises than with actual aid, the chancellor's subsequent hedging was not appreciated. Bismarck's tactic of offering more aid than he was prepared to give was in the long run an added strain on Russo-German relations.[56] He was regarded as a fair-weather friend.

Judging from Shuvalov's report of his conversations with Andrássy, his mission was not so unsuccessful as both told the British. He was careful enough to tell the French that he had

---

[54] Miliutin, iii, entry for 20 October; C. & B. Jelavich, 'Bismarck's proposal for the revival of the *Dreikaiserbund*'; Reuss to GFO, Vienna, 11 November, tel. 193, GFO, IABq 133.

[55] Bülow to Reuss, 12 November, tel. 224, GFO, IABq 133.

[56] Medlicott, 'Bismarck and Beaconsfield', p. 237.

gone to Vienna for the fun of it.[57] Although Shuvalov felt that
his report would not satisfy the Tsar, he believed he had
garnered all that was obtainable. He was right on both counts.
Andrássy had stressed repeatedly and, as the Russian diplomatist thought, sincerely his desire for a revived *Dreikaiserbund*.
At the same time Andrássy clearly insisted on strict adherence
to the Treaty; he was especially interested in seeing a speedy
evacuation by the Russian forces. Besides this, he showed
understanding for Russia's predicament. He thought, though,
that a term of three or four weeks would be ample and suggested
that Russia could propose to the Porte a date for the surrender
of Podgorica, mentioning that 'Southern Rumelia' would be
simultaneously evacuated. Shuvalov was pleased with this
suggestion. On the point of the proposed Russo-Turkish peace
treaty no agreement was reached. Since the Berlin Treaty had
only regulated those aspects of the preliminary Peace of San
Stefano which were of European interest, many questions were
still open. The Russians intended to conclude a final peace
treaty as a matter of right and regarded an eventual Turkish
refusal as a breach of contract. Andrássy thought it sufficient
if the Porte would give a simple declaration of intent to fulfil its
obligations. The difference was, therefore, not insurmountably
great. If Russia had no ulterior motives, an arrangement was
possible. Shuvalov asked Bismarck's opinion. He replied that
the Berlin settlement did not exclude the principle of a final
peace treaty to replace San Stefano; the content of it was the
important matter and he believed Russia would not necessarily
seek to make it offensive to the powers.[58] But the chancellor
failed to encourage an agreement. On the fugitive problem

[57] Reuss to Bismarck, Vienna, 14 November, no. 314 most confid., GFO,
IABq 133; Salisbury to Victoria, 26 November, SP, A/20; Waddington to St.
Vallier, Paris, 23 November, no. 168, FFM, Allemagne 26; Elliot to Salisbury,
Budapest, 16 November, no. 804 most confid., *FO* 7/936. Shuvalov, of course, had
an interest in describing his talks to the Germans as favourably as possible. He and
Andrássy wanted to scatter British fears of a revived *Dreikaiserbund*. Tatishchev, ii,
533, also thinks Austria was more reserved than Reuss' reports indicate; Miliutin's
diary (iii, entry for 8–9 November) shows that Shuvalov's report was disappointing
and led to a more severe line on Turkey.

[58] Bülow also tried to allay British and French suspicions of the proposed treaty.
Russell to Salisbury, 4 December, nos. 657 and 658 secret, FO 64/910; St. Vallier
to Waddington, 14 November, private, FFM, Allemagne M & D 166.

Andrássy stood firm but was conciliatory. For him the main thing was to obtain the rapid evacuation of the Russian troops. He suggested that when this had happened one of the Balkan commissions could look into the matter. To make this more palatable Andrássy promised to urge the Porte to restore order in the troubled areas.

Thus, Andrássy was willing to cooperate, but he was not prepared to tolerate infractions of the Berlin Treaty. Although Shuvalov disclaimed any intention of departing from its stipulations, Russia wanted in reality support for a more ambitious policy, and Shuvalov's work, which could have served as a first step in the direction of a *rapprochement*, did not make an impression in Livadia.

Bismarck advised the Porte to 'deprive Russia of all excuse for delaying the evacuation', but clearly intended to maintain his reserve. He acknowledged the news from Vienna with the remark: 'Andrássy . . . wants the understanding to avoid the appearance of being influenced by us. It is at least one positive result that a revival of the understanding *à trois* would be appreciated.'[59] By the end of November Bismarck's state of agitation had subsided. His less irritated attitude was reflected in a despatch on the 25th to Hohenlohe, who was told that Germany's influence in favour of the peace was governed by the way the other powers regarded their obligations to the Treaty. 'If the powers do not wish to respect the Berlin agreements, it is not our duty to force their execution . . . We have no real interest in the question, and at most only the wish to find a way to prevent the conflict from assuming greater dimensions.' While stating the desire to let things take their course in the East, the despatch left room for the exertion of positive German influence.[60]

Bismarck's apparent belief a few weeks earlier that Russia really intended to attempt a conscientious execution of the Treaty had given way to mistrust. The Russians, who counted on Bismarck's support so much, took few pains to keep him accurately informed of their plans. When Münster reported on 3 December that Shuvalov seemed to consider himself almost

[59] H. Bismarck to Bülow, Friedrichsruh, 15 November, GFO, IABq 133.
[60] Bülow to Hohenlohe, 24 November, no. 594, GFO, IABq 133.

foreign minister and sent instructions to his colleagues, Bismarck's hopes for the success of his friend must have risen. But on the same day Schweinitz spoke with Giers who professed to give a strictly confidential account of his activities during the last three months. The German ambassador was told, among other things, that Alexander would at once withdraw his troops from the whole Balkan peninsula with the exception of the occupation army in the agreed strength when three conditions had been fulfilled: the conclusion of a definitive peace treaty, the execution of the stipulations concerning Montenegro, and the solution of the emigration question.[61] Bismarck remarked that this was neither very new nor confidential. Nevertheless, the despatch brought news of a serious departure from the Andrássy-Shuvalov talks. Shuvalov's work had collapsed and Russia had to go her own way.

The character of Russian foreign policy was vividly illustrated by the Russian chancellor himself as he travelled through Berlin at the beginning of December to resume his duties. In the presence of several members of the diplomatic corps Gorchakov attacked Károlyi,[62] the Austrian ambassador, as well as recent Austrian policy. He added that no power, including Germany, had done its duty towards Russia. They had neglected to press the Porte sufficiently. He naturally took an indignant line with Odo Russell,[63] but strangely maintained that his first efforts would be aimed at improving relations with England and hinted rather plainly that he was less concerned with Austria. It was characteristic that in audience with the Emperor he mentioned the service he had rendered Germany by maintaining the peace in 1875.[64]

Bismarck's views on the *Dreikaiserbund* in the period after Shuvalov's mission are unclear. It is conceivable that in spite

[61] Münster to Bülow, London, 3 December, most confid.; Schweinitz to Bülow, Petersburg, 4 December, no. 438 most confid., GFO, IABq 133; Russell to Salisbury, 4 December, no. 658 secret, FO 64/910.

[62] COUNT A. KÁROLYI (1825–89). Ambassador in Berlin, 1871; ambassador in London, 1879–88.

[63] ODO RUSSELL, LORD AMPTHILL (1829–84). Ambassador in Berlin, 1871–84.

[64] Bülow to Schweinitz, 18 December, no. 719, GFO, IABi 53; Russell to Salisbury, Berlin, 8 December, no. 664, FO 64/910; St. Vallier to Waddington, 10 December, private, FFM, Allemagne M & D 166.

of all the information to the contrary, he had really believed Russia and Austria more inclined to cooperate than they, in fact, were. It is hardly likely that he now laboured under this illusion. Russia had isolated herself from the western powers and Austria. Bismarck stood between the two, but was equally isolated. If in the following months he sided more with the majority against Russia, it is doubtful whether this entailed an abandonment of the idea of the *Dreikaiserbund*; but he was clearly not prepared to do much to revive it unless, as will be seen, he could dominate it. The increased tension between Germany and Russia hampered cooperation, but as long as Russia remained isolated, Bismarck had nothing much to fear and therefore made no haste to improve mutual relations. Russia would eventually come round, he thought, and then his own position would be so much the better.

Austria's relations with Russia were certainly no better than those of Germany. The only positive factor left in the *Dreikaiserbund* was the amicable relationship between Germany and Austria. It cannot be said, though, that Bismarck had so far shown Austria more consideration than Russia. On the whole he had supported Vienna more warmly, although not always very patiently. But Russia had asked for more and obtained more.

So by the end of 1878 the Three Emperors' League as a practical arrangement had almost completely disappeared. Disraeli's assertion that he had broken it up was not so far-fetched as it seems. Before and after the Congress England had helped to estrange Austria from Russia and the strong line taken with Russia made it difficult for Bismarck to balance between the two powers. It must not be forgotten, though, that the *Dreikaiserbund* was rapidly dissolving because of the divergent interests of its members. Tsar Alexander probably sincerely desired to adhere to the Treaty. He shunned armed conflict, but was determined to be firm with the Turks and so save at least some tangible achievements from his crusade to free the Balkan Christians. As the Russian troops began to withdraw, the refusal of the Turks to proceed with negotiations for a definitive peace treaty and the disorders which sprang up on all sides embarrassed him greatly and made him delay the evacuation.[65] But some of these disorders resulted from attempts by Russian agents in the Balkan peninsula to salvage what they could from the Treaty of San Stefano. Russia was willynilly pursuing aims which went beyond the treaty settlement.

Andrássy expected the Russians and Turks to adhere faithfully to the Treaty. Common opposition to the Porte tended to unite the Austrian and Russian governments in August, but a solid understanding could not be attained. Then, when the occupation of Bosnia had been completed and it was no longer necessary to press the Turks, parliamentary difficulties and simultaneous Russian obstreperousness induced Andrássy to approach England.[66]

Although Bismarck still favoured the *Dreikaiserbund* after the Congress, he failed to breathe life into it in the first weeks when Austria and Russia might have been able to come to terms. After returning to Berlin in mid-September he attempted to revive the League, but the steadily worsening situation in the Balkans made him cautious. He did not wish to sacrifice English friendship for a strengthened *Dreikaiserbund*, nor would it have been easy to reconcile Russia and Austria. And, if he could not dominate the resultant alignment, he felt that there was always the danger that his two partners could become too intimate. So he retired into the background. This dealt the death blow to the dying Three Emperors' League. At the same time Bismarck led a bitter press campaign against Gorchakov and his foreign policy. In private conversations his criticism of the Russian chancellor was as unstinting as his praise of Shuvalov. This achieved nothing except a marked cooling in the relations of the two empires.

After the Congress England and Austria had to bear the brunt of Russian ill will. And although the Russian government and press were sparing of recognition for German aid and not otherwise especially friendly, the press campaign against Germany did not reach serious dimensions until the beginning

[65] Viel-Castel to Waddington, Petersburg, 21 November, no. 72, FFM, Russie 257; Salisbury to Loftus, 11 December, private, SP, A/31; Seton-Watson, p. 534; Tatishchev, ii, 514–20. Medlicott writes that Russia had no intention of departing from even the letter of the Treaty on the broader issues of the Balkan settlement, *Congress*, pp. 186f.

[66] Cf. Elliot to Salisbury, Vienna, 12 December, no. 853 confid., FO 7/937.

of 1879. The immediate causes were not connected solely with the Berlin settlement, but Bismarck's activity in the autumn of 1878 had strengthened the mistrust of Germany. There was more than a grain of truth in Salisbury's facetious remark: 'If there is a *Dreikaiserbund*, is there a *Dreikanzlerbund*?'[67]

[67] Salisbury to Russell, 1 January 1879, private, SP, A/27.

CHAPTER II

The Source of a New Orientation

Towards the end of 1878 Bismarck adopted an increasingly passive attitude towards the main problems of the renewed eastern crisis. Throughout 1879 he attempted to maintain this relative disengagement which provided the freedom needed for handling two problems. Although the other powers were involved in these merely peripherally, the effect on the international situation was profound. The more important of the two was that of the future of Russo-German relations. The essential issue was Russian 'ingratitude' for German diplomatic support during the eastern crisis and the Congress of Berlin and the subsequent cooling of relations between the two neighbours. The manifestation of this was the struggle for diplomatic supremacy between Gorchakov and Bismarck—the 'two chancellors' war'—which reached a climax in the following months. It was in fact much more a political than a personal struggle, but the personal side added a note of bitterness and intensity which made it more difficult for either to give in, thus forcing both to go further than intended.

If the 'two chancellors' war' was the salient feature in the relations between Germany and Russia from the summer of 1878 to the spring of 1880, it was Bismarck's Rumanian policy which mainly coloured his relations with the western powers. A detailed study of his Rumanian policy in this period is interesting primarily for three reasons. It sheds light on Bismarck's tactics and his relations with the western powers, and, as the first determined effort of the German government to give political support to German capital in other countries, it is an important symptom of the chancellor's renunciation of economic liberalism, and perhaps the largest of the initial, unwitting steps on the road to imperialism.

I. BISMARCK, BLEICHROEDER, AND THE RUMANIAN RAILWAYS

It has often been pointed out that Germany had little material interest in near-eastern affairs, but there was perhaps more German capital invested in the Rumanian railways than in any other project beyond the imperial frontiers. The greater part of the railway system was owned by a company controlled by the bankers Hansemann and Bleichroeder. They were the heirs of Strousberg's risky venture which had only been made possible by support of highly placed personages who enabled him to attract the savings of thousands from all classes of German society. Strousberg's consortium collapsed in December 1870.[1] Ever since then the relations between the company and the Rumanian government had been particularly bad and protracted negotiations had been going on for the sale of the railway to Rumania. Both sides had been manœuvring for the better bargain. Although Rumania was more unscrupulous, the German company was also well versed in chicanery. Bismarck had originally obtained the support of Bleichroeder and Hansemann and was determined to see the problem solved in a manner suitable to them.[2] Thus began the elusive partnership which was to figure so prominently in the colonial movement of the eighties.

It is difficult to estimate the extent of Bleichroeder's personal influence on the formation of German policy on Rumania and, therefore, indirectly on German relations with other countries. On several occasions his correspondence undeniably precipitated government action; the role played by the chancellor's banker probably went beyond that of a simple catalysing agent, but, unfortunately, one cannot say for sure.[3]

[1] A. VON HANSEMANN (1826–96). Head of Diskonto-Gesellschaft. B. H. STROUSBERG (1823–84). Financier and railway builder. For this section consult Medlicott, 'Recognition'; Meisel, pp. 1–30; Aus dem Leben, iv, 86–153.

[2] Radowitz, i, 189–241; Aus dem Leben, ii–iv, passim; Radowitz to Bismarck, Pera, 3 December 1871, no. 113; 21 December 1871, tel. 35; Bismarck to German ambassadors, 21 December 1871, tels.; Bismarck to Bernstorff, 24 December 1871, no. 184; Thielau to GFO, Bucharest, 25 December 1871, tel. 23; Bülow to William, 26 October 1877; Bülow to H. Bismarck, 1 November 1877, no. 37, GFO, IABq 104.

[3] See Leven, i, 212f; Hohenlohe, ii, 235; and Stern, pp. 37–46.

From the beginning of the dispute Bismarck had repeatedly used the lever of the Sultan's suzerainty and the intervention of the powers to pry concessions from the Rumanians who longed for formal independence.[4] Early in 1877 Alvensleben, the consul-general in Bucharest, was reminded to pay more attention to the railway, which, because of the German capital invested in it, was almost more important than political affairs.[5]

The importance of the railway question in the eyes of the German foreign office was soon to exceed that of general politics. In May 1877 Bucharest was told that the future of relations between the two countries would depend on the solution of this dispute. To allow no room for misunderstandings on the question of independence, Bismarck pontificated about the principle of *do ut des* and snorted that he could differentiate between friend and foe. In February 1878 Bleichroeder's complaints precipitated another step. Alvensleben was instructed to inform the Rumanian government that further injury to the railway company would not be accepted with indifference. He was to state: the unjust treatment of the company has created the impression that Rumania is bent on damaging German capital, and lacks, therefore, the trustworthiness which an independent state needs in international relations; it is questionable whether the recognition of independence and the abolition of a protective power, to which complaints may be made, are compatible with German interests.[6] Since on these occasions Rumania was pressing for support against Russia, the initiatives were well timed. But Alvensleben considered Bleichroeder's judgment of the situation too harsh and believed the Rumanian ministry would come to an understanding on all the points in dispute; further pressure, he thought, could be self-defeating. Bismarck remained suspicious, but agreed to let the matter drop.

[4] Radowitz, i, 230, 233; *Aus dem Leben*, ii, 208, 230f; N. Iorga, no. 224.

[5] F. J. COUNT VON ALVENSLEBEN (1836–1913). Consul-general in Bucharest, 1876–80; *chargé* in Petersburg, April to June 1879; envoy to Darmstadt, 1879–82; in The Hague, 1882; Washington, 1884; Brussels, 1886–1901; ambassador in Petersburg, 1901–05. Bülow to Alvensleben, 16 January 1877, no. 12, GFO, IABq 104. This despatch was occasioned by Bleichroeder's complaints.

[6] Bülow to Alvensleben, 17 & 22 May, 25 June 1877, nos. 107, 109, 128; 25 February and 2 March 1878, nos. 48 and 56; Alvensleben to Bülow, Bucharest, 24 May 1877, no. 143, GFO, IABq 104; Iorga, nos. 471 and 474.

Clearly, in 1877 the chancellor had already threatened the Rumanians with a refusal to recognize their independence unless they proved conciliatory in the railway question. The optimism of Alvensleben prevented the threat being repeated early in 1878, and during the next twenty-one months Bismarck did not again quite so openly link the two issues. Initially, the conclusion of a commercial convention had been shelved as a means of pressure in the railway question, but this partially successful tactic was abandoned on the understanding that the threat to refuse recognition of independence would be more effective.[7]

Until the Treaty of Berlin had been signed Bismarck was occupied with other problems and had no time for the railways. In the weeks after the Congress he was anxious to get away from near-eastern difficulties and, consequently, let things slide. His absence from Berlin and his inattentiveness in the Rumanian question lost him ground which he later regretted. The Congress act changed the political situation and made it desirable to abandon the explicit connection between the railway question and the recognition of independence. The Congress had made recognition dependent upon the emancipation of the Jews, a provision which had found much sympathy in England, France and Italy. Since it was unlikely that Rumania would willingly fulfil this condition, Bismarck could in the future push the Jewish question in the foreground as long as the railway quarrel lasted, thus indirectly securing western support for German interests. The western powers were in the dark for some time as to the real reasons for Bismarck's stubborn insistence on fulfilment of the Treaty clauses (article XLIV) concerning Jewish emancipation.

Berlin's interest in the fate of the Rumanian Jews was not wholly humanitarian. The railway company was controlled by the great Jewish banking houses of Bleichroeder and

---

[7] Alvensleben to Bülow, Bucharest, 5 & 12 March 1878, nos. 57 and 60; Bülow to Alvensleben, 26 September 1877, no. 234; 12 March 1878, no. 60, GFO, IABq 104; Bülow to Alvensleben, 2 December 1876; 19 April 1877; Bülow, 22 December 1876, memorandum, DZA, AA 10249; Reichardt, 23 June 1877, note; Bülow to Bismarck, 7 November 1877; Bülow to Hoffmann, 12 November 1877, DZA, AA 10250; H. Bismarck to Bülow, Friedrichsruh, 30 September 1877, FA, B–25; Böhme, p. 463.

Hansemann and many of the company's employees were Jews enjoying imperial protection. During the debates on the commercial convention with Rumania in late 1877 Bismarck had promised to secure equal rights for everyone under German protection in Rumania. The *Reichstag* had not yet ratified the convention.[8] Thus Germany had a material interest in both the emancipation and railway issues.[9]

A few days after the conclusion of the Congress the Rumanian government inquired whether the great powers would exchange ministers as diplomatic representatives. And at the end of September Prince Charles[10] asked for approval of his new title of 'Royal Highness'. Until the beginning of October the cabinets discussed these attributes of Rumanian independence without seriously stressing the necessity for the execution of the Treaty. Germany played an almost completely passive role. Austria, Russia and Turkey had little cause to withhold recognition. So the Rumanians could well afford to continue their dilatory policy which seemed to succeed.

On 2 October Bülow mentioned for the first time since the Congress that the execution of the Treaty was a condition of Rumanian independence. When Bleichroeder complained to Bülow on 4 October that the Rumanian government was tormenting the Jews, a stand on the question was finally taken. It was decided that the discussions on the exchange of ministers and the new title of the Prince could in no way facilitate recognition, which was dependent on the prior execution of the Treaty. Berlin felt that in this respect the Rumanian government had not only been completely idle, it had taken it upon itself to vex the Jews. Moreover, consideration for German public opinion was enough to oblige the government not to rush into recognition.[11]

It was Bleichroeder's complaint which had brought the

[8] Russell to Salisbury, Berlin, 8 March 1879, no. 152 secret, FO 64/932; Taffs, pp. 302f.

[9] But see Winckler, 'Bismarcks Rumänienpolitik', p. 63.

[10] E. F. Z. L. VON HOHENZOLLERN-SIGMARINGEN (1839–1914). Prince Charles of Rumania, 1866–81; King, 1881–1914. In this chapter no reference will be made to the routine correspondence on Rumania in GFO, IABq 24 and IABq 133 ix.

[11] Bleichroeder to Bülow, Berlin, 4 October, GFO, IABq 133 ix; Bülow to German ambassadors, 6 October; Bülow to Crown Prince, 2 October, GFO, IABq 24; Kogalniceanu, i, 596, 610ff.

German government out of its lethargy and from this point on the Germans were to press vigorously for the execution of the Treaty. As a first, entirely unnecessary, step Bleichroeder was asked to remind the French government of its obligations towards the Rumanian Jews.[12] When towards the end of October the Rumanian government asked for formal recognition, declaring that a constituent assembly would be called to regulate the emancipation question, Bülow insisted on prior emancipation and the establishment of complete religious equality. He personally thought the Rumanians were not inclined to make concessions to the Jews, but that they wished to obtain independence 'piecemeal' in order to avoid fulfilment of their obligations.[13]

Bismarck hoped for French, English, and perhaps Italian support against Rumania. He also thought Austria might demonstrate greater reserve. But the German cabinet had held back its views too long, for meanwhile Austria had recognized Rumania as an independent state. Since Rumanian goodwill would be handy in a confrontation with Russia, Andrássy had wanted to recognize from the beginning. Still, if Bismarck had pressed the matter earlier, Andrássy could not easily have avoided cooperation. Russia also would have been in less of a hurry. Gorchakov had not wanted to recognize Rumania before she fulfilled her obligations. Giers and Miliutin,[14] however, desired better relations with Rumania, and, following Andrássy's lead, they recognized the country.

The Italians wanted to follow suit, but a few days later they decided to wait for satisfactory explanations from the Rumanians before the newly designated minister presented his credentials. In the interlude the German ambassador was instructed to express official regrets that Italy was about to disregard a stipulation of the Treaty of Berlin which she had not only

[12] Leven, i, 284f, prints two letters from Bleichroeder to the *Alliance Israélite* in Paris. The first is dated mid-September, the second 18 September, but internal and external evidence suggests that the letters were actually written in October. Winckler, 'Bismarcks Rumänienpolitik', pp. 7of. Lyons to Salisbury, Paris, 1 November, private, SP, A/7; Mouy to Waddington, 4 October, no. 156, FFM, Allemagne 25.

[13] Bülow to Crown Prince, 27 October, GFO, IABq 24.

[14] D. A. MILIUTIN (1816–1912). Russian minister of war, 1862–81.

approved but attempted to make more stringent; he was to explain that because of sympathy for the Rumanian sovereign Germany would have had more reason for leniency than any other great power, but the German government had felt obliged to insist on execution of the Treaty before independence, as otherwise the evasion of the Treaty would be encouraged and the legal inequality of German nationals in Rumania made more difficult to remedy.[15] Bismarck was to use the warning against breach of contract consistently to keep Italy, England and France in line. These powers realized soon enough that he had ulterior motives, but were not quite sure what.[16]

Meanwhile the tension got the better of Bismarck. On 12 November he complained bitterly about the efforts of the powers to obtain support in matters which were no German concern. The issue of Rumanian independence was cited as an example of their unwillingness to insist on strict enforcement of the Treaty. Italy's behaviour was especially criticized; he openly complained of Italian treason and desertion. Rome had to play the unfortunate role of whipping boy. Some of the wrath Bismarck subsequently directed southwards was caused by the conduct of Russia and Austria, to whom, however, he would have to use more guarded language. He compared their attitude to that of two bidders at an auction with legitimate interests in the object for sale. Italy he consistently regarded as an intruder whose bidding would artificially raise the price for no reason except to please the Rumanians.[17]

Besides reprimanding the powers, the German cabinet continued to urge the Bucharest government to regulate the railway question and execute the Treaty loyally in order to obtain recognition. On 16 December, as a result of this hint, the Rumanian ministry decided to renew negotiations with the Berlin bankers on the purchase of the railway.

Bismarck's general nervousness at the beginning of November

[15] Bülow to Keudell, 8 November, no. 563, GFO, IABq 24.
[16] Salisbury to Lyons, 6 March 1879, private and confid., SP, A/26.
[17] Bülow to German ambassadors, 12 November, GFO, IABq 24. A letter from Bleichroeder complaining of the lot of the Rumanian Jews precipitated this despatch. St. Vallier to Waddington, 11 November, no. 190 confid., FFM, Allemagne 26; see also above Chapter I, v.

and his feeling that others were merely trying to use him can be additionally illustrated by his somewhat readjusted views on the Greek border dispute. The Congress had recommended to the Porte the cession of a sizable strip of territory. The other powers reserved the right of mediation in case of disagreement between the two countries.

Towards the end of September Waddington suggested multilateral cooperation to obtain from the Porte acknowledgement of the principle of a border rectification. He had championed the Greek cause at the Congress and despatched a squadron to Greek waters, but his enthusiasm had waned and he offered Bismarck the lead. After the failure of the *démarche* of 2 September the German cabinet had declared its reserve, so Bismarck hedged saying that with this step Germany had fulfilled her obligation as presiding power, but had complete trust in French leadership and would further the suggestion as much as possible.[18] Before a month had passed he was to regret this generous offer.

The French circular on Greece (21 October) asked for an identic and simultaneous communication to obtain the Porte's assent to both the principle of a border rectification and the actual appointment of commissioners to negotiate with the Greeks. Fearing resistance from England and Russia, Waddington wanted to be able to refer to previous German consent when recommending his proposal to the others. He asked whether Germany could support the suggestion in Petersburg. Bismarck purred like a kitten to the French, but to his colleagues he protested that he was not prepared to write circulars *à deux* with France; however, since the principle of a territorial regulation was part of the Berlin Treaty, he agreed to help.[19] The suggested recommendation in Russia was irksome. Bismarck certainly had this in mind when complaining some days later of the attempts by the powers to use Germany for their own purposes.

In reply to a query by the Crown Prince, who favoured the

[18] H. Bismarck to Bülow, Varzin, 25 September; Bülow to Wesdehlen, 5 October, no. 498, GFO, IABq 133 viii.

[19] Bülow to Bismarck, 28 October, no. 1; H. Bismarck to Bülow, Friedrichsruh, 29 October, GFO, IABq 133 viii; St. Vallier to Waddington, 3 November, private, FFM, Allemagne M & D 166; *DDF*, ii, nos. 357–8.

Greeks, as to what should be done in case the step miscarried, Bismarck defined his policy more closely. He argued that Germany had reserved her freedom of action for the future, but would continue to follow the French lead—partly because of the thing in itself and partly because the peace would be more secure if the attention of France could be diverted from Alsace-Lorraine; it would be wise to give moderate support to this French inclination, thus offering France and Europe proof that Germany was a friendly neighbour in all matters which did not jeopardize her own security.[20] Bismarck hardly wished the French much success; he merely desired to see them busily doctoring the reopened near-eastern 'sore'. Another reason for favourably regarding the French views on Greece was to provide an equivalent for support on Rumania.[21]

Thus, Bismarck's support for far-flung French aspirations was, initially, mainly a tactical manœuvre which enabled him to remain reserved, while verbally demonstrating goodwill for France. Then, he suddenly realized the advantages which French preoccupation with the Greek border dispute offered. In the following months the situation changed rapidly. The increasing tension between Germany and Russia as well as the stubbornness of the Rumanians forced Bismarck out of his reserve. Consequently, the role of France became more important and Bismarck's casual tactic was developed into a consistent policy.[22]

Meanwhile, towards the end of October Salisbury grew restless and wanted to hasten the recognition of Rumania. He was concerned about the willingness of the Russians to evacuate the peninsula in the coming spring. From his point of view this was the main obstacle to the execution of the Treaty. Recently he had learned that the Russians were attempting to secure an extension of the time limit set for their right of way through the Dobrogea and were strengthening the fortifications of the mouths of the Danube. He was willing to sacrifice the clauses

[20] Bülow to Frederick William, 10 November, GFO, IABq 133 viii; Pasetti to Haymerle, Berlin, 8 July 1880, private, WS, PA III 121.

[21] DDF, ii, nos. 360–1; cf., Winckler, 'Bismarcks Rumänienpolitik', p. 74; and 'Aufhebung des Artikels V', p. 491.

[22] This discussion is continued below, p. 102.

concerning Jewish emancipation in order to keep Rumania out of the arms of Russia.

England now replaced Italy as the object of Bismarck's indignation. Münster, the ambassador in London, was immediately instructed to repeat the reasons for withholding recognition and to argue that the clauses on Jewish emancipation were based on humanitarian, not political, considerations. Bismarck added that Germany had been exhorted from all sides to insist on execution of the Treaty in those cases where she was not bound to fulfil any part of it herself, but rather to check the performance of others; England certainly should not ask Germany to serve as an example of noncompliance in one of the few cases where she was to cooperate actively in the execution of the Treaty.[23] Then, a few days later, when Bismarck thought that Italy was also on the verge of recognition, he took a stand which amply illustrates the importance he attached to the question. He informed the German ambassadors that those powers who opportunistically dissociated themselves from the Treaty could no longer expect Germany to show further interest in its execution.[24]

Meanwhile the question suddenly lost its immediacy. On 24 November the Russians denied any intention of demanding further military concessions from Rumania. With this Salisbury's main worry disappeared and he became more ready to postpone recognition. The piece was over, but there was a rather strident postlude. Bülow wrote to Münster that although he was glad to see that Salisbury had returned to his original position, he would not so easily forget the incident. It seemed that the English had not displayed quite the consideration due to an international agreement of such importance. While England had requested support in Petersburg on various questions concerning the Treaty, the astonishing discovery had been made that she was prepared opportunistically to renounce the clear and unambiguous obligations of the Treaty, whose execution the German government valued solely in the interest

[23] Münster to GFO, London, 12 November, tel. no. 219; Bülow to Münster, 13 November, tel. no. 160, GFO, IABq 133 ix; Russell to Salisbury, 16 November, private, SP, A/9.

[24] Bülow to German ambassadors, 25 November, GFO, IABq 24; Russell to Salisbury, 22 November, no. 632 confid., FO 64/910.

of humanity. Münster was asked to express these sentiments in London and to display a certain amount of sensitivity.[25] This incident shows that the question of Rumanian independence had rapidly become prominent in Bismarck's foreign policy. It became, in fact, too important, and by February 1879 he was anxious to terminate the affair.

Until the end of 1878 the involved Rumanian question had brought Bismarck nothing but trouble and disappointment. Just after the Congress he had failed to make known his conditions for recognition. Then after three states had taken this step and England and Italy wanted to, he became indignant and stubborn. German relations with these two countries became strained. Waddington's firm stand beside the chancellor was the only positive factor. German support for France in the Greek border dispute had certainly helped to keep the French foreign minister toeing the line. Bismarck saw the connection between the two questions at an early date; and after hinting at this to the French in November, he openly admitted it by the middle of 1879, stating that support for initiatives in the Greek dispute would be linked to French support for the German views on Rumania.

It must be remembered that one of the main reasons for Bismarck's nervousness at the beginning of November 1878 was the pressure from various sides to take a stand against Russia, which he refused to do. Still, the Rumanian question did not improve Russo-German relations. In general, but for different reasons, Germany and Russia were united in mutual disregard for Rumanian feelings, but just as Bismarck hardly appreciated Russia's early recognition, so Russia could not approve of the emphasis on Jewish emancipation, since her own Jews were unfree.

Another unfortunate factor in German-Russian relations complicated the matter considerably. The international delimitation commission for Bulgaria had reached a deadlock on the point of departure towards the south-east of the Rumanian-Bulgarian border east of Silistria, a town on the right bank of the Danube. The German delegate, Colonel Scherff, had rather prominently opposed the Russians in this

[25] Bülow to Münster, 27 November, no. 625, GFO, IABq 24.

affair. Bismarck was greatly annoyed and Scherff was reprimanded. Although his instructions were rather vague, it was clear enough that he was supposed to maintain his reserve, which he repeatedly forgot.[26] If the British were puzzled by his conduct, the Russians were exasperated, believing, quite naturally, that he was acting on instructions.

Thus, questions involving Rumania had strained Bismarck's relations with Russia as well as with England and Italy and made him more dependent on Waddington's goodwill. In the following year Bismarck certainly regretted the gulf created between him and the other powers over this problem and would have liked to see it bridged. Yet he chose not to construct the bridge himself, but to depend more and more on cooperation with Austria.

2. THE ORIGINS OF THE 'TWO CHANCELLORS' WAR'

The other, more important, determining factor in Bismarck's foreign policy in 1879 was his struggle to undermine Gorchakov's position as foreign minister.[27]

Bismarck and Gorchakov first met at the Frankfurt diet of the German Confederation as representatives of their governments. Gorchakov, who was also accredited in Stuttgart, was seldom in Frankfurt except when serious trouble arose between Austria and Prussia. Then he attempted to mediate, often in a manner favourable to Austria. Bismarck, apparently, did not appreciate his activity; he regarded the Russian minister, his senior by seventeen years, as gifted and amiable, but clownish —'a fox in wooden shoes'. Gorchakov was, he thought, a mediocre diplomat who would not advance beyond the rank of envoy.

As a young man Gorchakov had been very promising; in the 1820s and 1830s he had occupied important positions in London, Berlin, and Vienna. There seem to be two reasons why he had not advanced beyond Stuttgart and Frankfurt by

[26] See above, p. 40 and correspondence in GFO, IABq 133 i; Salisbury to Russell, London, 1 January 1879, private, SP, A/27.

[27] The references for the first part of this section are in my essay 'Bismarck and Gorchakov'.

the early 1850s. First, he had been on bad terms with Nesselrode ever since he entered the diplomatic service. This was due partly to the rivalry between his protector, Capo d'Istria, and Nesselrode,[28] but perhaps mainly to his own tactlessness and anti-Austrian line. While at the Vienna embassy Gorchakov vigorously challenged his government's pro-Austrian policy. He had also been indirectly implicated in the Decembrist plot, a circumstance which Nicholas I could never forget. It is said that in the files of the third section alongside his name there was the remark: not without ability, but does not love Russia. Gorchakov's advancement had therefore depended on the disappearance of his two mighty opponents.

In 1859 when Bismarck was sent as Prussian envoy to Petersburg his old acquaintance was already firmly installed as foreign minister, a position which gave much more scope to a statesman with Gorchakov's gifts. Bismarck now saw him differently—less clownish and more competent and adroit.

Throughout his long term as foreign minister Gorchakov liked to deal with promising young members of the diplomatic corps. He patronized them, sometimes giving kindly advice in eloquent monologues, and sometimes scolding and chiding them. He was generally repaid with admiration for his intelligence and dexterity. In 1859 Bismarck was his grateful protégé. For many years afterwards Gorchakov regarded Bismarck as his most promising pupil, but only as Raphael could be considered Perugino's pupil, as he later magnanimously put it. Bismarck accepted his role, initially out of gratitude, later out of calculation.

There is little wonder that Gorchakov and Bismarck could get along well together. They had much in common. They both had extremely fertile minds and wide-ranging knowledge. Conscious of such gifts, these two self-confident and vain men made every effort to display them. Gorchakov and Bismarck wrote polished prose and talked well, almost compulsively; neither was a good listener. Essentially sensitive and volatile, both could be charming or devastating, just as they chose.

---

[28] K. V. COUNT VON NESSELRODE (1780–1862). Foreign minister, 1816–56; chancellor, 1845. JOHN CAPO D'ISTRIA (1776–1831). Secretary of state for foreign affairs, 1815—22; president of Greece, 1827.

Bismarck had greater will-power and energy; Gorchakov, the courtier, was less determined, but he was not so weak as some historians have thought. In an attempt to appear as a loyal servant of his master, he likened himself to a sponge which when squeezed by the hand of the Tsar yielded the liquid with which it was filled. But in fact he was remarkably independent and persistent. He was merely more supple than Bismarck, and his methods were more devious.

As statesmen, the Prussian *Junker* and the Russian *grand seigneur* owed much to the cabinet diplomacy of the eighteenth century. They were practitioners of *raison d'état*. Their policy was guided by the welfare of the state, rather than that of the nation or even the monarchy. They were, of course, monarchical and conservative, but if reason of state required, they did not hesitate to oppose the conservative sentimentality of their masters. Both also wished to restrain the aggressiveness of the generals and the military party.

As cabinet statesmen, Gorchakov and Bismarck concerned themselves mainly with the activity of other cabinets. For both the role of personalities with their likes and dislikes was extremely important. Political opponents were personal enemies who should be defeated or replaced at all costs. Neither fully realized that the days had passed when personal feuds could be fought between cabinet statesmen without having any important long term effects on the policy of the states involved.

Gorchakov and Bismarck took a short term view of diplomacy; they regarded it as a series of manœuvres on constantly shifting terrain. Any combination was theoretically possible. That is why both were as much concerned with keeping the rest of Europe in a state of 'balanced tensions'[29] as they were with winning friends and allies for themselves. This meant that allies should not be allowed to become too friendly with one another, or with anyone else. In order to insure the preservation of a healthy state of tension, both Gorchakov and Bismarck had to indulge in involved and not dissimilar tactics. Allies were encouraged to cooperate with one another when they were not inclined to do so; but, when they seemed to be too friendly, support was withdrawn and friction stimulated.

[29] Medlicott, *Bismarck, Gladstone*, p. 41.

Gorchakov and Bismarck were conservative cabinet statesmen at the dawn of a new age: both perceived the revolutionary
trends of nationalism and liberalism—if not their ultimate
consequences—and attempted to use them for their own ends.
But, inevitably perhaps, they were only partly successful. For
both statesmen 1848, its aftermath, and the Crimean War
were the decisive influences in the formation of their own
particular kind of *raison d'état*—essentially a development of
eighteenth-century diplomacy which sought to use, but not to
make, important concessions to the rising current of nationalism. Both felt their states had been humiliated by their natural
ally against revolution, the Austria of Schwarzenberg and Buol.
In reaction to this both adopted an approach to statecraft
similar to that of Schwarzenberg and used it against Austria.
Thus the wave of political realism after 1848 became a tide
which neither Bismarck nor Gorchakov had turned, but both
helped to swell.

Both statesmen were well acquainted with the culture of the
most important European states; neither was much interested
in or concerned with the non-European world. From a political
point of view, Europe for them was little more than the field
on which balance of power diplomacy was carried out. Nevertheless, they were both 'European' statesmen, not in the sense
that they were willing to make sacrifices for some ideal of
European harmony or unity, but rather in their belief that the
ambitions of the several states were strictly limited by the vital
interests of the others. This concept of Europe was widely
different from, for instance, Peter Shuvalov's conservative
European ideal, or the liberal and cosmopolitan Europe of
which Gladstone dreamed. Both Bismarck and Gorchakov
talked of conservative solidarity when it was advantageous to
do so, but when their own interests or those of their states
required an alliance with the revolutionary forces of the day,
they were among the first to advocate it. Gorchakov's repeated
invocation of 'Europe' and Bismarck's oft quoted rebuttal, 'qui
parle Europe a tort; notion géographique', have tended to
obscure this basic similarity. In this respect the essential difference between the two was their attitude towards a congress,
the incorporation of the 'Concert of Europe'. Gorchakov was a

warm advocate of the 'congress' idea for practical reasons, that is, to prevent other states from increasing their power, or to sanction changes he had already made. Bismarck opposed congresses; he felt that, if necessary, concerted action could be achieved by other, less showy, but more effective means. Thus, even regarding the idea of a European congress Bismarck and Gorchakov (except for the last few years of his career) were guided primarily by practical considerations. In this respect Bismarck was outspoken enough, but behind Gorchakov's illusive eloquence was a similarly practical approach.[30]

How can one explain the subsequent quarrel between these two evidently very close and in many ways quite similar statesmen?

Initially *raison d'état* suggested cooperation, but later the cooling of Russo-Prussian relations. As long as cooperation was mutually beneficial, the bonds of trust and friendship were strong enough to withstand easily several minor disagreements. Even after 1866 when the mutual advantages of continued cooperation became increasingly problematical, friendship was formally maintained, but as Russo–German rivalry began to develop their relationship became based on calculation. Ostensibly cordial personal relations were maintained on this level throughout the early 1870s in spite of repeated signs of opposition in the material interests of Russia and Germany.

In 1875 the cordiality came to an abrupt end, and shortly thereafter, the feud started. There were several reasons for this. In the late sixties and early seventies Gorchakov had abundantly shown his dislike of the rapid extension of Prussian power and was sceptical about any further conquests; he also strongly disapproved of the liberal trend in Bismarck's domestic policy which, he thought, endangered the monarchical principle. Bismarck strove to secure continued cooperation by the use of flattery (but not always tact), the emphasis on the conservative character of Germany, and by the promise of support for Russian ambitions in the East. This presupposed a *quid pro quo* in the West. These efforts culminated in the Radowitz mission at the beginning of 1875. A new method, that of indirect intimidation, was tried in the 'war-in-sight' crisis which was the

[30] For Bismarck and Europe see Schieder; Novotny, 'Berliner Kongress'.

result of the relative failure of Radowitz's mission. The desire to force Gorchakov to take sides against France was probably one of the reasons for provoking this crisis, but just the opposite happened.

Some of Gorchakov's personal motives for the role he played in this episode have often been stressed, but both he and Alexander had good political reasons for wanting to show Bismarck that he had gone too far. They were worried that he might do something rash; even Bismarck's friend Shuvalov thought that he was a little out of his mind at the time. Gorchakov realized that a powerful Germany could be a valuable ally and a counterweight to Austria and France, but any further aggrandizement would threaten Russia. This is why in Berlin in 1872 and 1875 he spoke out firmly for France, not because he was pro-French, but because he was Russian, a fact he loved to stress.

Bismarck was, of course, extremely upset by the intervention, and especially by the manner in which it was carried out. He was disappointed because his gamble had failed; still, neither the substance of the Russian position nor Gorchakov's attitude can have surprised him since 'friendship' between the two statesmen had for some time been largely formal. Beneath the surface of cordial relations, there had been considerable tension. Alexander's antagonism may very well have disturbed him more because in the past he had attempted to circumvent Gorchakov by appealing directly to the Tsar, recalling the traditional friendship of the two monarchs and the need for conservative solidarity, an indirect thrust at the Russian chancellor, who, incidentally, used the same tactics on him. At any rate, Bismarck did not immediately begin to show great irritation about Gorchakov's intervention. If it had not been for other factors, the 'war-in-sight' crisis might very well never have marked a turning-point in Russo-German relations. What were these things?

Shortly after the 'war-in-sight' alarm the eastern crisis of 1875–8 broke. It is interesting to note that Bismarck did not begin to show consistent signs of irritation about Gorchakov's role in the spring of 1875 until Russia was obviously becoming involved in Balkan affairs. In his countless stories about the episode the role he assigned to Gorchakov gradually assumed larger proportions, reaching its most extreme form by 1878.

Before 1871 it was in the interest of both countries to cooperate closely with one another because both hoped to alter the international *status quo*. Between 1871 and 1875 neither had ambitious schemes, but, owing to the strain on relations with France caused by the annexation of Alsace-Lorraine, Bismarck needed Russian support more than Russia needed his. That is why the suspicious Gorchakov could take a firm line, whereas Bismarck was on the defensive. Towards the end of 1875 the situation was reversed. Bismarck, remembering Gorchakov's activity not only in 1875 but in the whole period since 1866, was determined to give as little as possible unless Russia agreed at least to guarantee Alsace-Lorraine, that is, to accept German ascendency. Gorchakov would ideally have liked the re-establishment of German dualism; he was unwilling to make a concession which, he thought, was not in Russian interests. The more Russia became involved in the Balkan crisis the better was Bismarck's bargaining position, but Gorchakov refused to give way. Thus began another, unique, phase in the age-old struggle for European hegemony; it was the last of such battles waged as a feud between cabinet statesmen.

Why did this political struggle lead quickly to a bitter personal feud between Gorchakov and Bismarck? Part of the answer can be found in the manner in which Gorchakov used his relatively advantageous position between 1866 and 1875. Up to a point his policy was justified, but Bismarck felt personally injured just the same.

The role played by Peter Shuvalov explains much. He was a hard-headed, conservative Russian statesman and a formidable opponent of Gorchakov. In the late sixties and early seventies he had been, perhaps, more influential than Gorchakov, but was outmanoeuvred and 'put on ice' in 1874, that is, sent off to the embassy in London. Shuvalov did not willingly go abroad and had a personal interest in repaying his powerful rival. One of the main weapons in his arsenal was his friendship with Bismarck, whom he convinced that Gorchakov was Germany's greatest enemy and that once he, Shuvalov, was established in power mutual relations would immediately improve. Bismarck had great faith in him, but the Russian ambassador was by no means as trustworthy and pro-German as Bismarck and others thought. Whether once foreign minister he would have followed this line is an open question. Among other things, his betrayal to the French of Bismarck's alliance offer to Russia in 1876 does not quite fit into the picture.[31]

When an envoy in Petersburg Bismarck had admired elegant and sophisticated Russian society; until the end of his life he remained attracted to it. But he also was quite aware of its weaknesses which in the years 1859 to 1862 were particularly apparent. Subsequently the situation had become less precarious; but by the mid-seventies serious signs of disruption were again in evidence. It was partly through Shuvalov that Bismarck's attention was drawn to the rapidly worsening situation which could be dated from the Russian's dismissal as head of the third section, or more accurately, from the beginning of the eastern crisis. Particularly in the second year of the crisis, public opinion seemed to run away with the government. Bismarck was determined to take advantage of these weaknesses, at first in the hope that a little bloodletting would bring Russia to her senses (that is, turn more conservative and follow his leadership), and then in the belief that a change in ministers might bring about the desired alteration. For Bismarck it must have seemed quite logical to hope for Gorchakov's final embarrassment and the accession of the sensible, conservative, and supposedly pro-German Shuvalov. His approach had a positive side, but it eventually miscarried. Until the summer of 1879 when Bismarck finally realized that Shuvalov's candidature had failed he hoped for a turn for the better in Russia. He thought that a determined conservative government would be able to stop the process of decomposition. Afterwards, however, he lost faith in the possibility of a recovery and sought refuge in a policy of expedients. Throughout the 1880s Bismarck became increasingly pessimistic about Russian conditions. Towards the end of the decade he apparently expected a real improvement in mutual relations only if Russia were to disintegrate.

The change in Bismarck's relatively optimistic Russian policy

[31] Le Flô to Waddington, Petersburg, 9 August 1878, no. 45, FFM, Russie 257.

to an increasingly pessimistic line is an interesting symptom of
the change in the general character of his domestic and foreign
policy at the end of the seventies, for the things which disturbed
him on the Russian scene also made him apprehensive in
Germany. Can one not assume that the abandonment of
liberalism in this period was partly an attempt to prevent the
situation at home from deteriorating in the same way as in
Russia? And does not his domestic policy in the 1880s reflect
the same kind of pessimism about the future? At any rate, his
advocacy of Shuvalov's candidature and its subsequent failure
mark the most important turning point since the establishment
of the Empire, not only in Bismarck's Russian policy, but also
in the whole fabric of his domestic and foreign policy. A period
of relative optimism and liberalism was followed by one of
conservatism and pessimistic expedients.

Starting with December 1875 Bismarck's previously sporadic
displays of irritation at Gorchakov's policy or behaviour
assumed the proportions of a campaign against him. Originally
the personal feud was but one aspect of a larger and subtle
struggle for leadership. Bismarck did what he could to involve
the Russians in difficulties so that they could not threaten
German security, but would themselves be grateful even for
Platonic support. Thus Germany would remain on good terms
with England, Austria and Russia, without being under serious
obligation to any of these powers. Isolated Russian involvement
in war with Turkey was ideal for this purpose. Bismarck also
hoped by this policy—which amounted to a short-term
weakening of Russia—to induce the Tsar to strengthen and
reform the government. Gorchakov, therefore, had to go. In
1876 Bismarck dropped any pretence of cordial personal
relations. In private conversations he criticized him and praised
Shuvalov. Using tactics reminiscent of his struggle with Austria
in Frankfurt, he complained to Gorchakov and the Tsar about
Russian breaches in international etiquette. Parallel with this,
partly in order to disguise his hostility to Gorchakov and
partly to aid Shuvalov, Bismarck gave assurances of support if
Russia were to become materially involved in the eastern crisis.
In fact, this was merely non-committal talk and was interpreted
as such by the Russians. It backfired when in the autumn of

1876 he was pressed to take a definite stand; he had to refuse to confirm his promise in precise language. Although his ambiguous policy became transparent, he was not deterred; but the subtlety which characterized his approach to Alexander in the late summer of 1876 was dropped; from December onwards he simply urged the Russians to go to war, perhaps all the more willingly, because at the beginning of 1877 Gorchakov and other Russian statesmen were peacefully inclined. Bismarck hoped that the war would weaken Russia and completely embarrass Gorchakov, thus bringing Shuvalov and a conservative policy to the fore.

The war, however, did not seriously compromise Gorchakov, because although until the summer of 1876 he had opposed it, he then adroitly drifted along with the current of public opinion and the whims of the Tsar. He carefully prepared the war, but when it broke out he retired to enforced but fortunate isolation. He was not personally identified with the ill-considered peace of San Stefano, of which he did not approve. Therefore, in the negotiations leading to the Congress of Berlin, and also thereafter, he could easily play the role of a moderate but fervent Russian and good servant of the Tsar, just as he had done after the Crimean War. Shuvalov, on the other hand, had been too 'European' throughout the crisis. The weakness of his position was that he could not preach moderation in the name of the Tsar and the nation because he had not been willing to go part of the way with them; but Gorchakov had, and the fact that he was not suspect greatly aided him in the ensuing struggle. Nevertheless, in the period between the Treaty of San Stefano and the Congress of Berlin it was generally held that Shuvalov would soon be appointed foreign minister. Gorchakov was ailing and had apparently lost favour with the Tsar. In the pre-Congress negotiations Bismarck made little attempt to hide his dislike for his rival; and although the Tsar was treated with courtesy, and Bismarck gave some spontaneous help as a mediator, his brusque rejection of Gorchakov's rather abrupt demands for substantial support was regarded in Petersburg as a sign of ill will. Shuvalov, who counted on Bismarck's assistance in his own private feud with Gorchakov, received little more than mere sympathy.

Even before the Congress Bismarck's policy of opposition to Gorchakov and Platonic support for Shuvalov was problematical. If this was so in Shuvalov's heyday, it was even more so after the Congress when his star began to fade.

The 'two chancellors' war' was begun when Bismarck learned that Gorchakov would represent Russia at the Congress. He told Shuvalov: 'Tout est changé; nous resterons personellement amis pendant le congrès; mais je ne permettrai pas au prince Gortschakoff de monter une seconde fois sur mes épaules pour s'en faire un piédestal.'

From the Congress in mid-1878 to the beginning of 1880 the 'two chancellors' war' remained the central feature in Russo-German relations. Since both Gorchakov and Bismarck wanted to play the leading role in Europe, each sought to discredit the other. But the feud rapidly assumed such proportions that the character of Russo-German relations was changed much more than either had wanted at the outset: the struggle for hegemony led to the estrangement of the two neighbouring countries.

Gorchakov wanted to return to the days of Nesselrode, when Russia had been the arbiter of German affairs; he felt that Bismarck alone kept the German Emperor from following a pro-Russian line. Bismarck wanted Russia to recognize the altered balance of power and follow his own lead; he believed that his rival sabotaged Alexander's Germanophile policy in favour of the French. Each chancellor regarded the other as unreliable and dangerously radical.

At the Congress of Berlin Bismarck assumed the initiative and retained it till the beginning of 1880; Gorchakov retaliated as best he could. Schüssler has viewed the conflict in terms of a battle for emancipation from Russian tutelage. Although Germany was already 'emancipated', Bismarck probably regarded his struggle in a similar light. The chancellor—as many Germans—was perhaps unduly sensitive to what he regarded as unreasonable treatment reminiscent of the days of national weakness. He thought it was not enough to stand firmly and ward off unjustified demands. But the exclusion of the possibility of their repetition was a goal which could only be attained by a significant victory over Gorchakov. In other words, it was not 'emancipation' that Bismarck wanted, but acknowledgement of his leadership.

Bismarck's Russian policy during and after the Congress had two distinct sides, each with its personal and political aspect. The negative side, the predominant one, was the personal campaign against Gorchakov and the refusal to support what he considered as Russia's dangerously immodest and irresponsible claims. The positive side was reflected by his support of Shuvalov and what he regarded as Russia's rational and just claims. By means of this complicated scheme Bismarck hoped to see Shuvalov replace Gorchakov; the change of personnel was to be the testimony of the renunciation of irresponsible diplomacy. In 1878 and 1879 Bismarck expected great things from such a change; later he grew increasingly pessimistic. This rather involved policy did not date merely from the Congress, but since then it was intensified and had a greater effect on the international political scene. How did Bismarck conduct his feud and how did Gorchakov react?

In poor health when he arrived in Berlin for the Congress, Gorchakov made a particularly bad impression on most of the participants. Shuvalov, with hardly loyal frankness, did what he could to reinforce this impression. He assured Andrássy, for example, that 'the old man [Gorchakov] is full of arrogance and vanity, and will spoil everything'.[32] Bismarck ostentatiously supported Shuvalov in several major and minor issues, but treated the Russian chancellor with a minimum of formal courtesy. He hoped in this way to secure a sizable diplomatic victory for Shuvalov who could then brush aside Gorchakov. As if to make his point perfectly clear, Bismarck granted an interview during the Congress to the well-known *Times* correspondent, Blowitz, in which he is reported to have said, 'But for the affair of 1875, he [Gorchakov] would not be where he is, and would not have undergone the political defeat he has just experienced.' Immediately after the Congress Bismarck wanted the German press to point out Gorchakov's mistakes and stress that he was 'a calamity for Russia and her friends; not even the best intentions of the latter would suffice

---

[32] Novotny, 'Graf Peter Andrejewitsch Schuwalow', no. 20; Miliutin also thought Gorchakov senile, iii, entry for 15 July.

to make up for the consequences of his foolishness'.[33] This introduced a new note into the government press which had hitherto been regarded in Germany as rather pro-Russian.

By the time Blowitz's article appeared on 7 September Bismarck was more composed and had the government press disavow it, arguing that although Russia's diplomacy had made him wary, his policy had not changed. He also publicly questioned the veracity of *Times* correspondents. At the same time, however, he privately admitted that the 'revelations' were essentially accurate; he affirmed that he had intentionally spoken with Blowitz, thinking it necessary to draw attention to Russia's mistakes.[34] What bothered him was, in fact, not their substance, but the direct attribution of Gorchakov's defeat in Berlin to his own activity. In the following twelve months he wished this line to be held fast by the press. Then, when German policy obviously had changed, this was to be attributed to the irresponsible and threatening attitude of Russia, not to a personal grudge.

Clearly, the newspaper campaign against Gorchakov was instigated by Bismarck during the Congress.[35] Then, when in August Gorchakov went on a long leave, it was continued in the hope of giving him the *coup de grâce*. The result was different.

On the other hand, Bismarck did everything he could at the Congress to support what he thought were Russia's just claims as advocated by Shuvalov. This enabled him to pose as a well-wisher and at the same time insure that far-reaching Russian aims would be defeated. Whether Bismarck could have helped Russia more without straining German relations with England and Austria is debatable. At any rate he had little inclination to take this risk. As a result relations with Austria, France, and

[33] Le Flô to Waddington, Petersburg, 9 August, no. 45, FFM, Russie 257; *GP*, no. 440; Carroll, ch. iv; Holstein, *Erinnerungen*, pp. 118ff; Bülow, *Denkwürdigkeiten*, iv, 444. Gorchakov said that Bismarck had spoken to him in a similar way at the Congress. Langenau to Andrássy, Petersburg, 14 August 1878, private and confid., WS, PA X 71.

[34] Bismarck to GFO, Gastein, 13 September 1878, tel. no. 37, GFO, IABq 128; Bülow to Schweinitz, 11 November, no. 665, GFO, IABi 53; *GW*, xi, 604; cf. M. Busch, ii, 394.

[35] Windelband, p. 52, wrongly regards Bismarck's interference in the press campaign as a defensive measure dating from the beginning of 1879. Cf. Winckler, 'Aufhebung', p. 482.

England were probably improved. But Bismarck's support had fallen short of Russian expectations. Immediately following the Congress the Russians thought of Germany as a friend who had let them down. The Tsar's first impression had not been altogether unfavourable, but influenced by his entourage, public opinion and the private reports of Gorchakov, he began to look at the Congress as 'a European coalition against Russia under Bismarck's direction'. The Tsar's rage resulted from a general feeling of frustration and he also treated Gorchakov with a minimum of grace.[36]

It was in this mood that Shuvalov and Gorchakov found Alexander when they returned from the Congress. Shuvalov probably portrayed the achievements of the Congress and Bismarck's support in a favourable light, but he received very little recognition. He complained to Radowitz that although Alexander was disappointed with Gorchakov, he did not want to dispose of him. Shuvalov told also of his great concern with the state of the Russian press. Even the official and semi-official papers spread the most flagrant untruths. The authorities hesitated to take action against certain trends which appeared patriotic or popular. They preferred to let the public think that Russian interests had been harmed by foreign powers and not by the mistakes of Russian diplomacy.[37]

The initial outbursts of the Russian press against the Berlin settlement were directed against the obvious targets, Austria and England.[38] But the hostility and the didactic tone of the German newspapers after the Congress seemed to substantiate Gorchakov's argument that Bismarck was really to blame. The

---

[36] Berchem to Bülow, Petersburg, 17 July, GFO, IABi 53; Berchem to [Radowitz], 29 July, secret, GFO, IABi 53 secreta; *GP*, no. 440; Windelband, pp. 51, 56ff; Nolde, pp. 197, 209f; Wittram, 'Bismarcks Russlandpolitik', p. 173, following Miliutin, underestimates, perhaps, the influence of Gorchakov at this time. See Zaionchkovskii's introduction to vol. iii of Miliutin's Diary. One source indicates that Gorchakov was initially not displeased with the results of the Congress. Ado, p. 135.

[37] *GP*, no. 440; Reuss to Bülow, Vienna, 13 September, GFO, IABi 53 secreta; Werder to William, Tsarskoe Selo, 6 August, no. 21; Berchem to Bülow, Petersburg, 17 July; Berchem to Bismarck, 22 July, no. 215, GFO, IABi 53; Langenau to Andrássy, Petersburg, 1 & 9 August, private and confid., WS, PA X 71; Miliutin, ii, entries for 5 & 15 July; see also Novotny, 'Schuwalow', no. 27.

[38] Grüning, p. 62; Ado, *passim*; Loftus to Salisbury, Petersburg, 19 July, no. 653, FO 65/1005.

criticism of the German papers failed to achieve Bismarck's objective, because the Russian press refused to discuss the 'mistakes' supposedly committed by its own government, choosing instead to make ironic observations on the 'services' rendered by Germany. At the beginning of 1878 Katkov had advocated an alliance with Germany, but by mid-August he was blaming her for Russia's defeat in Berlin.[39] If Bismarck had been a little more hesitant in stimulating this press campaign against Gorchakov, Russo-German relations could have been better because at the same time he did offer considerable support in the detailed questions of the execution of the Treaty.

Bismarck's plan was to continue the press campaign and privately to foment ill will towards Gorchakov, while supporting Russia in essential matters. Thus, in a rather roundabout manner, it would be clear who stood in the way of better relations. Bismarck wanted Shuvalov as Russian foreign minister, but, realizing that German praise would hurt, he hesitated to draw him into the campaign.[40]

The publication of the Blowitz article fanned the flames. Referring to it, Bismarck directed the foreign office on 13 September to have the non-governmental press point out how much in the previous five years Gorchakov's fondness for France had strained his trust in Russian friendship. Then Bismarck decided to speak more plainly when he learned that part of the Russian press attacked him and that another part minimized the importance of Blowitz's article, saying that *The*

[39] Berchem to Bismarck, Petersburg, 1 September, no. 315, GFO, IABi 53; Mayr to Andrássy, Petersburg, 16 September, private, WS, PA X 71; Trauttenberg to Andrássy, Berlin, 14 September, WS, PA III 113; Langenau to Andrássy, Petersburg, 9 July, no. 28 A–B, WS, PA X 72; Plunkett to Salisbury, Petersburg, 3 August, no. 684; 25 September, no. 813, FO 65/1005–6; Viel-Castel to Waddington, Petersburg, 26 September, no. 58, FFM, Russie 257; Grüning, pp. 56ff.; Winckler, *Bismarcks Bündnispolitik*, p. 46; Nolde, p. 206; Vogüé, entry for 13 September; Windelband, p. 52, has pointed out that Grüning overemphasizes the friendly character of the Russian press in the months following the Congress.

[40] Schweinitz to Bülow, Petersburg, 7 May, no. 132; Berchem to Bülow, Petersburg, 17 July, GFO, IABi 53; Berchem to Radowitz, 27 July, secret and private, GFO, IABi 53 secreta; cf. *DDF*, ii, no. 345; Plunkett to Salisbury, Petersburg, 15 November 1879, no. 592, FO 65/1048; Haymerle to Andrássy, Rome, 29 November 1878, confid., private, WS, PA XI 87; Kálnoky to Haymerle, Petersburg, 24 March 1880, no. 18–D secret, WS, PA X 75; Mayr to Andrássy, Petersburg, 8 October 1878, private, WS, PA X 71.

Times probably wished to injure German-Russian relations. He drafted an article which appeared on 22 September 1878 in the *Norddeutsche Allgemeine Zeitung*, a government newspaper. The new element in this article was the emphasis on the diplomatic skill of Shuvalov which next to the bravery of the army had assured the Russians their great gains from the war.[41]

The Russian press fully understood the significance of this hint, but did not draw the conclusions from it which Bismarck had hoped. The reaction of the *Golos* was probably typical; it maintained indignantly that the powers would not let Germany influence their choice of diplomats.[42]

The position of the previously not particularly anti-German *Golos* is worthy of note. Hitherto attacks on the outside world had been led by the nationalistic Moscow press; just after the Congress of Berlin the *Golos* regarded Bismarck as Russia's 'only true friend'. In 1879 the liberal Petersburg press guided by the *Golos* was in the front rank in the battle with Bismarck. This was partly due to his break with the Liberals and advocacy of a protective tariff; but it was also due to official inspiration. The result was that the nationalist opposition to Germany was strengthened by the Liberals. The Conservatives were the only important group which remained, temporarily, aloof. When in the 1880s they fell under the spell of the nationalists, anti-German feelings in Russia were well-nigh universal amongst the leading classes.

For five months from the end of September 1878 there is no evidence that Bismarck continued to inspire the press in favour of Shuvalov. He confined himself to praising him in informal conversation[43] and later in despatches to the German ambassadors, the contents of which were intended for communication. True, Bismarck's support of Russia in the details of the

[41] Bismarck to GFO, Gastein, 13 September, tel. 37; Bismarck, 20 September, dictation, GFO, IABq 128.

[42] Berchem to Bülow, Petersburg, 28 September, no. 352, GFO, IABq 128; Viel-Castel to Waddington, Petersburg, 26 September, no. 58, FFM, Russie 257.

[43] Mouy to Waddington, 4 October, no. 157, FFM, Allemagne 25; St. Vallier to Waddington, 3 November, private, FFM, Allemagne M & D 166; Lyons to Salisbury, Paris, 19 November, no. 924 most confid., FO 27/2316; Russell to Salisbury, 29 November, no. 643 secret, FO 64/910; *DDF*, ii, nos. 398 and 406; Lucius, p. 143; Taffs, p. 249.

execution of the Treaty was calculated to strengthen Shuvalov's position, but any farther-reaching support was purely vocal. Instead the chancellor became increasingly concerned with the removal of Gorchakov from office.

Despite reports that Shuvalov was losing ground with the Tsar, Bismarck probably still believed his position had improved, so all that was necessary was to rid himself of Gorchakov. In October a further step was taken in his feud: he complained in Petersburg about the constant flirtings of the Russian press with France. Gorchakov was still away on leave, so this activity was attributed to Jomini, his protégé in the foreign ministry.[44]

It was quite important that the Russians should not attribute Bismarck's relative coolness to personal resentment. This point was repeatedly stressed in his despatches, but even the friendliest Russians found it hard to believe. The emphasis on the flirting with the French was not very convincing, to be sure, but in November he sallied forth again. Schweinitz, the ambassador in Petersburg, was instructed to argue that Gorchakov had not only flirted, but had gone quite far with the *pourparlers* for an alliance. It was therefore the law of self-preservation which bade him keep the doors open for Austria-Hungary and for England. The purpose of these historical reminiscences was to add weight to Bismarck's case, but since at that time such accusations were groundless, his position must have seemed insincere. Gorchakov's personal inclinations for the French are sufficiently well known and just after the Congress he said the usual nice things to the French ambassador and complained of Bismarck's Machiavellian politics. Waddington did not want to listen, although this was music in the ears of Le Flô, the ambassador. But he was replaced in March 1879 by the initially

[44] Berchem to Bülow, Petersburg, 17 July; Werder to William, Tsarskoe Selo, 6 August, no. 21, GFO, IABi 53; Berchem to Radowitz, 27 July, private, secret, GFO, IABi 53 secreta. The French and Austrian ambassadors were also sceptical of Shuvalov's chances; *DDF*, ii, no. 345; Holstein, 7 December, note, GFO, IABi 53; Langenau to Andrássy, Petersburg, 31 July, private and confid; 4 December, private and confid., WS, PA X 71; Bülow to Berchem, 11 October, no. 595, GFO, IABi 60; Russell to Salisbury, Berlin, 9 November & 21 December, private, SP, A/9; see also Busch, ii, 394. For Jomini's somewhat impracticable ideas in the autumn of 1878, see C. & B. Jelavich (eds.), *Russia and the East*, Jomini to Giers, 14/26 September; 9/21 October.

reserved Chanzy,[45] and from September to December 1878, when he was on leave, the *chargé*—Viel-Castel—was rather suspicious of the Russians. So it is virtually certain that in late 1878 no negotiations had been initiated, or for that matter, in 1879 when Bismarck revived this complaint.[46] In fact, Franco-Russian relations after the Congress were at a low point. Bismarck's attempt to seek reassurance by discrediting Gorchakov was unnecessary.

Bismarck's desire to see Gorchakov whisked away was stimulated by the belief that, if Balkan problems were to fade, the attention of the powers would be drawn towards Alsace-Lorraine. This rather unlikely eventuality was not very enticing as long as his powerful rival was in office and the spectre of a Franco-Russian alliance haunted him. Indeed, the despatches to the Petersburg embassy display a vastly exaggerated pre-occupation with a Franco-Russian alliance. There is also, despite all Bismarck's contrary assertions, a note of personal resentment. On the other hand, it would be wrong to say that Bismarck was governed only by personal feelings. Here personal resentment and misconceived reason of state coincided. But the campaign against Gorchakov did not seem to succeed. As far as Bismarck was concerned the year ended rather discordantly. At the beginning of December Gorchakov returned to Petersburg to resume his duties. On the way he passed through Berlin and reprimanded the Austrians, as well as the Germans.[47] The Russian chancellor had lost none of his self-confidence, but in other respects he had degenerated considerably. Those who saw him in Berlin were impressed by his recovered physical condition, but almost everyone doubted his ability to direct foreign affairs.

Gorchakov's return to office and the failure of the attempt to secure his retirement was a defeat which Bismarck would

[45] GENERAL A. LE FLÔ (1804–87). Minister of war, 1870–1; ambassador to Russia, 1848–9 and 1871–9. GENERAL A. CHANZY (1822–83). Ambassador to Russia, March, 1879–82.

[46] Berchem to Bismarck, Petersburg, 29 July, no. 229; Bülow to Schweinitz, 11 November, no. 665, GFO, IABi 53; St. Vallier to Waddington, 11 November, no. 190 confid.; 3 November, private, FFM, Allemagne 26 and Allemagne M & D 166; Le Flô to Waddington, Petersburg, 28 July and 9 August, nos. 44 and 45, FFM, Russie 257; Viel-Castel to Waddington, Petersburg, 23 September 1879, no. 44, FFM, Russie 259; Medlicott, *Bismarck, Gladstone,* pp. 68f.

[47] See above, p. 50.

have done well to take with good grace. It was one thing to conduct a 'whispering campaign' against a minister who was not actually in charge of affairs himself. But it was another and much more delicate matter to carry on the same campaign against one who was in a good position to retaliate. This did not deter Bismarck. By the end of 1878 he had already done what he could to combat Gorchakov personally. He treated his Russian opponent with a minimum of formal courtesy; in private and official conversations he praised Shuvalov and indulged in tirades aimed at discrediting Gorchakov, associating him with the revolutionary principle, and ridiculing him and his foreign policy; he had mobilized the press and kept it supplied with ammunition; and he had gone so far as to complain about him in Petersburg. If Bismarck intended to continue the battle in 1879, he would have to use heavier weapons. But until the end of 1878 he had not reached this stage. In the coming year it became increasingly clear that Bismarck had set about ridding himself of Gorchakov at all costs. At first the only visible result on the Russian side was that Gorchakov, his circle and the Tsar grew more irritated. The Russian chancellor, although he may have been aged and weak, was not incapable of returning the fire.

The personal aspect of Bismarck's policy was unfortunate, but aside from this it would be difficult to suggest an essentially different one. He sincerely desired to aid Russia where she followed a moderate course, but support for an active Russian line would have damaged his relations with the other powers. Certainly, he could have chosen to drop either Russia or the others, but this was exactly what he wished to avoid.

The advancement of Shuvalov and his views, the positive side of Bismarck's policy, was no more successful. On Christmas day he learned that Shuvalov, who was just as dismayed as Bismarck at Gorchakov's return to power, had formally offered to resign. Shuvalov had good reason to be disappointed, because, according to the German ambassador in London, before Gorchakov's return he had almost been conducting himself as foreign minister.[48] Now that he had forced the issue it was

[48] Münster to Bülow, London, 23 December, private, GFO, IABi 53 secreta; 3 December, most confid., GFO, IABq 133.

hardly probable that the Tsar would decide in his favour.
Bismarck's open praise was certainly not well calculated to
help him, nor was the rather weak support in the detailed
questions of the Treaty execution enough to matter much.
What was needed was a little more active support for those
things with which Shuvalov was most identified—especially
his two missions to Vienna to obtain Austrian support. And
now at the very end of the year Bismarck refused to participate
in a mixed occupation plan.[49] Shuvalov was later to stake his
future on the success of this scheme, but his position had been
compromised unwittingly by Bismarck from the beginning.

In the coming year the international situation rapidly
changed although Bismarck's basic approach to Russia did not.
As his goal—a moderate Russia led by Shuvalov—drifted
farther away, the scope of his policy widened and the campaign
against Gorchakov grew more intense. One cannot admire
Bismarck's wisdom, but one can his tenacity and ingenuity as
he steered into the crisis.

[49] See below, pp. 117ff.

CHAPTER III

Casual Austro-German Cooperation and Russian Exasperation

The first six weeks of 1879 were extremely important for the future orientation of German foreign policy. Accident and design converged to overturn the careful balance Bismarck had striven to maintain. It has already been pointed out that the salient feature in Bismarck's foreign policy was his effort to have Gorchakov, and what he was supposed to represent, removed from the political scene, while at the same time maintaining sufficiently good relations with Russia to enable a new start with a more promising programme when the chancellor was replaced by a more 'sensible' man. Gorchakov's return to power marked the failure of the first phase of this policy and made it well nigh impossible to continue in the same vein. It can hardly be assumed that the meaning of Bismarck's policy escaped Gorchakov, or that he was not determined and able to defend himself.

Then, three new questions arose which, in their origins at least, were only indirectly, if at all, related to the main trend of German-Russian relations. They were first, the publication of the revocation of part of article v of the Treaty of Prague; secondly, the Austro-German measures against an outbreak of the plague in Russia; and thirdly, the German tariff bill. The last question was initially completely independent of Bismarck's Russian policy. But it had effects similar to the latter and so attained exaggerated significance. The second was originally of no political consequence; but very quickly it became probably the most important of the three as a factor determining the future direction of German-Russian relations. The publication of the revocation of part of article v of the Treaty of Prague at this time was caused primarily by the agitation accompanying the Cumberland marriage project and the Anglo-German tension which resulted from it. Berlin wanted to stress cooperation with Austria, which was not necessarily incompatible with amicable Russo-German relations. It is worthwhile noting, however, that Bismarck had in the past thought of annulling the embarrassing part of article v as a first step to an alliance. When rejecting the Austrian alliance feeler in the autumn of 1876 he had hinted that an 'organic alliance' would be conceivable at some later date and that this would be the way to approach it. Andrássy's readiness to concede this point when he again approached Bismarck for an alliance in early 1878 cleared the way for the final dual alliance. Still, one must be careful not to read too much into this episode; it is more instructive for the continuity of Andrássy's than Bismarck's foreign policy.[1]

The coincidence of these three factors at this particular time caused a tremendous amount of Russian ill will and great national indignation. This is certainly what Bismarck had hoped to avoid. The campaign against Gorchakov which he had been conducting for the previous few months could only be carried out effectively when there were no heavy clouds on the horizon. But clouds had overshadowed his positive efforts and darkened the negative side of his policy. The few light spots could hardly be perceived. As a result Bismarck stepped up the tempo of his campaign against Gorchakov and grew more intimate with Austria, the only power with sufficiently similar interests to help him out of his isolation. Nevertheless, until the summer of 1879 he did continue to support Russia in the same manner as before.

I

During the negotiations preliminary to the Congress, on 13 April 1878, an agreement was signed between Austria and Germany revoking that part of article v of the Treaty of Prague (1866) which provided for the possibility of a border rectification in northern Slesvig, a predominantly Danish area. Neither Andrássy nor Bismarck wished for publication at the time and

[1] See below, p. 176.

the agreement stipulated that for one year the revocation of this section of article v could not be made public without consent of both. In November 1878, however, as a result of the engagement of the duke of Cumberland to Princess Thyra of Denmark, agitation for the cession of Slesvig, or part of it at least, gathered momentum. Andrássy was asked whether he would agree to the publication of the Treaty. Why? Certainly the press agitation for a settlement of the Slesvig question in favour of Denmark bothered Bismarck; more important for him was the fact that the duke of Cumberland was the pretender to the throne of Hanover. Thus, the Slesvig and the very delicate Guelf question became linked. A demonstration of Austro-German unity implied by the publication of the revocation would stop the North Slesvig agitation, prevent further trouble from arising out of the non-execution of this Treaty paragraph, and also deal the Guelf party a severe blow. [2]

The Guelf question itself had recently caused international complications and there was some indication that it would become entangled with the North Slesvig dispute. After the death of George V, the last King of Hanover, earlier in 1878, the duke of Cumberland, his son, [3] issued a statement reasserting all his rights to the succession. The Guelf sympathisers, on their part, heartened by this brave if unwise stand, increased their agitation against the empire. The Prussian government may have been prepared to make a partial settlement with the pretender, but only after a total renunciation of his supposed rights. The duke was not prepared to go this far, although he seems to have been willing to make some sort of *de facto* recognition of the territorial *status quo*. Queen Victoria had taken a fancy to him and, not without reservations, interceded on his behalf. In two letters, one to her daughter, the

---

[2] M. Winckler, 'Aufhebung', pp. 486–97, overstates the weakness of the German position after the Congress; see also his two articles in *Die Welt als Geschichte*. A. Scharff's criticism in 'Zur Problematik der Bismarckschen Nordschleswigpolitik', p. 214, seems justified. He doubts whether the 'reservation' concerning North Slesvig could have provided a platform for an 'extremely dangerous' European coalition. Scharff's further article, 'Bismarck, Andrássy und die Haltung Österreichs', is a devastating criticism of Winckler's work. For this section consult the documents printed by Platzhoff and Friis & Bagge.

[3] GEORGE V (1819–June 1878). King, 1851–66. ERNEST AUGUST, DUKE OF CUMBERLAND (1845–1923).

Crown Princess, and the other to the Crown Prince, she attempted to discover the least which would be acceptable to the Prussian government. 'An actual renunciation of his rights no one I think can ask.' She also hinted at his willingness to reach some sort of *modus vivendi* by emphasizing his love for his fatherland. Although the English government made no official move, the German cabinet regarded Victoria's step as interference in internal matters and was very upset. It was feared that an official *démarche* would follow. Then, as the engagement was announced, a *Times* article on 9 November, based on details which, according to Bülow, could only be known in court circles, suggested that the time was ripe for the 'good offices' of a friendly power. [4]

Victoria's intercession on behalf of the duke and the *Times* article indicated the possibility, if not probability, of official intervention. It is in this light that the instructions to Reuss on 13 November should be viewed; the motive given for requesting the publication of the revocation of the reservation on Northern Slesvig was the necessity to terminate the press agitation. The *Times* article and the suggestion of 'good offices' are mentioned explicitly. Reuss was told further that such proof of intimacy between Berlin and Vienna would have an advantage which perhaps would surpass the direct interests of both. Clearly, it was in the first instance English, not Russian, intervention which Bismarck sought to forestall. At this point the emphasis on Austro-German intimacy was meant to impress England. [5] After the journey of the Russian Grand Duke Alexis[6] to Copenhagen in December, the front changed.

In mid-November, Anglo-German relations were none too good. The conduct of Victoria had rankled, but Bismarck was also quite disturbed over English intentions regarding Rumania which have been discussed in the previous chapter. It is probably right to say that, in general, relations improved after

[4] Ponsonby to Salisbury, Buckingham Palace, 7 August, SP, A/1; M. Winckler, 'Aufhebung', p. 487; Scharff, 'Bismarck, Andrássy und die Haltung Österreichs', p. 239.
[5] Cf. A. Friis, 'Aufhebung' and Platzhoff, p. 50. Both assume that Bismarck desired the revocation and cooperation with Austria in view of the tension with Russia.
[6] ALEXIS, third son of the Tsar (1850–1908).

the Congress, but this improvement did not set in immediately.[7] For the next two weeks German relations with England remained strained because of the differences in the Slesvig and Rumanian questions. Then, rather suddenly, both were cleared up, the first for good, and the second for the next few months.

On 15 November Odo Russell announced that he had been charged to receive any communications concerning the duke of Cumberland, and that the Queen of England, who was the *executrix testamenti* of George V, suggested the payment of an annual pension to George's sisters.

Official intervention seemed to be just around the corner. Bismarck must have been still unaware that Victoria's apparently impudent behaviour had been all along encouraged by the German Crown Prince. So he expressed surprise at her suggestion:

When one sees that the English carry their consideration for Rumania to the point of disregard for the Treaty of Berlin, and at the same time are so impertinently inconsiderate with this Hanoverian suggestion, one must suppose that they regard the Germans as good, simple, and timid people. A show of indignation as well as some explanations in accordance with the Three Emperors' League would be advisable, so that the English will become more careful and courteous.[8]

This reference to the Three Emperors' League has a strange ring if one remembers how little Bismarck had done to revive it after the Congress. Nevertheless, it gives us a hint as to the possible direction of German foreign policy had England decided to intervene in the question. On the other hand, Russia would hardly have shown great enthusiasm for this particular question and her goodwill would have had its price. Fortunately, Bülow's more diplomatic wording of the final despatch enabled Münster to achieve an easy success without offending, because Salisbury had no intention of taking further action: he even denied knowledge of Russell's step. Victoria seems to have waged the campaign for the duke on her own without informing the cabinet. Although henceforth there was

[7] Cf. Windelband, p. 57; but also *DDF*, ii, no. 358; and Cecil, ii, 336f.
[8] Friis & Bagge, iv, no. 1590.

no danger of English interference, Bismarck's minutes on Münster's report of his conversation with Salisbury show that he was still upset.

Meanwhile, the agitation for the cession of North Slesvig continued and the journey of Grand Duke Alexis to Copenhagen seemed to herald Russian intervention. Bismarck grew uneasy again. Reuss had been unable to carry out his instructions in November because of Andrássy's absence from Vienna. Towards the end of December he was asked to revive the question. This time his instructions were more urgent. In order to facilitate Andrássy's consent, Reuss was asked to counter a possible objection that the opposition would interpret the move as subservience to Germany by saying that the publication of the agreement would have a salutary effect on German public opinion in Austria and increase trust in the loyalty of the government. In addition, Reuss was told that Germany valued publication in view of the demonstrative journey of Grand Duke Alexis. Bismarck also wished to complain to Petersburg about it, arguing that, if the action had originated with the Tsarevna, a Danish princess, it would be a hint of what could be expected in the future.[9]

The chancellor's rage, previously directed at the English, was vented on the Russians. The differences with Britain had not been great, Salisbury had shown a conciliatory disposition, and thus Anglo-German relations became more genial. With Russia, however, the differences mounted. The Russians returned Bismarck's ill humour in kind and every little disagreement was magnified.

It was mere accident that Andrássy had not been asked in November to sanction publication of the agreement on Northern Slesvig when this was aimed at countering English intervention. At that time consideration for England and Andrássy's weak parliamentary position could hardly have made him enthusiastic for the proposal. Later, publication had acquired an anti-Russian nuance and Andrássy's parliamentary position was stronger. Moreover, the nationality principle was inimical to the existence of the Habsburg monarchy, so he readily agreed, provided that the treaty was postdated. Bismarck made

[9] Platzhoff, no. 343.

no objection. Since he was mostly concerned with connecting the Cumberland marriage to the alteration of article v, he pressed for the earliest possible disclosure of the revocation. Andrássy, who wanted the treaty postdated to avoid the reproach of having bought German support at the Congress, desired to forestall such an inference. Accordingly, the treaty was dated 11 October 1878, before the engagement was announced. It was published officially on 4 February 1879 and the Germans could maintain that the Cumberland marriage project had influenced the publication, even if not the conclusion of the treaty.

In spite of the later date, the Austrian concession in the treaty was considered as payment for services rendered at the Congress. Although no country was prepared to protest, the Danes had the sympathy of all. The Russians were disturbed the most. The act itself was only of indirect concern: its importance lay in the demonstration of complete Russian isolation. Until this point Russian diplomats had counted on German support, or at least indifference, in near-eastern affairs and had taken a stubborn line against England and Austria. The revocation of article v was immediately interpreted as Austrian payment for German support in the Near East. It was believed to shed a flood of light on the character of Austro-German cooperation since the Congress. The joint Austro-German measures against the plague and the new German tariff policy seemed to fit into the same pattern. It looked very much as if Bismarck had decided to take sides with the English and Austrians in the crisis to be expected in the spring and that he had secured his interests in advance. The Russians were especially sour because, while continuing to profess friendship, the Germans seemed to be joining hands with the enemy.[10] Even Shuvalov, regarded as pro-German, was disturbed by the extent of Austro-German cooperation. Gorchakov's views were quite moderate. Although he sympathized with the Danes, he realized that interference was inexpedient and he encouraged them to accept their lot quietly. The main political importance of the revocation he saw in the

[10] Loftus to Salisbury, Petersburg, 12 February, private, SP, A/14; Grüning, pp. 63ff; Tatishchev, ii, 534–6; Vogüé, entry for 15 February.

intimate *rapprochement* between the central powers. He concluded that Shuvalov's policy was abortive; the Three Emperors' League had ceased to exist because of Austrian and
German activity; Russia would have to rely on herself in the
future. He seems to have believed in the existence of a secret
treaty.[11]

In Britain hardly anyone outside court circles was troubled
by the revocation. As a whole, public and official sympathy
was on the Danish side. Bismarck fell in the public esteem as a
result of the law against the social democrats, the tariff, the
'muzzle law', which restricted freedom of speech, and, then,
the partial revocation of article v.[12]

Le Flô, the French ambassador in Petersburg, understood
the potential danger of a strong Austro-German *entente*, but
Waddington was no more inclined to interfere than anyone
else. His desire and need for tolerable relations with Germany
confined him to the role of spectator.

It was fortunate for Bismarck that the revocation of article v
came at a time when the powers were occupied with other
problems and were all, in one way or another, dependent on
German support. Thus no power dared protest. The effect of
the revocation in France and England was minimal. Neither
wished to jeopardize German friendship for the sake of the
Danes. The Russian cabinet maintained its reserve for the same
reason. Meanwhile another question had excited the Russians
even more.

II

Schweinitz wrote in 1883: more than anything else it was our
duty-bound security measures against the plague in Vetlianka
which aroused the most hatred, and marked a turning point in

[11] *DDF*, ii, no. 392; Tatishchev, ii, 534-6, states that Oubril and Novikov had
pointed out for some time that the *Dreikaiserbund* no longer existed, but that
Gorchakov's illusions were only completely dispersed when he saw that the German
delegates in the various commissions 'constantly' supported the Austrians, and
Germany cooperated with Austria in revoking article v, as well as in imposing on
Russia the quarantine against the plague. Tatishchev quotes extensively from
Gorchakov's despatches to Oubril (17 January, 1 & 18 February, 10 March) and
a despatch to Novikov (14 February); cf., however, B. Nolde, pp. 210f, who
prints part of the despatch to Novikov.

[12] Salisbury to Russell, 1 January, private, SP, A/27.

public feeling towards the Germans.[13] Indeed, it would be difficult to over-emphasize the effect of the measures against the plague which the Russians found so injurious to their national pride.

The plague had actually broken out in October 1878 in Vetlianka, a Cossack village on the lower Volga. Diagnosis was difficult and the local authorities mistook the sickness for a form of typhus. In December it took a sudden murderous turn and, although the local population had no doubts as to the real character of the disease, Petersburg still held to the original diagnosis. By the time the news finally reached Europe on 9–10 January the plague began to vanish as quickly as it had appeared. The last death in Vetlianka itself occurred on 24 January and the last death in the area on 9 February. The total number of victims was in the vicinity of 425, including several doctors.[14]

When the first alarming reports reached Berlin on 10 January Bismarck wished to know if the imperial health office thought it necessary to take steps to prevent the introduction of the disease. It is not clear what his motives were. At this stage it could hardly be said that he was pressed by public opinion which was not yet excited. A letter written to Bülow on 28 January may contain the key. In it Bismarck expressed the justified desire to protect the empire from what was then thought a very real danger. The promptness of his reaction betrays, however, a deep-seated mistrust in the ability and efficiency of the Russian government. This mistrust was shared by his countrymen, and now that it appeared that the bad habits of the Russians would endanger Germany the press became vindictive. Russian slothfulness and corruption were widely commented on. Throughout Europe excitement mounted rapidly. While in Russia the government continued to speak of a typhus epidemic, which it was making every effort to control, public opinion proclaimed it the plague and doubted the official assurances.[15]

[13] Schweinitz, ii, 40; cf. also Langenau to Andrássy, Petersburg, 16 July 1879, no. 32 A–C confid., WS, PA X 73.   [14] See Zuber, Hirsch and Sommerbrodt.

[15] Bismarck to Bülow, Friedrichsruh, 28 January, DZA, AA 19846. See, for instance, *Bürger Zeitung*, 28 & 29 January. The daily German correspondence on the epidemic is in DZA, AA 19844–55.

The carriers of the disease were then unknown and reports of the plague recalled images of the Black Death and subsequent epidemics. Until about 1720 the bubonic plague had appeared sporadically in Europe. At the beginning of the eighteenth century the last great epidemic originated in the East and swept westwards almost depopulating parts of Lithuania and East Prussia. Later, in 1770, in spite of rigid quarantine measures, a more localized epidemic had ravaged Moscow, being carried there by soldiers returning from Galatz. Since this time Europe had for the most part been free of the plague, although it occasionally made its appearance in Asia Minor, Egypt and Persia. The memory of this mysterious and frightful disease lived on. The appearance of the plague in Astrakhan was disturbing for still another reason. In the nineteenth century cholera, previously confined to India and other areas in the Far East, began to migrate. It had reached Europe by either of two routes: by sea via Egypt, or by land via Persia and Astrakhan. In 1830 a great wave of cholera had swept Europe via Astrakhan. Further epidemics followed the same path. It seemed as if the plague was taking the same route. The public reaction was all the more intense because the recent extension of the Russian railway network to Tsaritsin (now Volgograd) meant that the disease could, conceivably, be virtually everywhere within a few days.

Although much of present-day European sanitary legislation resulted from the fear of cholera, by 1879 little had been undertaken. Conferences at Paris (1852), Constantinople (1866), and Vienna (1874) had attempted to reach an understanding on uniform action, but without success. Nevertheless, the resolutions of the Vienna conference did serve as the point of departure for some of the subsequent security measures.

On 14 January 1879 a report arrived from General Werder, the German military representative attached to the Tsar, stating that there was great excitement in Petersburg about a sickness which had broken out near Astrakhan and which bore all the symptoms of the plague. Of 139 sick persons, 111 and 5 doctors had already died. Werder reported that the most stringent quarantine had been ordered and medical personnel greatly increased, but, unfortunately, the sickness had spread to the neighbouring villages.[16] On 15 January Bülow informed Bismarck that he expected Austria to assume the initiative since in the last five years Vienna had taken the greatest interest in such things. But nothing was heard from this quarter, so on 19 January Dr Finkelnburg, acting director of the imperial health office, decided to leave for Vienna in order to attempt an understanding on joint security measures which he believed would be more efficacious than isolated action. The Austrians and Hungarians were glad that Germany was willing to cooperate, and after detailed conferences of experts a protocol[17] was drawn up on 24 January which provided for:

1. an embargo on certain goods that the experts had considered as germ carriers,
2. disinfection of other suspicious articles as they crossed the border,
3. pass checks with the provision that travellers must prove they had not been in infected areas for twenty days,
4. sanitary inspection of ships from Russian ports,
5. despatch of a medical commission into the infected areas.

These resolutions were immediately made public in order to calm aroused emotions, but the German government had no official notification until Finkelnburg returned on 27 January. On the same evening a committee of experts recommended the measures, and on the 29th the import embargo was passed by the *Bundesrat*. The decree was published on 31 January. A few days later (2 February) the pass restrictions were decreed and went into effect on 10 February; several days afterwards (20 February) the sanitary inspection of ships was proclaimed. On 29 January Schweinitz was instructed by telegraph to prepare the Russians for the pending embargo; on the 31st he was telegraphed to ask permission for the sending of the joint medical commission, but he did not do this, because the

[16] GENERAL B. WERDER (1823–1907). Military plenipotentiary of the German Emperor, 1869–86; ambassador in Petersburg, 1892–5. Werder to William, Petersburg, 9 January, no. 3, GFO, Russland 61. On 16 January Loftus reported 273 victims, Loftus to Salisbury, no. 28, FO 65/1041.

[17] See correspondence in FO 7/983; Poschinger, *Volkswirt*, i, 181; Winckler, 'Aufhebung', p. 498, wrongly states that Germany forced Austria to support her embargo measures; but see correspondence in WS, PA 296 F 34 SR. Also Schulthess, (1879), p. 602, thinks Germany took the lead; and *GW*, viii, no. 228. Scharff, 'Bismarck, Andrássy und die Haltung Österreichs', p. 241.

Russians themselves intended to invite foreign specialists. Then on 1 February Schweinitz was telegraphed to prepare the authorities for the pass and baggage check which was to start on 10 February.[18]

Meanwhile the rumours of the plague had caused increased excitement; in Vienna and Budapest there was a great deal of panic. Russian securities suffered severely and the whole stock market was hit. Methods of combating the plague were aired in the press. So the impact of the eventual measures was felt in Petersburg before they had gone into effect. Part of the Russian press vigorously attacked the German and Austrian governments. On the other hand, many Russians hoped that the proposed measures would force their government to act more energetically.[19]

This was the state of the question when Oubril, the Russian ambassador in Berlin, visited Bülow on 2 February. Oubril communicated the measures approved by the Tsar for the suppression of the plague. The state secretary, in turn, mentioned the pending pass and baggage checks. Oubril applauded Schweinitz's instructions to inform the Russian government of this and added that he had an unpleasant communication to make. He said the way Germany had handled this matter, without explaining her intentions, had made an unfortunate impression. Alexander was 'very dissatisfied' and *froissé*, because of Germany's lack of consideration for Russian commerce and finance. He, Oubril, had been instructed to say this. Bülow answered that his official position forbade him to accept a communication of this kind and added that, if Oubril meant that his government regretted not having been informed more completely of the German measures, he would have to protest. He asserted that Schweinitz had always been informed as completely and as quickly as possible. Oubril then gave way a

[18] Protocol, Berlin, 27 January; *Reichsgesetzblatt*, 2 February; *Reichsanzeiger*, 20 February, DZA, AA 19844, 6, 9; Bülow to Bismarck, 3 February, no. 21, GFO, Russland 61 secreta.

[19] See correspondence in GFO, Russland 61 and Russland 61 secreta; WS, PA 296–7 F 34 SR. Loftus to Salisbury, Petersburg, 9 & 26 February, nos. 88 and 137, FO 65/1041–2; 30 January & 12 February, private, SP, A/14; Russell to Salisbury, 1 February, private, SP, A/9; Vogüé, entries for 29 January & 15 February; Vogüé to Waddington, Vienna, 27 January, no. 7, FFM, Autriche 525.

little and said this was not so important as the fact that Germany had permitted herself to be misled by Austria to the approval of measures which were so harmful and unpleasant. The whole business was an Austrian intrigue aimed at discrediting and weakening Russia. The plague would of course be suppressed. But the restrictions on travellers and the blocking of Russia from the outside world were surely a matter for complaint. Bülow answered that when he had reliable information that Russia had done her part he would gladly discontinue the precautionary measures which were also unwelcome for Germany. But as the situation had been two weeks previously, he had had the responsibility to take immediate steps in view of the common danger and the geographical position of Germany.[20]

It is easy to imagine the effect on Bismarck of Bülow's memorandum of his conversation. The chancellor covered the piece with bitter remarks. That Oubril had been instructed to state that Alexander was 'very dissatisfied' he accepted philosophically, saying that Gorchakov had often used this expression with German officials, but the *froissé* he found 'rather coarse'. He was indignant that the Russians expected Germany to nurse their commerce and remarked that the Austro-German blockade of the frontier did not amount to one tenth of the Russian blockades against Germany. Bülow attributed the whole thing to Gorchakov, stating that Russia was deliberately slow in making communications to Germany which had been made much more promptly to Austria. He also maintained that Schweinitz and Oubril had been adequately informed at all stages. Bismarck needed no prompting to believe that Gorchakov was the author of this step. In answer to Bülow's question whether Schweinitz should be instructed to use similar language in Petersburg, he remarked: 'Gorchakov's language is so brutal that, if we were to take the complaint officially, the senile nonsense would have serious repercussions. The language is similar to Napoleon's New Year's salutation to Austria in 1859.' Schweinitz was instructed, however, to mention Gorchakov's language in the course of light conversation at the

[20] Bülow, 2 February, memorandum, GFO, Russland 61 secreta; Schüssler, p. 13; Tatishchev, ii, pp. 534f; Miliutin, iii, entries for 23 & 27 January. Langenau to Andrássy, Petersburg, 3 March, tel. no. 14, WS, PA 296 F 34 SR.

proper place and to inform General Werder of the matter to enable him to make use of the material in the presence of the Tsar.[21] In what form these instructions were carried out is unknown.

From a technical point of view the Austro-German measures were justified. The reports from Russia were contradictory, but it was obvious enough that nothing had been seriously undertaken, although the plague had been in existence for some months. At this stage European public opinion was universally against the Russian government. The French ambassador in Petersburg had unswerving trust in the efficiency of the Russian authorities, but he was an exception. It was probably only owing to the energetic measures proposed by Austria and Germany and the activity of the Tsar's own physician, Professor Botkin, that the government agreed to take vigorous measures against the plague.[22]

The Russian complaints were not groundless, but in view of the earnestness of the situation they were out of place. Cholera had swept across Europe several times in the previous fifty years: why not the plague? The measures themselves were not immoderate; embargos, later recognized to be ineffectual, were common and considered useful. The consul-general in Petersburg reported that he did not believe Russian trade would be seriously affected by the German measures.[23] Disinfection of suspicious articles was customary, and, at most, vexatious for those involved. The pass restrictions, which applied to Germans as well, merely required all travellers to prove that they had not been in infected or suspicious areas for twenty days. But since the Russian government allowed no one to leave the country without permission and travel was slow in winter anyhow, it is doubtful whether the restrictions were a significant hindrance to anyone.

[21] Bülow to Bismarck, 3 February, no. 21; Bülow to Schweinitz, 4 February, no. 56 confid., GFO, Russland 61 secreta; Windelband, p. 53.

[22] Langenau to Andrássy, 29 January; 12 February, no. 16 A–C, WS, PA 296–7 F 34 SR; St. Vallier to Waddington, 3 March, no. 47, FFM, Allemagne 27; Le Flô, reports in FFM, Russie 258.

[23] Brauer to GFO, Petersburg, 4 February, DZA, AA 19847. Wood and grain were not prohibited, but cf. Eyck, iii, 315f. About 8 per cent of Russian trade with Germany was covered by the embargo, Brauer to GFO, 10 February, DZA, AA 10472.

Even the official Russian reports continued to be contradictory, but by the end of January it was clear that the plague had at least almost disappeared in the places that were initially infected. On the other hand medical authorities believed that in the spring a new outburst was not unlikely, and numerous cases of the plague were falsely reported in various cities ranging from Salonika to Petersburg. A certain amount of caution was advisable, and in reaction to Oubril's complaints Bismarck's concern for the safety of the Empire mounted. Although the experts and public opinion advised even stronger measures, he continued to resist them. On the other hand he was not willing to withhold those measures which had been planned, but not yet put into effect.

The medical experts had agreed in Vienna on 24 January to an inspection of ships arriving from Russian ports. The conference on cholera in Vienna in 1874 had provided for either quarantine measures or inspection in the case of threatened epidemics.[24] The Austrian and German governments agreed on the milder alternative. Other states, however, for instance Greece, Italy, and France, declared more or less severe quarantines, and when cases of the plague in Salonika were erroneously reported, a quarantine was adopted in Trieste.

Schweinitz was instructed to inform the Russians that the sanitary inspection would go into effect. It is an interesting indication of the state of mind in Petersburg that Giers—usually composed and moderate—received this communication with 'pained surprise'. Alexander is reported to have said that the plague chicanery was nothing more than Bismarck's revenge for Gorchakov's telegram in 1875 which after his intervention in Berlin during the 'war scare' proclaimed that peace was assured. Russian newspapers spoke of Germany with enmity. Schweinitz himself believed that the measures against the plague were too inconsiderate. The new restrictions seemed to fit into a pattern of gratuitous hostility. For some years the exportation of cattle to Germany (and elsewhere) had been difficult if not virtually impossible owing to sanitary restrictions on the spread of rinderpest. British restrictions were the most severe; Berlin argued that its measures (which

24 *Staatsarchiv*, xxvii (1875), pp. 258–82.

also applied to Austrian cattle) were meant to forestall the exclusion of German cattle from the British market. From the Russian point of view this looked hypocritical. The cattle restrictions gave German producers protection. Was that not the real intention of all this? What would be the next step?[25]

Giers's remark infuriated Bismarck, who by this time, it appears, would truly have been glad of new signs of the plague in order to torment the Russians.[26] But by the beginning of March Bismarck had it on good authority that the plague was virtually extinguished. As soon as the first favourable report from the medical commission arrived in mid-March Germany, taking the lead, lightened some of the protective measures; Austria followed with reluctance. It had evidently been planned to abandon the rest as soon as the medical commission sent conclusive evidence, but owing to the slowness of communication and the undesirability of waiting longer, by 31 March all measures had been withdrawn except the embargo on such things as unclean bedlinen and rags. Henceforth, the sanitary inspection was applicable only to ships from the Black Sea ports.[27] The Austro-German passport restrictions were continued with only slight modifications. The excuse for their retention was the necessity to combat the nihilist danger. Bismarck stressed the need to erect an Austro-German 'cordon' against the 'socialist plague' and the 'slav-celtic danger'. He refused to consider cooperation with Petersburg because of the unreliability of Gorchakov. Andrássy, too, wished to avoid concerted action with Russia.[28] Was the German government really so concerned about the socialists and other agitators? Surely the concern was authentic to a certain extent, but it is

[25] Schweinitz to GFO, Petersburg, 19 February, tel. no. 21, DZA, AA 19849; Schweinitz to Bülow, 4 February, no. 27 secret, GFO, Russland 61 secreta; Busch to GFO, Budapest, 10 December 1879, copy, DZA, RKA 212; Langenau to Andrássy, Petersburg, 26 February, no. 9 B, WS, PA X 73; Schweinitz, ii, 41–5; Medlicott, *Congress*, p. 371; Tatishchev, ii, 535f; Matlekovits, pp. 38f, 46; Lotz, p. 179.

[26] Bülow to Schweinitz, 27 February, tel. 23; Schweinitz to Bülow, 5 March, DZA, AA 19850; Schweinitz, ii, 44; St. Vallier to Waddington, 3 March, no. 47, FFM, Allemagne 27.

[27] Reuss to Andrássy, Vienna, 19 & 23 March and 1 April; Andrássy to Reuss, Vienna, 27 March, WS, PA 297 F 34 SR.

[28] Bülow, 8 April, note; Bülow to Hofmann, 22 April; Bülow to Alvensleben, 24 April, tel. 58; 16 May, DZA, AA 19854–5; Bülow to Reuss, 13 February; 24 March; Reuss to Bülow, Vienna, 7 April, GFO, IAAa 39.

hard to avoid the conclusion that the real reason for the continued restrictions was repayment for Russian discourtesy.

On reviewing the incident one has the feeling that neither side was completely in the wrong, although both made mistakes. The Germans were justifiably and genuinely concerned about the plague, but their quarantine measures were executed abruptly. The Russians felt injured by this display of distrust and reacted with excessive passion which the Germans repaid with stubbornness and apparent vindictiveness. Bülow had the objectivity to remark that Russian malcontent was, in some respects, understandable. The advance notification of the embargo, which was the important thing, amounted to two days. Although the measure had been discussed in the press for several days and Bülow had made some preparatory statements to Oubril, it had only been finally decided on 29 January. Then Schweinitz was immediately telegraphed to inform the Russians.[29] Thus, technically Bülow was right—a warning had been given. It might be a legitimate question to ask, however, if Berlin would have acted as decisively and as quickly, if political relations with Russia had been better. The Russians, on the other hand, were more at fault; they were slow in reacting to a danger which had alarmed Europe. They had also been warned that decisive steps were going to be taken if they did not act quickly. But nothing was done until after the Austro-German measures had been agreed. The execution of the Russian measures was slow and uncertain. Oubril's complaint in Berlin was a major diplomatic error. This was, no doubt, Gorchakov's retaliation for Bismarck's agitation against him, but he went too far. The cooperation of Germany with Austria had hitherto been of a haphazard and accidental nature; soon it was to become deliberate.

III

As long as joint Austro-German measures were being discussed in the press and had not gone into effect, the brunt of Russian public ill will was directed towards Austria. At the same time

---

[29] Bülow, 2 February, memorandum, GFO, Russland 61 secreta; Tatishchev, ii, 534, wrongly maintains that there was no advance notification.

the new German tariff and finance bill became the subject of widespread debate. The idea suggested itself that the plague was a convenient pretext for a tariff war. In government circles many believed that Germany had merely hastily sought a means of embarrassing Russia.[30] Accordingly, Russian animosity turned increasingly against Germany.

The primary reasons for the tariff—a means of improving the financial situation of the empire and combating the economic depression, while at the same time shoring up the social *status quo* and strengthening Bismarck's personal position of power as chancellor—lie within the realm of domestic policy.[31] Originally he had probably thought merely of a financial tariff intended primarily to raise revenue, but, faced by French export premiums, the unfavourable duties of other countries and the prospect of higher barriers in the future, he quickly broadened the basis of his scheme to include retaliatory tariffs. The increase of the Russian tariff in January 1877 convinced him of the necessity and justification of such means in order to force concessions, since he thought negotiation useless, especially in view of the gathering momentum of the protectionist movement in Europe and America.[32] First he contributed to the growth of the protectionist cause in Germany. Then, as it became more popular, he sought its support so as to inaugurate the reform in such a way as to consolidate his own position. This seems to have been the decisive factor in his

[30] Bülow to Schweinitz, 4 February, no. 56 confid.; Schweinitz to Bülow, Petersburg, 4 February, no. 27 secret, GFO, Russland 61 secreta; Windelband, p. 53; Grüning, p. 63. For this section consult Poschinger, *Volkswirt*, i, 112–249; *Aktenstücke*, i, nos. 133–81.

[31] Maenner, pp. 24, 56. German historians agree as to the domestic origins of the tariff reform, but they are not sure whether economic or political motives were more important. For example, Bussmann, pp. 190, 195, stresses economic motives, but Bergsträsser, p. 147, emphasizes the political reasons for Bismarck's conversion to the tariff. For a Marxist view, see Rathmann. As an external political motive Maenner says that Bismarck advocated the grain tariff in order to preserve an independent bread supply in time of war, pp. 37, 69. Bussmann sees a connection between the tariff, aimed at strengthening the empire, and the diplomatic security system, inaugurated by Bismarck with the Austrian alliance, p. 195.

[32] *GW*, xi, 405; Lambi, pp. 150ff, 163f. Maenner, p. 27, maintains that the retaliatory tariff idea existed from the beginning. The development of Bismarck's thinking is shown in Böhme, pp. 388, 410–12, 422–4, 432–4. Here Bismarck appears as an early advocate of a protective tariff. Hardach's contention that Bismarck and Germany led the movement for protection is unsubstantiated, pp. 53–64.

resolution to propose a general tariff on all goods passing the frontier.[33]

In spite of his encouragement of the movement for protection, Bismarck's initiative must not be overstressed. His argument that 'we should obtain through our own legislation the security for German production which we cannot find in the benevolence of foreign governments' formed the bridge between *laissez-faire* and protection and seemed so sensible that even his liberal advisers accepted it in essence. He allowed his opponents to isolate themselves through lack of realism and advanced relatively cautiously, although the Emperor probably would have preferred more decisive action. He did not forge ahead until the spring of 1878.

His handling of the negotiations for the renewal of the commercial treaty with Austria illustrates this point. In October 1876 Austria gave notice to terminate the treaty of 1868 and wished to replace it with one establishing higher tariffs for Austria and lower rates for Germany. Bismarck insisted on 'true reciprocity' and took a liberal, *laissez-faire* stance in the negotiations. He had little faith in a positive result and remained suspicious of Austria throughout. So he was probably glad that the Austrians proved difficult; but they were the ones who had wanted an early termination of the original agreement and their protectionist demands prevented an understanding on a liberal basis. In addition, the negotiations clearly demonstrated—also to his liberal advisers—the futility of bargaining from a weak position.[34]

---

[33] Bergsträsser, pp. 147f; Maenner, p. 34 and *passim*; cf. Bussmann, p. 191. Maenner, p. 63, says that the attack on the National Liberals was the main reason for the protective tariff and the only reason for an all inclusive tariff; but cf. Hallgarten, *Imperialismus*, i, 188f.

[34] Böhme, pp. 436f, 450–2, 461–70; Bismarck to Stolberg, 27 February 1877; Jordan, 12 April 1877, memorandum; Bülow to Jordan, 13 April 1877; Hofmann to Philipsborn, 27 June 1877; Bismarck to Dönhoff, 2 July & 23 November 1877; Stolberg to GFO, 12 July 1877, confid.; Bismarck to GFO, Varzin, 22 July 1877; Hasselbach *et al.* to Bismarck, Vienna, 25 September 1877; Bülow to Hasselbach *et al.*, 28 September 1877; Bülow to O. Bülow, 4 October 1877; Bismarck to Hasselbach *et al.*, 19 October 1877; H. Bismarck to Bülow, Varzin, 6 November 1877; Bismarck to Bülow, 9 December 1877; Károlyi to Bülow, 29 May 1878; Philipsborn, 1 August 1878, memorandum; Bismarck, Kissingen, 12 August 1878, note, DZA, AA 9929–41; Bülow to H. Bismarck, 23 November 1877, FA, B 23; H. Bismarck, Friedrichsruh, 30 April 1878, FA, B 25.

Böhme underlines the complexity of Bismarck's motives and stresses the necessity to avoid attributing too much tactical consistency to him. He himself, however, credits Bismarck with remarkable single-mindedness as to ultimate goals. He insists that neither the agricultural nor the industrial tariff was decisive. Bismarck's aim, from the early seventies on, was to establish solidarity between the wealthy agrarians and industrialists and to bind them to the monarchical state—which he wished to turn into a conservative welfare state—by satisfying their economic demands: thus Germany would rest on two solid pillars instead of one, the agrarian, as had Prussia. Such an interpretation does shed much light on the situation—why Bismarck originally liked the idea of a financial tariff, encouraged the movement for protection, and then advocated a general tariff—but in emphasizing the constructive elements in Bismarck's thinking it overshoots the mark. The concept of the welfare state was surely peripheral; in stressing the desire to reconcile the wealthy landowners and industrialists and fashion them into the two pillars of the state, Böhme overlooks the fact that Bismarck often opposed these groups when they did not do his bidding. Böhme, it would seem, does not sufficiently take account of Bismarck's will to dominate and the consequent importance of tactical considerations. The same would apply to Wehler, but his view of Bismarck's turn to protectionism as part of a concentrated effort to combat the Great Depression and preserve the social *status quo* is, on the whole, a little more convincing. He thinks that the depression, largely caused by overproduction, stimulated a process of concentration and the elimination of competition on all levels; Bismarck's protectionism and later imperialism must be regarded in this light as signs of anti-cyclical behaviour.[35]

Although the tariff reform was mainly due to internal economic and political considerations, Bismarck undeniably regarded a tariff as an excellent means of reprisal, not necessarily only or even mainly against Russia. In public utterances, however, he mentioned especially the necessity of this sort of retaliation against the empire to the east, and he probably

[35] Böhme, pp. 378, 410–12, 419f, 537f. Hardach, pp. 185ff. Wehler, pp. 22, 25, 51, 93, 95, 99f, 105f, 111, 123, 185f, 413–500; cf., Rosenberg, chs. v and vii.

believed open threats would have a greater effect on Russia than on France or Austria. In addition, it is not at all impossible that Bismarck's wish to tax all goods crossing the border was intentionally phrased so as to make at least part of the transit trade, mainly Russian products, subject to customs.[36] But until the end of 1878 Bismarck's statements of his own views were kept so general that it is difficult to say what he intended in particular.

At the beginning of January 1879 the special *Bundesrat* committee charged with the elaboration of the tariff bill started its deliberations and the situation began to clarify immediately. The proceedings of the committee were kept secret, but communications about its progress were made public from time to time.[37] A lively discussion began which grew more detailed as the work of the committee progressed.

The Russian press, of course, took an active part in the discussions, but did not display an increasingly greater aversion for Germany and Bismarck as the depressing details were gradually revealed. The initiation of serious consultations on the tariff in January 1879 sufficed to upset the Russians, because it seemed to offer a ready explanation for other German behaviour. From this point of view Bismarck's subsequent conduct and the actual stipulations of the bill verified the first impression, for the chancellor himself took a prominent part in the discussions and, although the bill as a whole was not particularly prejudicial to Russia, he identified himself with those aspects of the tariff (and the accompanying bill for the regulation of railway freight rates) in a way which seemed to justify their reproaches. Bismarck could hardly have overlooked this, and one might assume that his insistence on some aspects of the tariff was influenced by the Russo-German tension and was calculated either to irritate his neighbour, or bring her to her senses by a demonstration of power. Thus the Russian censure that Bismarck was aiming at a tariff war was, while exaggerated, not without the proverbial grain of truth.

---

[36] Schulthess (1879), 3 April; *Staatsarchiv* (1880), xxxvi, nos. 7014, 7015, 7020, 7021; Maenner, pp. 27f.

[37] For a competent survey of the discussions leading up to the enactment of the bill, see Lambi.

In order to understand more completely the sharp reaction
to the tariff discussions it is necessary to call to mind briefly
the trend of Russo-German economic relations. Throughout
the century the Russian tariff was higher than that of Prussia
although in Russia, too, there was a relative slackening parallel
with the general European free-trade movement. As Germany
became progressively industrialized, trade with Russia and
capital investment there also developed, especially in connection with the construction of a railway network. So in the
eyes of contemporary Russians the post-war boom and subsequent depression affected their country as a German impor-
tation. In the lean years German industrialists redoubled their
efforts to sell in Russia. The Tsar's subjects for their part
were keen to export grain to, or through, Germany on the new
railway lines and industrialists naturally clamoured for and
obtained more protection. The proposed German tariff increased the feeling of exploitation and frustration, for the
exportation of grain, by far the best source of foreign exchange
for economic and military recovery, was to be hindered and
German domination apparently secured. So it is understandable that the Tsar immediately appointed a commission to
discuss tariff revision. The higher tariffs introduced in mid-
1880 and January 1881 on the whole made German imports
noticeably dearer.[38]

When on 3 January 1879 the *Bundesrat* committee began its
work, Bismarck at once started forceful agitation for the grain
tariff. The Russian press interpreted his interest in this special
field as an oblique attack on Russia whose main export to
Germany was grain. The justification for this seemed obvious
because in the past Bismarck had taken advantage of the Tsar's
weak diplomatic position to threaten publicly the imposition
of retaliatory grain tariffs. But there were sufficient other
reasons for championing agrarian interests to suggest he was not
initially aiming at provocation. There is even some evidence
that at this stage Bismarck advocated a lower tariff for rye
than wheat. Whereas at that time America was the chief

---

[38] See Böhme, pp. 438–41, 444, 467, 498, 526, 543, 587f, 601. Alvensleben to
GFO, Petersburg, 25 April 1879, DZA, AA 10473; Mendelssohn *et al.* to ministry
of trade, 19 February 1881, BA, R2/1688.

supplier of the latter, Russia's main export to Germany was rye.[39] But by April, at least, he had become more demanding in this respect.

His endeavours to obtain a unified regulation of rail freight rates ran parallel to these efforts to secure a tariff on agricultural products. Because of the numerous small rail lines competing with one another, it had hitherto been easy for importers of Russian grain to secure substantial rebates often several times as high as the planned tariff rates.[40] The ostensible reason for this measure was to protect German agriculture by preventing the private railways from counteracting the tariff and granting correspondingly greater rebates so as not to lose their trade.[41] This was all quite logical from the German point of view, but one cannot argue that Petersburg received any special consideration.

Whatever the causes of Bismarck's initial activity in these two aspects of the tariff his continued agitation, together with his exertions in two other questions of detail, suggest an increasingly anti-Russian tendency. Both questions—the transit and retaliatory tariff—appeared in the public discussion after the bill had passed the *Bundesrat* on 3 April 1879 and found their chief exponent in Bismarck. Neither was inspired by the immediate Russo-German tension. The retaliatory tariff was one of Bismarck's points of departure for the general tariff and was, in principle, directed as much against France and Austria as Russia. Also the transit tariff was probably conceived at least as early as October 1878. It is significant, however, that

[39] Langenau to Andrássy, Petersburg, 1 January 1879, no. 1 E, WS, PA X 73; Stumm to GFO, Petersburg, 9 January, no. 8, DZA, AA 6962; Alvensleben to GFO, Petersburg, 27 June 1879, DZA, AA 10473; *DDF*, ii, no. 406; Grüning, p. 67. Poschinger, *Volkswirt*, i, 202. Here Bismarck is reported to have desired 25 pfennige for rye and 50 pfennige for wheat. L. Rathmann, pp. 931ff; A. Sartorius von Waltershausen, p. 319. Germany imported in 1880 24 per cent of her wheat from Russia and 39 per cent from America, but 62 per cent of her rye from Russia and 29 per cent from America. Hardach estimates that in the late seventies larger percentages were imported from Russia, and correspondingly less from America, pp. 81f. In the 1880s Austria was the chief supplier of wheat for the German market.

[40] *Staatsarchiv*, xxxvi (1880), nos. 7015, 7017; Schulthess (1879), 18 March, 2 & 16 April; *GW*, vi–c, no. 136.

[41] It was also a means to control the railways since the attempt at nationalization had failed. The duties on wheat (4.6 per cent) and rye (6.3 per cent) offered little protection, Hardach, p. 134.

the transit tariff, which in this case was a kind of reprisal, was meant to be applied first to the shipment of Russian grain and wood,[42] and that he campaigned earnestly in favour of the adoption of both measures, although in vain; the transit tariffs were completely discarded by the *Reichstag* as was the important clause of the retaliatory tariff paragraph which would have allowed Bismarck to raise the tariffs against any state that levied considerably higher duty than Germany. Although this stipulation could have been applied to many other countries as well, Russia was clearly his main preoccupation. Within five months he was again considering retaliatory and transit tariffs designed to put pressure on the Tsar.[43]

While Bismarck was pursuing these two issues he continued to push his plan for the regulation of the railway rates, also without success. In addition, he expressed his discontent with the rather modest cattle and grain customs—this time especially emphasizing the tariff on rye. He only succeeded in obtaining a doubling of the grain customs.

One might conclude that when the public discussion started, the tariff itself probably had only a slight point against Russia. The sudden appearance of serious tension with Russia, however, made Bismarck more inclined to support the rapidly strengthening agrarian interests in Germany and less willing to permit his activity to be inhibited by consideration for the Tsar. By April 1879 he was prepared to expose himself as a proponent of measures which could easily be interpreted as anti-Russian. That Bismarck did not confine himself to the role of a supporter, but rapidly adopted that of a crusader for agrarian interests seems difficult to understand if one considers only the internal political situation and not the irritation with his neighbours. Indeed, those aspects of the tariff bill which Bismarck advocated were calculated to create a position of strength against Russia. St. Vallier was oddly misguided in believing at this time that the chancellor's apparent favours

[42] Neither product was 'transit' in the strict sense of the word, since both were stored for some time, and the grain was mixed with German grain to be resold with the somewhat misleading labels of 'Danzig', or 'Stettin mixture', etc. *Staatsarchiv*, xxxvi (1880), no. 7020.

[43] Scholz to Hohenlohe, 7 June 1880, no. 79; Bismarck to Scholz, 16 June 1880, DZA, AA 6966.

for Russia were compensation for the tension caused by the new trade policy.

Bismarck's contention was that one should only use economic means to achieve economic ends, political means for political ends. It might be assumed, therefore, that the anti-Russian tinge he wished to give the tariff was aimed partly at forcing tariff concessions. But it seems unlikely that this was his only or even his main aim. The fact that he took such a prominent part in the discussions[44] and the severity of the economic measures he advocated were surely influenced by the political tension, and it may be assumed that Bismarck expected more than the improbable trade concessions from this demonstration of force.[45] He had used economic weapons in the past to attain political goals and he would do so in the future.

[44] In the same period Germany had trouble with Austria over the commercial treaty and Bismarck made sure that the Austrian foreign minister learned of his irritation, but the public was less involved because Andrássy assuaged the Viennese press. Reuss to Bülow, Vienna, 21 May, no. 218; Bülow to Reuss, 26 May, no. 393, GFO, Österreich 70; Reuss to Bülow, 1 February, DZA, AA 6962; 29 May, confid.; H. Bismarck to Bülow, Varzin, 2 June, DZA, AA 9948; St. Vallier to Waddington, 8 April, no. 73, FFM, Allemagne 28.

[45] The new German protective tariff was also inimical to English commercial interests. In December 1878 Salisbury called it a 'broadside against the free trade citadel'. A halting attempt to query some aspects of the tariff was quickly rebuffed. See FO 64/914 and 940; Jordan, 21 May, note, DZA, AA 6964; Taffs, p. 257. Despite this there is no evidence that the political relations between the two countries were prejudiced.

CHAPTER IV

The 'Two Chancellors' War' and the Near Eastern Settlement: January—April 1879

Although the new factors mentioned in the preceding chapter had completely changed the setting of the 'two chancellors' war', Bismarck continued his double policy towards Russia, broadening and intensifying the negative side without correspondingly increasing his support. It would be wrong to see a decisive turning away from Russia at this point; even though it was not easy to stand by her without irritating the other powers, until June 1879 Bismarck offered important support in some essential matters. But relations with Russia deteriorated just the same. Although Russia's isolation had increased since the Congress, making good relations with Germany more desirable, by mid-February 1879 even the moderate and conciliatory Giers and the pro-German Tsar were thoroughly irritated. This was probably why Bismarck stressed the negative aspects of his Russian policy. He tried to increase and take advantage of Russia's isolation. Advice to France to take Tunis, a hint to Odo Russell that his sympathy was with the British in Egypt, and growing intimacy with Andrássy, helped to turn all these powers away from Russia. As the year progressed the pattern of an all-embracing manœuvre to increase Russia's isolation clearly emerges. Simultaneously, Bismarck increased the direct pressure on Gorchakov, his circle, and his policy. The Tsar and the 'moderates' were spared, but without much avail. In the end the massive direct and indirect pressure moulded all forms of opinion into one anti-German cast.[1]

[1] For this chapter consult Medlicott, *Congress*, pp. 198–261.

I

As a counterbalance to the negative side of his diplomacy, Bismarck gave Shuvalov some weak and rather maladroit assistance, and offered the Russians quite solid support in two closely connected questions which were of great importance to them. These were the problem of majority decision in the Balkan commissions and the dispute over the Silistria boundary.

The position of the German delegate to the Eastern Rumelian organization commission at the beginning of 1879 illustrates clearly the extent of support for Russia as well as the weakness in the German line. He had instructions to maintain strictest reserve and only participate in discussions concerning the two actual tasks of the commission: the drafting of a project for the administration of the province and the provisional administration of the finances.[2] This generally worked to the advantage of the Russians, because the other representatives attempted to extend the scope of the commission's activities. On the other hand, the silence of the German delegate also hampered some of the less scrupulous Russian activities. And at one point, towards the end of December 1878, in the face of continued panslav chicanery, Bismarck even threatened to recall his delegate; but this seeming determination to hinder ambitious Russian schemes was actually only a passing pique because shortly afterwards he rejected a suggestion by Emperor William to make a formal complaint about this subterfuge. Apparently, Bismarck's intention was to offer no support, but also little opposition to a policy of extreme obstruction. This incident served as ammunition for those Russians who felt that Bismarck had left their country in the lurch. In fact, it accurately documented the gradual cooling of his attitude towards Russia and the continued, nervous, care to avoid unnecessary provocation. Bismarck wanted to embarrass Gorchakov but avoid giving obvious justification for the criticism of meddling in affairs which did not concern him. It is worth noting, too, that if he had been aiming at an alliance with Austria while hesitating

[2] Cf. above, pp. 30 and 40f. Bülow to Hatzfeldt, 1 December, tel. no. 129; 7 December, no. 456, GFO, IABq 133 iv.

because of his Emperor's sympathy for Russia, he missed an excellent opportunity to draw him over to his side.[3]

A suggestion that decisions in the commissions should be taken by majority (instead of unanimously) resulted from Andrássy's attempt to get the majority vote of the Bulgarian delimitation commission pertaining to Silistria adopted by the powers. The commission was to draw the line of the Rumanian-Bulgarian border from a point 'to the east of Silistria' towards the Black Sea. The Silistria decision had gone in favour of the Rumanians and at the end of January 1879 they occupied the provisional frontier including the fort Arab-Tabia, near Silistria. The Russians demanded their withdrawal. This strengthened Bismarck's determination to avoid assisting Rumania and enabled him to aid Russia. The way he attempted to solve the problem of pressing Rumania and thereby aiding Russia, without at the same time estranging Austria, illustrates the direction of German policy in the following months.

Bülow argued that Rumania's conduct seemed to have been tumultuous, and Bismarck added that she could not count on German support or deduce rights from the Treaty until she had herself complied with it.[4] Russia then proposed as a compromise that the troops should withdraw a certain distance from the tentative border, and Andrássy said this ought to depend on Russia's acceptance of a majority decision in a re-examination of the Silistria border. Bismarck discarded the idea. Andrássy was told that he wanted to avoid helping Rumania and that Russia was unlikely to regard the military satisfaction of a Rumanian withdrawal as enough to justify acceptance of the principle of majority decision; one should not make a suggestion if its refusal were almost certain. Andrássy weakened. On 17 February the powers recommended evacuation. Rumania, isolated, gave way immediately.

[3] H. Bismarck to Bülow, 20 December 1878; William, 23 February 1879, note; Bülow to Schweinitz, 24 February, no. 97 secret, GFO, IABq 133 iv. Schweinitz, ii, 42, 44, 58, believed Bismarck was trying to provoke the Russians; also Medlicott, *Congress*, p. 371.

[4] Bülow, 4 February, memorandum, GFO, IABq 133 i (the routine German correspondence on the majority vote issue is in this file); Russell to Salisbury, 4 February, no. 72 confid., FO 64/931.

Berlin informed Vienna that it had not displayed sympathy for the Tsar; but Schweinitz in Petersburg was told just the opposite. This, it was pointed out, was proof that Gorchakov's haughty bearing and certain childish and senile whims of his had not caused irritation or lessened support of Russia.[5]

Bismarck's move gave Russia support in an important matter, but it is questionable whether it would have been given had it not been in line with his Rumanian policy. Russia, at first unaware of Bismarck's help, was most reluctant to show gratitude. The Tsar's government even feared that Germany and Austria were growing intimate with Rumania. This apprehension resulted partly from the joint sanitary measures the three powers were taking against the plague in Astrakhan. Rumania willingly cooperated, but there was no solidly united front and Berlin discouraged Bucharest from provoking Russia.[6]

Andrássy continued to press the idea of majority decision and, in the middle of March, Bismarck finally agreed to back the suggestion. Andrássy, obviously irritated by previous opposition, did not accept the concession with good grace, so it was withdrawn. The reason Berlin gave for this reversal was that, if the central powers pushed Russia to accept the majority principle, Shuvalov's cause would be impaired and Gorchakov's strengthened. The latter could then mount 'his highest Ukrainian horse' and maintain: 'That is the policy to which we have to submit if we want to reach an understanding with Germany and Austria.'[7] Andrássy, exasperated, asked Berlin at least to abstain from actively opposing his proposal. Bismarck tried to salvage something by offering his best wishes. Fortunately for him, the Russians grew more amenable and agreed early in April to accept a majority vote in the details, reserving unanimous decision only for questions of principle. Vienna also showed less rigidity, and Bismarck took the opportunity to applaud the conciliatory attitude of his two neighbours.

[5] Bülow to Reuss, 16 February, no. 85, GFO, IABq 133 i; Müller, nos. 29 and 31; also p. 67; for this section on Silistria and Rumania see *Aus dem Leben*, iv, 160–89.

[6] Schweinitz to GFO, Petersburg, 19 February, no. 46; Bülow to Schweinitz, 27 February, no. 107, GFO, IABq 133 i; see correspondence in WS, PA 296–7 F 34 SR.

[7] Bülow to Reuss, 23 & 26 March, nos. 182 and 197, GFO, IABq 133; St. Vallier to Waddington, Berlin, 27 February, no. 39, FFM, Allemagne 27.

The Russian concession on majority rule did not signify the end of the Silistria or other border squabbles, although it did facilitate negotiation. Equally important was the fact that the solution of this knotty problem helped to untangle the threads of the question of the recognition of Rumanian independence. Until this point Bismarck had been able to pose as the bene-factor of Russia by linking these two disputes to the recognition question. Afterwards, he had to come out in the open. More-over, the necessity of resisting one of Andrássy's pet schemes no longer existed.[8]

Even before this point the powers were obviously with-holding recognition largely in deference to Germany. The Rumanian dispute was assuming rather serious dimensions. Outwardly Bismarck followed a firm line, making only two slight concessions. He realized, however, that German relations with the powers would suffer if he could find no exit from the quagmire. Consequently, he urged Bleichroeder to strive earnestly for a settlement.

During the discussions on Silistria Salisbury again suggested recognition of Rumanian independence, probably as a kind of implicit compromise. Bülow replied that recognition would set a precedent for evasion of the Treaty for 'Serbia, Bulgaria, Eastern Rumelia, and a far greater power'. But he conceded that he did not expect all Jews of questionable nationality to receive all political rights at once; however, German nationals had to be relieved of restrictions based on their religion. Bis-marck wished ideally for 'full and formal recognition by Rumania of the principles laid down in the Treaty of Berlin', but English pressure had caused him to beat a retreat. As cover, he spoke disparagingly of the Rumanians. He had as much concern for them, he said, as for his glass when it was empty.[9]

At the beginning of March the British obtained a further concession. Bismarck agreed to make recognition dependent

---

[8] Reuss to GFO, Vienna, 10 March, no. 96; Reuss to Bülow, 21 March, GFO, Rumänien 1; 29 March, no. 132, GFO, IABq 133 ix.

[9] The routine German correspondence on this question is in files GFO, IABq 133 ix, IABq 104 and Rumänien 1. Bülow to Münster, 10 February, no. 76, GFO, IABq 133 ix; St. Vallier to Waddington, 26 & 27 February, nos. 38 and 39 confid., FFM, Allemagne 27; Meisl, p. 36.

only on conscientious legislative preparation of legal guarantees for religious freedom.[10] But the point was less substantial than it appears because the Rumanians found even a display of goodwill difficult.

Pressure from the powers continued. Paris and Rome also hinted that Rumania might be treated more leniently. The Italians spoke perhaps a little too openly in favour of Bucharest, and, as in other matters, reaped a harvest of wrath. Berlin had information that Italy was preparing to recognize. Because of the rapid tacks in Italian foreign policy, Bismarck and Bülow were always sensitive to such reports. Both complained of this conduct to the French, and the usual stiff despatch was sent to Rome. But before the Italians could be rebuked, they again gave way. This ended the tension for the next two months after which the quiet was broken by renewed signs of Italy's desire for precipitate recognition.

In March all the powers, even France (hitherto the most reserved), had pressed for recognition. It was clear by the beginning of April that at the first good opportunity the powers would desert Bismarck unless they could somehow be kept dependent on German goodwill. In addition to this external pressure, the Kaiser had recently shown himself indifferent to the Jewish cause. In the future his gentle but stubborn pressure in favour of recognition was a factor to be taken into account.[11]

Meanwhile, at the beginning of February the negotiations between the railway company and the Rumanian government had stalled. Bismarck hoped to get them moving by taking advantage of Rumania's embarrassment with the Arab Tabia affair and her partial dependence on German goodwill. And to add weight to his policy he needed active cooperation from another power. To secure this, he was forced to play a more important part in near eastern questions.

In the complicated Silistria affair Andrássy had sympathized with Rumania. But Austria had already recognized the country and was consequently not so anxious as England

[10] Bülow to Münster, 9 March, tel. no. 18, GFO, Serbien 1.
[11] Bülow to William, 14 & 16 March, GFO, IABq 133 ix; Meisl, pp. 44ff, seems to exaggerate the difference between Bülow's and William's views at this stage.

about offending it. So on 13 February Andrássy was asked to
intercede for Germany. He was told that Berlin would gladly
recognize Rumania, but could not because of the systematic
injuries to German enterprises; the railway negotiations had
been fruitless apparently owing to obstruction aimed at forcing
the company to abandon its property. In this, the cheapest,
way Bucharest hoped to gain possession at the cost of the ruin
of the shareholders. Berlin had protested in vain and would
assume a grave responsibility towards public opinion if it
were to make political concessions to Rumania. According to a
good recent source the shareholders, in view of these difficulties,
had considered selling to a Russian company, an eventuality
which would hardly be welcome in Vienna. Finally, Andrássy
was told that Germany wished to go hand in hand with Austria
in this as in the other near eastern questions; so on political
grounds Andrássy ought to facilitate this by clarifying what
could be expected from Rumania. Andrássy accommodatingly
promised to do his best; Austrian commercial relations with
Rumania were also unfortunate, and he could perfectly understand the German view. The hint about the sale of the railway
to a Russian company had the desired effect.[12]

The hitherto slightly haphazard and accidental cooperation
between Austria and Germany seemed to become more deliberate. Bismarck was soon to ask for more than a mere
reconnaissance mission; in fact, he subsequently got Andrássy
to accept some of the responsibility for achieving his own
political aims.

Since the Rumanian question had decreased the chancellor's
freedom of movement, he was understandably glad to hear at
the beginning of April that the Rumanians seemed more willing
to negotiate for the purchase of the railway. This information
was relayed to Bleichroeder. Bismarck remarked that the
question was becoming very ticklish and consideration for other
important national interests could prevent further support for
German capital; in any case it was politically desirable for
everything possible to be done to reach a settlement. In view
of previous unfortunate experiences with Bucharest, it would
be best to come to terms quickly because in the future the

---

[12] Bülow to Reuss, 13 February, no. 80, GFO, Rumänien 1.

opportunities could be less favourable and German influence diminished.[13]

The seeming willingness of the Rumanian government resulted probably from the Austrian *démarche* for Germany. Despite this no progress was made until the beginning of June when Bismarck decided to force the negotiations. Thus, in April and May, while tension between Russia and Germany continued and Bismarck needed freedom from obligations, the question of Rumanian independence remained essentially unchanged.

Towards the end of 1878 the idea of a mixed occupation of the Turkish areas to be evacuated was being discussed by London and Vienna. The Treaty stipulated that the Russian occupation should last till 3 May 1879. In order to expedite the evacuation of the Balkan peninsula and ensure the maintenance of order, Andrássy had suggested at the Congress that the Russian troops might be replaced by contingents from various nations. The Congress had found the idea impracticable, but the fear of serious trouble after evacuation was widespread and most statesmen felt that something would have to be done. When Shuvalov learned that the scheme had been revived, he hesitated for a moment and then promoted it energetically. But Bismarck renewed the opposition he had shown at the Congress; he logically refused participation when the idea was mooted in December because it looked like a manœuvre to force the Russians to withdraw promptly, and Bismarck's reserve might be interpreted as a refusal to contribute to Russia's embarrassment. But, after all, his policy was to support Shuvalov where he could, and the failure of the mixed occupation scheme was partly his fault.

When St. Vallier visited Bismarck in Friedrichsruh early in January 1879, he was told that Germany would never send a man, nor a *sou*. St. Vallier agreed with every word, and both made an unnecessary appeal to Waddington not to participate.

---

[13] Bülow to Bleichroeder, 4 April, GFO, IABq 104; Medlicott, 'Recognition', p. 575; Taffs, pp. 302f. No evidence has been uncovered that Bismarck instructed Bleichroeder and Hansemann to offer the railway to the Austrian and Russian governments.

Not willing to limit himself to a purely negative approach, Bismarck revived the idea he had toyed with before the Congress of an Austro-Russian occupation.[14] The motives for this suggestion are not clear. Certainly he wanted the powers to discuss a solution which would not involve Germany. But, in addition, he seemed to be confident that the scheme would be generally acceptable; his role would then be, he told St. Vallier, to demonstrate to Russia and Austria that, if one should attack the other, he would throw his weight on the side of the victim. Why did Bismarck seem so ready to mediate, even arbitrate, between Russia and Austria? He was otherwise quite anxious to maintain his reserve in Balkan questions. Conceivably, he was just thinking aloud; it is more likely that he would have welcomed a state of tension between the two which would make both more dependent on German assistance. The tension would increase Russian isolation and in turn aid Bismarck in his campaign against Gorchakov. Chances were equally as good, however, that Bismarck would be left sitting between two stools.

Until the idea of a mixed occupation was abandoned in April Andrássy continually urged Germany to take part. Bismarck firmly refused, but refrained from further ridicule and expressed approval of whatever the other powers accepted. From the start, the middle of January 1879, Andrássy continually repeated that support for the scheme would aid Shuvalov[15]—an argument Bismarck must have found tantalizing. Apart from Austria, no power was very enthusiastic. Had Bismarck put his weight behind the idea, they might have come round, but he rightly refused to be tempted; the position of Germany between Russia and the other participating powers would surely have been delicate.

Bismarck's idea that Russia and Austria should carry out the occupation impressed Waddington; on 25 February he encouraged Germany to come forth with the plan. The

[14] Bülow, 27 December 1878, memorandum, GFO, IABq 133 iv; Russell to Salisbury, 15 April 1878, no. 269 secret, FO 64/904; St. Vallier to Waddington, 26 December 1878, private, FFM, Allemagne M & D 166; *DDF*, ii, no. 371.

[15] Bülow to Reuss, 20 January, no. 39; Reuss to Bülow, Vienna, 15 January, no. 22 confid., GFO, IABq 133 iv. For this section see the correspondence in GFO, IABq 133 vii.

chancellor hesitated for a moment because, as he affably explained to St. Vallier, although Andrássy's burning desire was to snatch Saloniki and the German plan would move him nearer that goal, he was like an amorous woman longing for her lover's kisses, but afraid to receive them. Bismarck decided to try his luck anyhow. Accordingly, Andrássy was cautiously sounded; he was informed that the initiative was French; Bismarck would make no proposals; he wished merely to harmonize his with Austrian policy when the time came for evacuation.[16] His circumspection is partly explained by the fact that he had opposed Andrássy on the question of majority decision in the commissions and was anxious not to make an awkward suggestion. In fact, Andrássy was unimpressed, but Bismarck persisted with his idea which he modestly continued to call the French proposition. When Andrássy finally rejected the scheme, the chancellor also dropped it and confined himself to defending his refusal to participate.

Meanwhile, Shuvalov persuaded the Tsar to suggest a mixed occupation. And Schweinitz reported that Shuvalov had actually—for the second time—taken over the direction of Russian foreign policy. The German and British ambassadors thought that a change in favour of Shuvalov was certainly possible if the powers accepted his proposal.[17]

Andrássy again attempted to persuade Berlin not only to take part, but to have a German general assume command. Playing Bismarck's tune, he harped on the theme that this would aid Shuvalov. Such importunity grated on Bismarck's nerves,[18] although he tried to save Andrássy from outward signs of his displeasure. Vienna was informed that his main reason for abstaining was the difficulty in participating without constantly 'taking sides'; this would lead to the accusation of arbitrariness because Germany had no material interest in the question. The danger would only be aggravated if the command of the troops were assumed. Even if Germany were to remain

[16] Bülow to Reuss, 28 February, no. 112 secret, GFO, IABq 133 vii; St. Vallier to Waddington, 26 February, no. 37, FFM, Allemagne 27.

[17] Dufferin to Salisbury, Petersburg, 2 April, private, SP, A/14; Langenau to Andrássy, Petersburg, 1 April, no. 15 D réservé, WS, PA X 73; Schweinitz, ii, 56f.

[18] Széchényi to Andrássy, Berlin, 6 April, no. 15 A–B confid., WS, PA III 119; Taffs, p. 346.

reserved the other powers would take this amiss. Bismarck had been unable to avoid this pitfall at the Congress and, as a result, his longstanding good relations with Russia had suffered. On the other hand, he would be prepared to further an understanding amongst the powers, and Austria would certainly have no cause to complain of his disregard for her interests. In this spirit of mutual understanding and peace Germany wished Shuvalov success, but in view of the present mood in Petersburg it would be best not to mention this because Shuvalov himself had the feeling he was regarded as the candidate of Germany.[19]

The English, at this time, agreed to a mixed occupation, but appended a condition which eventually doomed it—the participation of Turkish troops. The main point for the Russians was the exclusion of the Turks from the occupation, but Münster, the German ambassador in London, had actually been told that Germany did not object to this point. The Russians learned of this and were quite upset. Then, Münster was instructed that Germany would only accept Turkish participation if all the powers agreed to it. Bismarck had apparently wanted to give Shuvalov some slight support in London, but the matter was bungled and the misunderstanding contributed to the anti-German sentiment in Petersburg; in this respect the damage could not be completely repaired.[20]

With such indifferent backing the mixed occupation scheme was discarded, and after the first week in April England and Russia began negotiating on alternative proposals. Realizing this, Bismarck wished to see the blame pushed on to other shoulders than his own. Reuss, in Vienna, was instructed to insinuate that the antagonism of Gorchakov, his organs (the panslav press), and a group of French agents in the East were the real cause of failure. Andrássy was certainly not happy about Bismarck's refusal to cooperate, but he spontaneously attributed the miscarriage of the scheme to Gorchakov. The fact that the Russians were negotiating separately with England was not reassuring. He feared that they were merely manœuvr-

[19] Bülow to Reuss, 26 March, no. 195; Reuss to Bülow, Vienna, 23 March, no. 116, GFO, IABq 133 vii.

[20] Schweinitz to Bülow, Virballen, 3 April, private and secret, GFO, Russland 61 secreta; Schweinitz, ii, 47, 58f.

ing for a prolongation of their own occupation. These remarks encouraged Bismarck to speak more boldly. Vienna was informed that Russia's conduct in the negotiations was an ill omen for a peaceful future. The sudden decision for a quick evacuation made him suspicious; this was merely another example of a policy reversal resulting from unreliability and impatience.[21]

Bismarck's attempt to blame Gorchakov for the failure of the mixed occupation plan was based on the tactical desire to shift suspicion from himself. But he was also genuinely irritated with Gorchakov for many reasons. He drew closer to Austria as a result.

The defeat of the mixed occupation idea was a great blow for Shuvalov. Gorchakov was now, at least formally, secure in his position. His influence, of course, had dwindled steadily[22] and Russia had turned more conciliatory, but it was Giers and not Shuvalov who was to guide the new line. He was generally regarded as a sensible man but without the necessary calibre. Since Bismarck had less confidence in him than in Shuvalov he leaned more heavily on Austria.

Before he finally stepped from the stage Shuvalov had one last problematical triumph. According to the Russian ambassador, Andrássy wanted to see him in Vienna on his way to Britain. He was instructed to proclaim Russia's faithful adherence to the Treaty so as to obtain approval of the retention of a division of Russian soldiers for the maintenance of order in Eastern Rumelia. He also sought support in the delimitation of the Bulgarian-East Rumelian border. Shuvalov arrived in the Austrian capital on 23 April. Andrássy received him with a 'whole arsenal of bitter reproaches' and their first conversation ended unsatisfactorily. Shuvalov felt that Andrássy's self-confidence had risen too sharply. He imagined this disturbing

[21] Bülow to Reuss, 9 & 12 April, nos. 247 and 257, GFO, IABq 133 vii. Reuss was also told that 'in more than one respect' it would be desirable, if Bismarck's arguments were to appear in the Viennese press. Cf. *DDF*, ii, nos. 409 and 411.

[22] Schweinitz to Bülow, Petersburg, 24 February, no. 55 most confid.; 13 March, no. 69; Alvensleben to Bülow, Petersburg, 23 April, no. 132, GFO, Russland 61; Schweinitz to Bülow, 27 February, no. 61 confid., GFO, IABq 133 i; Salisbury to Dufferin, 9 April, private, SP, A/31.

phenomenon resulted partly from the security offered by his friendly relations with Germany.[23] No doubt, this was true. But on the following day Andrássy was much more conciliatory and a tentative agreement was reached on the 29th. Andrássy affirmed his belief in Alexander's determination to evacuate promptly and agreed to leave the details to Russia. In return, he asked for completion by 3 July. Shuvalov promised to recommend this heartily to his Emperor, but, if he did, his eloquence fell on deaf ears because the Tsar held to 3 August as the final date. Andrássy also accepted the Russian view in the delimitation question, but refused to agree to the retention of a division in Eastern Rumelia. Here Shuvalov gave way readily. Both statesmen had good reason to be satisfied with their conversations, but both feared the results could be compromised by unforeseen events.[24]

Shuvalov's mission to Vienna was a success. He did not achieve the maximum, but at least he had discovered that no effective understanding, to say nothing of an alliance, existed between England and Austria. Also Andrássy had been more than usually conciliatory, probably because England and Russia were meanwhile working out a solution to the Balkan problems, and excessive rigidity on his part would have led to isolation. For this reason he immediately tried to sow distrust between the two. The Anglo-Russian understanding was also largely the work of Shuvalov, who had persuaded the Tsar to declare that after the evacuation of Eastern Rumelia he would leave its inhabitants to their fate.

Thus Shuvalov's mission and the Anglo-Russian agreements mark the end of the worst tension which had lasted the winter over. He had helped to initiate the more conciliatory trend in Russian diplomacy, but this was his last triumph. His policy unfortunately always seemed to involve uncomfortable concessions. When present in Petersburg he was capable of persuading Alexander, but as soon as he left other influences gained the upper hand and the Tsar appears to have had quite enough

[23] Münster to Bismarck, London, 7 May, no. 49; Reuss to Bülow, Vienna, 25 April, no. 181, GFO, IABq 133; 27 April, no. 184 confid., GFO, IABq 133 i.

[24] Reuss to Bülow, Vienna, 28 & 30 April, nos. 189 confid. and 192, GFO, IABq 133 i; 28 April, no. 186, GFO, Bulgarien 1; 7 May, no. 201; Andrássy to Károlyi, Vienna, 2 May, GFO, IABq 133; Medlicott, *Congress*, pp. 374f.

of what he regarded as humiliating concessions. Shuvalov himself realized this, and although he believed that he had accomplished much during his stay in Petersburg, he told Reuss that 'l'empereur ne veut pas de moi', and that he had urgently requested his recall.[25]

From the point of view of German diplomacy the Shuvalov mission had another meaning. It was the ambassador's first faint success achieved by means of an Austro-Russian agreement and could have been used as a point of departure for further cooperation. But Shuvalov was used up, and although the tension slackened between the two countries, distrust continued. In the first half of April Bismarck had spoken in favour of the *Dreikaiserbund* and criticized Andrássy's lukewarm attitude towards it,[26] but during Shuvalov's visit to Vienna he refused even Platonic support. He could hardly have seriously feared an intimate Austro-Russian understanding, but by this time he seemed to have no interest whatever in advising them even *pro forma* to reach an agreement. Evidently the tendency of Austria and Russia at the end of March and the beginning of April to make mutual concessions, when there was no other sensible way out, had made him wary.

II

Germany's relative unconcern for the main problems involved in the execution of the Treaty is probably the underlying reason for Bismarck's failure to respond to the more conciliatory turn in Russian policy dating from about the signing of the definitive peace treaty with Turkey on 8 February. The significance of the conclusion of the Treaty as a demonstration of Russian goodwill towards Europe was understood by Bismarck; he welcomed it as an indication of greater sympathy for

[25] Alvensleben to Bülow, Petersburg, 20 April, no. 124 most confid.; 20 April, private, GFO, Russland 61; Reuss to Bülow, Vienna, 28 April, no. 183 most confid., GFO, Russland 61 secreta; Dufferin to Salisbury, Petersburg, 26 March, private, SP, A/14; St. Vallier to Waddington, 12 March, tel., FFM, Allemagne 27. Shuvalov had so successfully taken matters in his own hands that Jomini, Gorchakov's *protégé*, extolled him in the presence of the German *chargé*. Alvensleben to Bülow, 19 April, no. 119 most confid, GFO, IABq 133 iv.

[26] Bülow to German ambassadors, 5 April, GFO, IABq 133; Russell to Salisbury, Berlin, 16 April, no. 210 secret, FO 64/932; *DDF*, ii, 406; Taffs, p. 346.

Shuvalov's views. On the other hand, Gorchakov was still in office and there were signs that he was playing an active, if not always the most important, role in the foreign ministry and that he continued to do so until Tsar Alexander journeyed to Livadia on 24 April leaving him behind.[27] Gorchakov's mere physical presence in Petersburg was for Bismarck sufficient to make a *rapprochement* with Russia difficult, if not impossible. But the German chancellor had other reasons for refusing to conciliate Russia. Ominous reports about Russian army increases began arriving and other information seemed to confirm that they were intended to facilitate war with Germany. But something else disturbed Bismarck even more.

In February 1879 Waddington, French foreign minister since December 1877, formed a cabinet. Most of his attention was devoted to balancing between a radical assembly and a conservative senate. He was seemingly unable to control the newly awakened independence of some of the French representatives in the Balkans who from January to March had taken it upon themselves to cooperate more closely with the Russians than hitherto.[28] The weakness of Waddington's cabinet, which could be replaced by one dangerously radical and more ambitious in foreign affairs, was a cause of worry, and so was the fact that, if Russia continued to demonstrate goodwill in the Treaty execution, she could soon escape from her isolation. This worry seemed all the more justified when the Russian press lashed out against Germany and reports arrived of wide-spread flirting with France.

As a result of these apprehensions Bismarck began to deploy his heaviest armour against Gorchakov; he also cultivated more intensively his relations with Austria. Not only did he assure Andrássy of German friendship, he sought to go hand in hand with Austria in questions where the interests of the two countries were similar, and even in those where they differed somewhat. Because of the protracted difficulties with Russia, Bismarck continued to pay particular attention to his relations with the

[27] Note, 8 February 1879; Bülow to William, 9 February, GFO, IABq 133; Alvensleben to Bülow, Petersburg, 23 April, no. 132, GFO, Russland 61.

[28] See Hatzfeldt's reports in GFO, IABq 133 iv; Bülow to German missions, 21 February, GFO, IABq 110; Russell to Salisbury, 15 & 21 February, private, SP, A/9.

western powers. And since his squabbles with Rumania stood in the way of better relations, he was anxious to dispose of that troublesome matter. Accordingly, a show of assistance to France and England was advisable, when possible, in such a way as to increase Russian isolation. France received more consideration, because she could be more dangerous. Bismarck tried to stimulate French interest in the Mediterranean region, so as to turn her attention from squabbles with Germany and cooperation with Russia, and turn it towards collaboration with England, with whom France should be a quarrelling friend, for he also helped to keep the British actively occupied there. The support Bismarck gave the British in Egypt was a service of questionable value, but he apparently wanted them to achieve some satisfaction with a drop of French vermouth.

Gorchakov keenly felt the attacks aimed at him since the Congress and he understood the significance of the German chancellor's political manœuvres. Seeking to make a virtue of necessity, he advocated and began to implement a policy of 'free hands'. After his return to office in December he organized the counter-attack. He spurred on the Russian and pro-Russian foreign press, displayed sympathy for Beaconsfield, made a fumbling attempt at a *rapprochement* with England and inspired a strongly pro-French movement in Russian government circles.[29] The Austro-German measures taken against the plague gave him the opportunity he wanted to repay Bismarck and to protest directly to him.

On the last day of February Valuev,[30] the Russian minister of imperial domains, visited Schweinitz. The Germans regarded Valuev as sober and reliable—perhaps because he had a picture of Bismarck in his office. The Russian conveyed his regrets at the discontent with Germany and the flirting with France which were increasing in many circles. As Schweinitz

[29] Skazkin, pp. 65–77; Grüning, pp. 63–7; *DDF*, ii, no. 392; Langenau to Andrássy, Petersburg, 21 May, no. 23 C, WS, PA X 73; St. Vallier to Waddington, 3 March, no. 47, FFM, Allemagne 27; Chanzy to Waddington, Petersburg, 29 March, no. 2, FFM, Russie 258.

[30] COUNT P. A. VALUEV (1814–90). Minister of imperial domains, 1872–9; minister president, 1879–81.

retorted that he found the tirades of irresponsible journalists not unduly alarming, Valuev answered that he had not meant the press, but other groups in which this flirting had quite recently mushroomed. He went on to say that in his opinion Germany had encouraged the Tsar a little too much to go to war, but her attitude during and since the war had been beyond reproach.[31]

It would be easy to imagine the impact of the report of this conversation in Berlin. Just what this flirting was, it was not said; but it was enough to know that criticism of Germany was paired with growing sympathy for France. The trend was attributed to Gorchakov, and Bismarck clearly feared its consequences if a crisis were to come in France. Up to a point his anxiety was justified. True, Russia was in no position for new adventures and Gorchakov had lost his ability for constructive diplomacy; still, he felt his frustration keenly and vented it in a peculiar manner. On 5 March Münster, the ambassador in London, reported that Shuvalov had told him Gorchakov was irritated about the revocation of article v and the measures taken to contain the plague, and believed that the Three Emperors' League had lapsed. He thought that Austro-German cooperation could threaten Russia. Shuvalov was instructed to ascertain whether London recognized this danger. The Russian ambassador believed that it would be unwise to draw attention to an alignment which the English would hardly consider disconcerting.[32] This view was correct without a doubt. Gorchakov's move was nothing more than a clumsy and misconceived attempt to undermine Bismarck's position with the English. On the other hand, his awkwardness was exceeded by the disloyalty of his agent who made no secret of his disapproval of practically everything Gorchakov was doing. Shuvalov had

---

[31] Reuss to Bismarck, Petersburg, 14 May 1872, no. 76, GFO, IABi 50; Schweinitz to Bülow, Petersburg, 28 February 1879, no. 62 secret, GFO, Russland 61; Loftus to Salisbury, Petersburg, 26 February, private, SP, A/14; Schweinitz, ii, 44. For an interesting example of flirting with France see Windelband, 'Bismarck über das deutsch-russische Verhältnis', p. 172.

[32] Münster to Bismarck, London, 5 March, private, GFO, Russland 61 secreta; Dufferin to Salisbury, Petersburg, 12 March & 30 April, private and confid., SP, A/14; St. Vallier to Waddington, 13 March, private, FFM, Allemagne M & D 166 bis; Friis & Bagge, iv, no. 1484; see also, DDF, ii, no. 392 for an indication that Alexander was becoming familiar with Gorchakov's way of thinking.

been equally disloyal at the Congress, and he clearly wanted to nourish Bismarck's suspicion of Gorchakov.

At about the same time (26 February) an article appeared in the Brussels *Nord*, a newspaper subsidized by Russia; it described the mood of official Petersburg circles in words unflattering for Germany. Bülow regarded the article as Gorchakov's 'unbosoming' of his 'yearning for more intimate relations with France'.

The information gained from Münster's letter and the article was relayed to Schweinitz. He was told that despite the difficulties caused by the Russian chancellor Berlin would not succumb to the irritation which he had desired at various times in the previous year for use as a means of agitation with the Tsar; nevertheless, Russia had threatened to ally with France where at the moment anything was possible, even the red flag prophesied by Treitschke. Such a threat at this time could perhaps serve as evidence that, if France had been ready in 1876, there would have been a Franco-Russian alliance instead of the Turkish war.[33]

The views of the press were a handy barometer for measuring the state of Franco-Russian relations. Bismarck would have been foolish to make no use of this instrument. But the surprising thing is not that some courting should go on—that was after all a natural reaction—but that there was so little of it.[34] Throughout the whole period covered by this study there was much mutual criticism and no sustained effort to improve relations. Bismarck must have realized this, or did he?

These incidents clearly show that the 'two chancellors' war' was having detrimental effects on the general diplomatic relations between their two countries.

Bismarck could not be sure that Gorchakov would confine himself to threats, and the activities of the Russian and French agents in Eastern Rumelia aroused suspicion. In March they became 'most intimate'. Waddington did not approve of this, but his position was so weak at the time that he was unable to

---

[33] Bülow to Schweinitz, 9 March, no. 122 secret, GFO, Russland 61 secreta; Széchényi to Andrássy, Berlin, 30 August, no. 24–B, WS, PA III 119.

[34] See for instance St. Vallier to Waddington, 27 April 1879, tel., FFM, Allemagne 28.

reprimand his agents. And Bismarck apparently feared that Fournier, the French ambassador in Constantinople and author of this subterranean activity, could easily become foreign minister. Fournier, at any rate, was planning to move into the Quai d'Orsay at the earliest possible date. St. Vallier was horrified at the thought and passed many an hour with Bismarck and others exchanging abusive stories about this impossible man.[35]

Bismarck thought that the French agents were merely acting on their own; he facetiously claimed that Fournier at his earlier post in Italy had learned the tactics of *fara da se*. Nevertheless, his uneasiness increased; he believed it was more likely that the Russian rather than the French government had its hand in the intrigues. However, a change in the French foreign ministry was possible any moment.

It is interesting to note that Bismarck wished to label Gorchakov as the chief intriguer, not the Tsar, to say nothing of France. He was not satisfied merely to air his complaints in London, Paris, and Vienna, but decided to reassure himself of Andrássy's sympathy, reopen the press campaign against Gorchakov, and take the bold step of complaining about him directly to Alexander. Also, when Bismarck learned that there was discussion about calling a conference in Berlin to expedite the execution of the Treaty, he refused to take part, arguing that he had experienced too much Russian ingratitude and, although he would never vote against Russia, he could not help as much as hitherto.[36]

In view of manifest Russian goodwill towards Europe since the conclusion of the Treaty with Turkey (8 February) the

[35] H. FOURNIER (1821–98). Envoy in Stockholm, 1862; Rome, 1872–3; ambassador in Constantinople, 1877–80. See Hatzfeldt's reports in GFO, IABq 133 iv; Bülow to Hatzfeldt, 25 March, no. 120, GFO, Türkei 135. The British were also troubled by Fournier. Lyons to Salisbury, Paris, 19 January 1879, private; 2 January 1880, private, SP, A/8; Salisbury to Lyons, 27 November 1878, private; 25 January & 2 April 1879, private, SP, A/26; Waddington to St. Vallier, Paris, 20 February, no. 21, FFM, Allemagne 27; numerous letters from St. Vallier to Waddington in FFM, Allemagne M & D 166–166 bis.

[36] Bülow to Münster and Reuss, 18 March, nos. 151 and 167 secret, GFO, IABq 133 iv; Bülow to Reuss, 26 March, no. 197, GFO, IAB 133; St. Vallier to Waddington, 26 & 27 February, nos. 37 and 39 confid., FFM, Allemagne 27; Müller, no. 30.

Russian ambassador's statement that the Tsar was *froissé* over the plague measures came at an awkward moment because it suggested that Germany was replacing England in the minds of the Russians as their chief opponent. In answer to this Bismarck became more responsive not in his relations with Russia, but with the other powers, primarily Austria. Accordingly, when Andrássy congratulated not only Tsar Alexander for the final conclusion of peace with Turkey, but also Gorchakov for his 'political stature', Bismarck was upset, perhaps all the more because the compliment was well received in Petersburg. He expressed doubt to Andrássy about the wisdom of such a demonstration. Gorchakov regarded ovations as natural tribute, he was told, and they merely increased his already highly developed self-confidence and made him even more intractable and pretentious. In the past Bismarck had attempted such gratification of his vanity as a sort of homeopathic cure, but only discovered that the antidote, which was necessary afterwards, had a worse effect than the medicine.[37]

Bismarck was obviously concerned about the possibility that Andrássy could seek better relations with Russia. Therefore, before taking the next step in his battle against Gorchakov, he wanted to ascertain Andrássy's views of his rival. But it was some time before a report arrived. Meanwhile the international constellation seemed to take a turn for the worse. So Bismarck, his patience worn thin, continued his personal war without waiting for an answer.

The wave of hostile articles appearing in the Russian newspapers had its effect. The press war continued. Some of the German papers seemed to be immensely enjoying the fray. Tongue in cheek, they argued that because of the danger of an Anglo-Russian alignment, the best alliance for France was one with Germany. Bismarck took a less frivolous view of the matter. On 1 January he had already inspired articles warding off excessive claims for support and affirming that Germany had, in fact, given more than the Russians had requested. Then, towards the end of February, he summoned Moritz Busch[38]

---

[37] Bülow to Reuss, 26 February, no. 103, GFO, IABq 133.

[38] MORITZ BUSCH (1821–99). Journalist; temporary assistant in German foreign office, 1870.

to his office and instructed him to write an article praising Shuvalov and attacking Gorchakov, but sparing the
Tsar. Busch was permitted to see the relevant correspondence
in the foreign office files. Bismarck himself provided the general
outline and read the proofs of the final article which appears
to have caused quite a stir.[39]

Shortly thereafter, in the middle of March, General Werder,
the German military plenipotentiary in Russia and intimate
friend of the Tsar, was in Berlin. Bismarck apparently believed
that the Tsar had asked Werder to sound him out as to the
possibility of more substantial support. This gave him the
opportunity he wanted to air his own views on the subject.
Deciding to take the gravest step yet in his battle, he authorized
Werder to tell the Tsar frankly that Gorchakov was ruining
Russian foreign policy, or at least relations with Germany;
Russia's fundamental mistake in the Balkan crisis had been the
alienation of Austria through failure to reach a timely understanding with her; the attempt to burden Germany with the
responsibility for the natural consequences of this mistake was
estranging Russia's powerful and perhaps only friend.[40] This
was certainly plainer than Alexander's insinuations against
Bismarck in August 1879, yet the Tsar is reported to have
received Werder's remarks indulgently, although the general
spoke with remarkable frankness, arguing that Russo-German
relations would be much better if Gorchakov were dismissed.
In his own words the conversation appeared like an indictment
of Gorchakov.[41]

This was a serious but vain step. Gorchakov did not accom-
pany the Tsar to Livadia in April, but this decision had been
made earlier. It was most likely Alexander's plan to let Gorchakov fade into the background without actually dismissing
him. His stubborn refusal to release his aged minister could
hardly have been altered by this massive pressure. On the

[39] Bülow to Hohenlohe, 13 March, no. 139, GFO, Bulgarien 1; H. Bismarck
to Bülow, Friedrichsruh, 1 January, GFO, IABi 60; St. Vallier to Waddington, 3
March, no. 47, FFM, Allemagne 27; Busch, ii, 390–6; *DDF*, ii, no. 406; Winckler,
Bismarcks Bündnispolitik, p. 35.

[40] Bülow to Reuss, 20 March, no. 174 most confid., GFO, Russland 61 secreta.

[41] Werder to William, Petersburg, 27 March, no. 14, GFO, Russland 61
secreta; Windelband, pp. 53, 67.

contrary, it made him all the more suspicious of Bismarck. Turning the tables on the Germans, he told Schweinitz that after the amicable letter from William in the autumn of 1876 he had expected more from his neighbour.[42]

Both the newspaper campaign and the Werder mission illustrate the trend of Bismarck's Russian policy. The tension with Gorchakov was so severe that the carefully maintained distinction between him and the government, or the Tsar, was becoming more and more unreal, for at the same time Bismarck's comprehensive diplomatic manoeuvres led to the isolation of the Russian empire itself. In comparison, his continued support in those matters where he thought Russian aims justified weighed but little; and although Shuvalov was praised again in diplomatic circles and the press,[43] Bismarck found it difficult to support him in the business of day to day diplomacy. It is strange that at just this moment the British ambassador in Berlin should have been so gloomy about the possibility of obtaining Bismarck's support in the disputes arising out of the Treaty. He wrote: unjustifiable as Russia's ingratitude certainly is, it must be admitted that Bismarck returns good for evil.[44]

Bismarck did not wait for Werder's report to reassure himself of Austrian goodwill. The harder he worked for Gorchakov's dismissal, the more he courted Andrássy. On 18 March Berlin finally learned that the misgivings about the effect of flattery on Gorchakov were shared; Andrássy believed that he had become completely inept and would probably soon be forced to retire.[45]

[42] Schweinitz to Bülow, Petersburg, 13 March, no. 69, GFO, Russland 61; Schweinitz to Bülow, Virballen, 3 April, private and secret, GFO, Russland 61 secreta; *GP*, nos. 230 and 446. Windelband, p. 53, cites the army increases as a sign that the Tsar was unwilling to consider Bismarck's criticism, but these increases were certainly well on the way towards execution by this time.

[43] Langenau to Andrássy, Petersburg, 26 March, private, confid., WS, PA X 74; Salisbury to Russell, London, 1 May, no. 244, FO 64/929.

[44] Russell to Salisbury, Berlin, 9 May, no. 241 secret, FO 64/933; 22 March, private, SP, A/9; Széchényi to Andrássy, Berlin, 10 May, private, WS, PA III 119. St. Vallier and the Austrian ambassador in Petersburg also still believed that the tension between Bismarck and Gorchakov was 'purely personal'. Langenau to Andrássy, Petersburg, 16 July, no. 32 A–C confid., WS, PA X 73; St. Vallier to Waddington, 27 March, no. 62, FFM, Allemagne 27.

[45] Reuss to Bülow, Vienna, 17 March, no. 105 confid., GFO, IABq 133.

This was good news, and Bismarck informed Vienna of Werder's mission. In addition, he confided that relations with Austria had become more intimate through his experiences since the Congress. As if to stress his good intentions, he reiterated that he had always advised the Russians—and still did—to reach an agreement with Austria and he, Bismarck, would subscribe to it. But this advice did not imply any suggestion that Austria should avoid intimate relations with England. Three weeks later, on 12 April, he went so far as to say that he would not regard an unwritten, or even a formal and permanent alliance between Austria and England as a disturbance, but rather as a further guarantee of the peace. The Austrian foreign minister nodded approval to the discussion of Gorchakov's mistaken policy and hoped that Werder's mission would bear fruit; he hailed the acceptance of good relations with England.[46]

On 5 April Bismarck saw Schweinitz, ambassador in Petersburg. The chancellor complained about Gorchakov's flirting with France, Miliutin's never-ending armaments, the cavalry positions near the German frontier and the frenzied language of the Russian press; all this had convinced him of Russia's unreliability—even the Tsar was less certain than he had been. Therefore, the other powers, especially England, must not be antagonized. With Austria one should strive for an organic relationship only to be dissolved with parliamentary consent.[47]

How seriously Bismarck meant these repeated assurances of friendship, the desire to walk 'hand in hand' with Austria,[48] it is difficult to say. It would be incorrect to dismiss them especially because Bismarck had talked earlier (January 1877) of an organic alliance with Austria under similar circumstances. The well-known conversation with Schweinitz can easily be construed to mean that Bismarck followed a carefully conceived

[46] Reuss to Bülow, Vienna, 23 March, no. 119 confid.; Bülow to Reuss, 20 March, no. 174 most confid., GFO, Russland 61 secreta; 12 April, no. 253, GFO, Österreich 70. At the end of February Bismarck had told Dufferin that he was not inclined to quarrel with his other allies, especially Austria, towards whom Germany was drawing more closely, for the 'beaux yeux' of Russia. Dufferin to Salisbury, Berlin, 28 February, private, no. 1, SP, A/14.

[47] Schweinitz, ii, 60.

[48] Bülow to Reuss, 3 March, no. 122, GFO, IABq 110.

plan culminating in the Austrian alliance, but this is unlikely. He had, after all—perhaps just as frequently—considered alliance with Russia. And it should not be forgotten that he regarded Schweinitz as somewhat too pro-Russian. The ambassador was therefore a good object on which he could profitably vent his spleen; his remarks were meant partly as chastisement for Schweinitz. At this stage he was probably merely looking for reassurance in his feud with Gorchakov. Bismarck's ill will had been assiduously directed against him personally; if he had been dismissed, which at the time was probably more likely than his retention in office, the way would have been clear for a *rapprochement*. On the other hand, the chancellor was obviously carefully considering the idea of an Austrian alliance.[49]

At any rate intimacy with Austria increased steadily, and Andrássy's attitude towards Russia became more independent. The French ambassador in Vienna cleverly described this, saying that Andrássy had an *entente confiante* with Germany and an *entente défiante* with Russia.[50] So the problematical nature of an alliance with Austria appeared even before it was concluded. Bismarck certainly wanted Vienna to adopt a firmer line, but he could not have wanted a general increase in Andrássy's self-confidence, since this would encourage independence from German guidance.

How Austria was to maintain good relations with Russia without neglecting England is an open question.[51] Probably Bismarck wanted Andrássy's relations with England to be good enough to prevent him from becoming either too friendly with, or dependent on, Russia. This would also keep the English from attempting to solve their problems with the Russians alone, as before the Congress, and, to a certain extent, in April 1879, when the mixed occupation scheme was dropped in

[49] See below, pp. 176ff.

[50] Vogüé to Waddington, Vienna, 26 March, no. 25, FFM, Autriche 525.

[51] Windelband, p. 53, states that Bismarck 'energetically' referred to the necessity for Austria to reach an agreement with Russia. In fact, he merely referred to his policy: that he would subscribe to anything on which Russia and Austria agreed. This must be seen in context with Bismarck's serious criticism of Russian diplomacy, his repeated references to his friendly disposition towards Austria, and thirdly, with the reservation concerning good relations with England.

favour of bilateral negotiations.[52] Gorchakov's ostentatious sporadic flattering of Disraeli during and since the Congress was an additional indication that England and Russia could, conceivably, come to terms.[53] So London was kept posted about German anxieties concerning Russia. But Bismarck could hardly have wanted the link between England and Austria to be forged too strongly; in the last analysis it was safer and easier to dominate a Three Emperors' League than an Anglo-Austrian alignment. Also the tendency to flatter Andrássy and to portray himself in a benevolent pose should not be overlooked. Bismarck needed Austrian support because of frosty Russo-German relations; but as the Russians became aware of the Austro-German *rapprochement*, they grew all the more bitter and the assurance that Bismarck gave Andrássy regarding his relations with England helped to undermine the community of interest—small as it was—between Austria and Russia.[54] This had been the necessary prerequisite to Bismarck's role as mediator between the two in the old Three Emperors' League.

The chancellor's approval of healthy relations between Austria and Britain thus fostered the establishment of an indirect link with England. So while remaining a theoretical adherent of the *Dreikaiserbund*, Bismarck pursued a policy which in practice served to estrange his two partners, the one from the other, and to establish at least the possibility of another diplomatic orientation.

[52] In January 1879 he had told Széchényi that the growing alliance between Austria and England was a guarantee of the general European peace which Germany much needed. *GW*, viii, no. 229. Bismarck was probably worried that England would object to his intimacy with Austria. Holstein, 15 March 1879, note, GFO, England 69. He had, therefore, attempted to disarm the British by encouraging their good relations with Austria. Russell to Salisbury, Berlin, 2 March 1879, no. 138 secret, FO 64/932.

[53] Langenau to Andrássy, Petersburg, 31 July 1878, no. 31 A–D, WS, PA X 72; 21 May 1879, no. 23 C, WS, PA X 73; Salisbury to Russell, London, 1 & 13 May 1879, nos. 244 and 265 confid., FO 64/929.

[54] Cf. Bülow to Reuss, 12 April 1879, no. 253; 26 May, no. 392, GFO, Österreich 70; but see also Bismarck's remarks to a friend in April 1879. Andrássy's statesmanship is criticized and especially his efforts 'to emancipate himself from the *Dreikaiserbund*', etc., Russell to Salisbury, 16 April, no. 210 secret, FO 64/932; *DDF*, ii, no. 406.

CHAPTER V

The Approaching Storm: Bismarck and the Russian Army

In the summer of 1876 the Tsar had appointed a commission to ascertain whether the Russian railway system corresponded to the economic, political, and strategic needs of the empire. On 9 March 1879 Lignitz,[1] the German military *attaché* in Petersburg, reported on the results of this study. Lignitz was able and ambitious; he looked on the Russian army with amused contempt and on the intentions of the Tsar and his advisers with constant suspicion. His views were regarded in Berlin as a healthy antidote to the less critical ideas of the other two German representatives in Petersburg, Schweinitz, the ambassador, and Werder, the military plenipotentiary. He pointed out that the Russian railway system was most carefully constructed in the area bordering on Prussia and that its carrying capacity was being steadily increased. He believed there was no real economic justification for this and that strategic considerations had been decisive. Lignitz emphasized that in the last war the troops had been mobilized long before the railway could transport them to Kishinev in the south-west corner of Russia. A concentration in Vilna would be completed with far greater, and increasing, rapidity. Lignitz thought compensatory projects would be necessary in East Prussia.[2]

Moltke was asked if improvements to the East Prussian railway were necessary in the light of Lignitz's report. The chief of staff was unmoved and stressed the necessity for

---

[1] MAJOR V. VON LIGNITZ (1841–1913). Writer, *attaché* in Petersburg, 1876–1885; general, 1896.

[2] Schweinitz to GFO, Petersburg, 26 July 1876, no. 172; Schweinitz to Bülow, 16 February 1877, no. 66, GFO, IABi 53; Lignitz, Petersburg, 9 March 1879, secret, GFO, IABi 57 secretissima; Limburg-Stirum to H. Bismarck, 31 October 1880, FA, B 70; Brauer, pp. 52ff.

increasing the capacity of the railways in western Germany instead. Bismarck supported Moltke's plans.[3]

One is tempted to stress the political motives of this Russian railway construction, but there were also good economic and geographical reasons for the lines converging on Warsaw. And the Prussian government itself had encouraged some of the building largely to open up the hinterland of the ports of Danzig and Königsberg.[4] Nevertheless, the railways could be used for military purposes.

More important for the understanding of Bismarck's reaction to the report is the fact that international tension was high at the moment and he was uneasy about supposed Franco-Russian intrigues in Eastern Rumelia and also, perhaps, continued Russian efforts to secure a large international loan. Then, on 21 March, a report by Schweinitz on the Russian army increases arrived. The ambassador stated that the cadres for twenty-four new reserve infantry divisions were being formed. This meant that the Russian army in wartime would have seventy-two divisions instead of forty-eight—an increase of about 400,000 men. In peacetime the increase would amount to about 58,000 men. Schweinitz's statistics were later verified by Lignitz and Andrássy, although Werder maintained that the increase was less and Moltke thought it was more significant. Schweinitz and Andrássy had not much faith in the proficiency of the Russian army and were not really alarmed by the increases. Miliutin, Schweinitz said, was afflicted by the modern mania of numbers and was turning the army into a militia, forgetting that there were not sufficient means to train, lead or service such masses. A year later, however, Schweinitz claimed that he had repeatedly drawn attention to the main danger of Miliutin's military reforms: the increase in the cadres coupled with a shortened service period allowed for rapid expansion in wartime.[5]

[3] COUNT H. VON MOLTKE (1800–91). Prussian chief of staff, 1858–88. Bülow to Moltke, 15 March; Moltke to Bülow, 20 March, no. 344 secret; Bülow to Maybach, 8 April, GFO, IABi 57 secretissima.

[4] Ames, pp. 64, 68; Reuss to Bülow, Petersburg, 18 July 1874, no. 192 confid., GFO, IABi 53; see also Reutern, pp. 183–207.

[5] Schweinitz to Bismarck, Petersburg, 16 January 1880, no. 19, GFO, IABi 57 secretissima.

Just as disturbing as the actual increases was what Schweinitz had to say about Miliutin, the man responsible for them. He was, Schweinitz thought, the Tsar's most influential adviser at the moment. He believed, however, that this would be merely a temporary arrangement since Alexander, although not strong enough to rule personally, was not so weak as to tolerate domination. At any rate it was possible for Miliutin to get all the money he wanted for his army reorganization schemes because the other ministers did not raise objections, partly on account of their own insignificance, age or lethargy. What his political aims were, Schweinitz could not say. He had known the minister of war for fourteen years, but had never been able to discover them. He did know that Miliutin had no particular sympathy for Prussia and believed that, although he was not very articulate, one might nevertheless draw some conclusions as to his aims based on past actions. It was he who was responsible for the development of the Russian railways in the neighbourhood of Prussia. His strategic railways were not built for a war with Austria, to say nothing of Turkey. Besides this he was responsible for the transfer of several cavalry divisions from more fertile provinces to inhospitable quarters on the Prussian border. In spite of it all Schweinitz did not believe that Miliutin was belligerent. He thought the Russian minister of war considered the army more as the school of the nation than as a weapon. Schweinitz mentioned that Miliutin was level-headed and never lost his self-control. Bismarck did not share the ambassador's uncomplicated views.[6] Like many others, he labelled the minister an extremist, but on the whole Miliutin's views were fairly moderate. On the other hand, no responsible German statesman could regard with complacency the railway construction in Russian Poland, the shifts in troop dispositions, and the army increases.

A patriotic liberal, but no democrat or exaggerated nationalist,

[6] Schweinitz to Bismarck, Petersburg, 22 March, no. 78 secret, GFO, Russland 61; Lignitz, Petersburg, 28 April & 8 June, reports; Werder to William, Petersburg, 21 April, no. 20; Reuss to Bülow, Vienna, 16 June, no. 245, GFO, IABi 57 secretissima; Schweinitz to Bismarck, 5 December 1880, no. 377, GFO, Russland 69 secreta; Russell to Salisbury, 16 & 26 April 1879, nos. 210 secret and 222 secret, FO 64/932; Windelband, p. 54; Miliutin, i, 46; Reichsarchiv, Weltkrieg, no. 6. The figures in DDF, ii, no. 411, appear inaccurate.

Miliutin intensely disliked the German Balts whose influence in the Russian army and civil service was still very strong. His aversion was all the greater because of their extreme conservatism—not necessarily because of their German ways. His views on the Baltic barons coloured his attitude towards the Germans inasmuch as they had similar traits. He was very concerned about the possibility of an attack from the west, but he must not be considered as especially anti-German. Like so many men of his age his thinking was both liberal and nationalistic. That is why he wanted to reform the army along lines developed by the French and Prussians three-quarters of a century earlier and to strengthen his country's defences, particularly with regard to Russia's most powerful neighbour, and that is why he had dreams of a final solution to the Eastern Question. But he was not a man to seek salvation through conquest. Werder admitted sometime later that many of Miliutin's arrangements did not square with aggressive plans. Nevertheless, this gives an indication of the problematical nature of Miliutin's lifework. A mass army modelled on liberal lines and patriotic in spirit was necessary for the survival of imperial Russia, but it invited misuse and was bound to challenge the autocratic foundations of the state.[7]

Besides these real or possible threats to the security of Germany, magnified by the immediate political constellation, there was an important structural weakness in the German defensive system which must have increased Bismarck's apprehension. It was Moltke's belief that the supposedly weak geographical position of Germany could best be countered by an extremely rapid mobilization and transportation of the army to the border where the enemy could be sought and decisively defeated. Only in this manner, it was thought, could Germany survive a war on two fronts against stronger enemies. As long as this was the official strategy, there would be a

[7] Reuss to Thile, Petersburg, 12 July 1872, no. 109 confid., GFO, IABi 46; Werder to William, Petersburg, 8 December 1880, no. 34; Schweinitz to Bismarck, Petersburg, 10 June 1880, no. 175 confid., GFO, Russland 61; 5 December 1880, no. 377, GFO, Russland 69 secreta; Manteuffel to Bismarck, Bromberg, 4 September 1879, GFO, Russland 65 i secreta; Kálnoky to Haymerle, Petersburg, 6 March 1880, private and secret, WS, PA rot 454 Liasse II; Jelavich, 'Diary of Miliutin', pp. 255–9; Miliutin, i, 5–72; Skazkin, pp. 143–8; Aus dem Leben, iv, 341.

serious temptation for preventive war, even in the pursuit of a
purely defensive policy. In fact, Moltke believed firmly that it
was not the power that struck first which broke the peace, but
rather the state which forced the other to defend itself. Aside
from this, however, constant watchfulness was necessary and
any increase in the ability of a possible enemy to concentrate
troops more quickly on the German frontier, or even to withstand the first decisive battle, was eyed with the greatest uneasiness; the strengthening of defensive fortifications—and this
seems to have been the chief aim of the Russians and French—
was almost as dangerous as actual offensive preparations.[8] Thus
every effort was made to increase the speed with which Germany
could force the decisive battle. The expansion of the German
railway system in the 1870s should be seen partly in this context.

On the other hand the Russians realized quite well the
military significance of these endeavours which they thought
threatened their own security. They did their best to counterbalance them by expanding their own railway system and
stationing larger numbers of troops on the frontier.[9]

United Germany had possessed undoubted military superiority on the continent in 1871, but the margin of superiority
had dwindled steadily, and with it the feeling of security. Thus
it is no surprise that the news of the Russian army increases
alarmed Bismarck. Yet he was not paralysed by alarm, but
sought to communicate it to others and so make it serve his
own purposes. On 20 March he told Chanzy, the newly
appointed French ambassador to Russia, of his fears, stressing
the anarchy in Russia and the rivalry between Shuvalov and
Gorchakov. The ambassador guessed that Bismarck sought to
arouse suspicion of Russia. Earlier in the month he had made
similar complaints to Odo Russell and Dufferin, the new
British ambassador in Petersburg. Russell believed that Bismarck's complaints were 'only blinds', whereas Salisbury
feared that he was 'clearing the decks for action'.[10] Of the three,

[8] Moltke, *passim*; Stadelmann, pp. 283, 297, 301, 303f, 326.

[9] Miliutin, i, 52–4; iii, entry for 29 January 1880.

[10] F. BLACKWOOD, MARQUIS OF DUFFERIN AND AVA (1826–1902). Governor
general of Canada, 1872–9; India, 1884–8; ambassador in Petersburg, February
1879–81; Constantinople, 1881–4; Rome, 1889–91; Paris, 1891–6. *DDF*, ii, no.
398; Medlicott, *Congress*, pp. 226f, 378.

Chanzy was closer to the truth, since Bismarck's aim was to increase the isolation and embarrassment of Gorchakov and his policy.

The chancellor's conversation with Schweinitz on 5 April was in a similar vein.[11] He stressed Russian belligerence and spoke of the need for better relations with England and an organic agreement with Austria. His anger continued, but there were some interludes when he was less preoccupied than usual. One of these moments was during Shuvalov's successful visit to Vienna in late April which marked the end of the winter's squabbles and the clear victory of a more conciliatory line in Russian foreign policy.[12] But simultaneously (23 April) Lignitz's report on further army increases arrived.

In March Schweinitz had written about the expansion of the wartime army by twenty-four reserve divisions. This would entail, he said, the formation in peacetime of the cadres for these divisions. Now Lignitz told of the formation of a fourth battalion in each of the four regiments of thirty-eight infantry divisions, or one hundred and fifty-two new battalions. He admitted that these increases had been planned for some time, but was surprised that they were introduced at a moment when imperial finances were strained and the army had not regained its equilibrium after the war.[13]

Lignitz's report must have made a vivid impression in Berlin, because it indicated that the peacetime strength would be increased by about 142,000 men—more than one third of the strength of the German army—at a single stroke, and this but one month after the formation of the cadres for twenty-four reserve divisions—about 58,000 men.[14] Bülow immediately wrote to Lignitz asking for a comprehensive account of the Russian army increases since the previous summer. When his report arrived on 1 May it turned out that the alarm was much exaggerated. Lignitz's earlier account had been incorrectly worded. Instead of 152 battalions, 152 companies, at peacetime

[11] See above, p. 132.

[12] See above, pp. 121ff.

[13] Lignitz, Petersburg, 20 April, report, GFO, IABi 57 secretissima; Windelband, p. 54.

[14] St. Vallier wrote, *DDF*, ii, no. 417, that Bismarck's 'confident habituel' (Bleichroeder) believed Bismarck less disturbed than previously about Russia.

strength, were being formed; and parallel to the formation of
the cadres for the reserve divisions there were reductions in
local troops. In sum, the increase in the army amounted to what
Schweinitz in March had said it was.[15] Thus, although the
worst fears were unjustified, this information was hardly
comforting.

It would be difficult to exaggerate the importance of these
armaments increases which demonstrated dramatically the
failure of Bismarck's previous Russian policy; not that the
increases themselves were of enormous significance, but because
of the context in which they were announced. Lignitz's report
arrived at a time when the tension over the Eastern Question
had definitely begun to slacken. So Russia was gaining while
Germany was losing independence of action. As Russo-German
relations worsened, Bismarck was less willing to aid his eastern
neighbour, but on the other hand, the Russians needed German
support less. Misunderstandings, mutual distrust, and stubbornness had made a large contribution to the tension, and hindered
the re-establishment of good relations. The situation was
dangerous for the German chancellor, but he evidently did not
see any reason to alter his political course, although the *rapprochement* with Austria could easily lead to a Franco-Russian agreement.[16] To strengthen his position in relation to Russia, he
also did his best to have England and France squabbling
elsewhere and tried to free himself from the aggravating
Rumanian difficulty.

Bismarck had attempted to differentiate carefully between
the policy of Gorchakov and that of Emperor Alexander, but
by this time the distinction was illusory.[17] Although Gorchakov
was rarely asked for advice, the Tsar shared his distrust of
Bismarck and was determined not to be dictated to. Any
further attacks on Gorchakov would now also involve Alexander
and Shuvalov.

It was not only by diplomacy that the chancellor sought to

[15] Lignitz, Petersburg, 28 April, report, GFO, IABi 57 secretissima.

[16] Windelband, p. 54, writes that the Russian military preparations added to the
danger of an anti-German coalition and formed the 'great new fact' that caused
Bismarck to reconstruct his diplomatic system.

[17] Tatishchev, ii, 538; Simpson, p. 48.

neutralize the detrimental effect of the Russian armaments increases. He began to consider the advisability of strengthening the German forces.

In March Bismarck had communicated to Moltke the symptoms of Franco-Russian cooperation. Moltke, in turn, had thought it necessary to rework completely his mobilization plan for the contingency of a war on two fronts—mainly because of the strengthening of the French forces. Previously he had planned to defeat France quickly, then to engage the Russians in battle. Now he reversed the plan and lowered his sights. It is indicative of the political situation that he counted on Austrian benevolent neutrality. In 1877 he had already feared France could be knocked down but not out. Two years later such fears seemed more justified than ever. The strengthened Russian frontline increased the risks of delayed action in the east, so Moltke decided to attack Russia first. Then he hoped to wear out both with alternating blows.[18]

Since the Russian armaments increases made the possibility of an early victory in the east more remote, Bismarck seems to have sent the details to Moltke who advised strengthening the German military force. His report included a comparative table on the reserves in trained manpower which revealed that both France and Russia had larger armies than Germany in peacetime and war. He proposed to increase the peacetime strength of the army, and provide the cadres of the reserve forces by expanding the officer corps.

Kameke, the minister of war, reporting at the same time, believed that since parliament would resist an increase in the size of the army, it should not be attempted. He suggested more intensive training of the reserves as well as a relatively larger officer corps to facilitate rapid expansion in time of war. Bismarck agreed with his suggestions, but wanted also to add to the peacetime strength of the army which had remained at 401,000 since the war with France, although the French and Russian forces had increased considerably. In addition, the German constitution provided for the establishment of the army at the level of one per cent of the population. The growth

18 Bülow to Moltke, 19 March, secret, GFO, IABi 57 secretissima; Moltke, pp. 65ff, 77ff, 109; Stadelmann, pp. 305ff; Kessel, pp. 649ff; Windelband, pp. 45f.

of the population since 1871 would allow for an extra 25,000 men.[19]

As a complementary measure to these initial preparations for the approaching army bill, Bismarck desired to enlighten England and Austria about the dangers of the Russian armaments increases. The reaction of London and Vienna is instructive for the alignment of the powers at the time. Münster reported that Salisbury had found the increases unexpected and perplexing. He attributed them to the slavic party which was behind the intrigues in Eastern Rumelia and striving for an alliance with France. He thought that Miliutin had given the slavic party in the army much assistance. The Russian army increases were not particularly dangerous to Great Britain and Salisbury did not appear especially worried. His remarks seemed calculated more to augment Bismarck's suspicions of the Russians.[20] This was not difficult, but Bismarck perhaps realized the intention of the English and did not return to the subject.

With Austria the chancellor was more persistent. Andrássy was not well informed and not particularly disturbed. He said Shuvalov had told him that Russia was hardly capable of forming eight or nine new divisions and that the armaments existed only on paper. Andrássy had adopted Shuvalov's way of thinking without further ado since it corresponded to his previous information on the psychological and physical condition of the Russian army. What he had noticed, he told Reuss, was that the Russians were annoyed with Austria and not particularly charmed by the Germans.[21] So initially Salisbury and Andrássy lost little sleep over the Russian armaments, but neither could avoid encouraging Bismarck's suspicion.

Not convinced by Shuvalov's theory of 'paper armaments', the German foreign office was more than a little puzzled and

[19] Reichsarchiv, *Weltkrieg*, nos. 6 and 7.

[20] Bülow to Reuss and Münster, 7 May, confid., GFO, IABi 57 secretissima; Münster to Bülow, London, 16 May, no. 54 confid., GFO, IABq 133 iv; Münster to Bismarck, 20 June, no. 71 most confid., GFO, Russland 61; Salisbury to Russell, 13 May, no. 265 confid., FO 64/929; Cecil, ii, 362.

[21] Reuss to Bülow, Vienna, 13 May, no. 212 most confid., GFO, IABi 57 secretissima.

instructed Lignitz to state whether he thought that the changes in the Russian army represented an actual increase in military might. The Germany military *attaché* continued to emphasize the danger of the 'slavic camp', and although he admitted the weakness of the Russian army, he claimed that the recent increases certainly strengthened it. As if to underline the connection between these two factors, he wrote that for several years the minister of war had been organizing the power of 80,000,000 people as if a new *Völkerwanderung* towards the west were intended.

The details reported by Lignitz were communicated to Andrássy who was taken by surprise; he had not realized the extent of the Russian army expansion and promised to check the figures with his own sources. Two weeks later he confirmed the German statistics, but still believed that the wartime strength could not be reached for several years and existed mainly on paper. Andrássy's awareness of the danger had been aroused, but he refused to take any practical steps in consequence. The slackening of the tension over the Eastern Question made him perhaps less uneasy about Russian intentions, and public opinion in Austria opposed a strengthening of the Habsburg army.[22]

Berlin abstained from further attempts to convince Vienna of the danger. At this stage the Russian armaments threat had made the German government extremely suspicious of its eastern neighbour, and cooperation with Austria had become closer, but the possible danger to central Europe did not in itself suffice to unite the two cabinets finally. Until the meeting of the Russian and German Emperors in Alexandrovo at the beginning of September the armaments question lay more or less dormant. Then Bismarck's earlier preoccupation returned, but in a much more serious context. The story of his efforts to induce the Russians to alter their troop disposition on the frontier will be continued in chapter ten.

[22] Lignitz, Petersburg, 24 May, report, GFO, Russland 61; Lignitz, 8 June, report; Bülow to Alvensleben, 17 May, no. 318 secret; Reuss to Bülow, Vienna, 29 May, no. 230 confid.; 16 June, no. 245, GFO, IABi 57 secretissima. The Austrian military *attaché* reacted more philosophically to the expansion of the Russian army. Bechtolsheim to Beck, Petersburg, 8 June, WS, PA X 74; Windelband, p. 54.

CHAPTER VI

Flanking Manœuvres: Tunis and Egypt

During the first months of 1879 the rift with Russia and the squabble with Rumania influenced Bismarck's attitude towards certain thorny questions concerning the Mediterranean, an area in which he had normally shown little concern. Since the beginning of the year his encouragement of French and British interest in that region helped to keep Russia isolated and assured him a minor, but important, role there, which the western powers could not overlook. Since in Egypt cooperation with Austria was stressed, she, too, became more dependent on German goodwill.

Both Tunis and Egypt were virtually independent of the Sultan, but in the course of the nineteenth century increasingly dependent on western European banking and business interests. This was the result of vast profiteering as much as sublime extravagance, and both sides were bound to turn to a more realistic attitude. If left alone the local rulers could probably have evolved a working arrangement with the money lenders and businessmen, but the Europeans were partly backed and partly used by powerful rival governments. Inevitably, the authority of the Khedive and Bey crumbled; a scramble to fill the power vacuum ensued.

Since the days of Napoleon France had dominated Egypt, but after the construction of the Suez Canal England began to challenge her. By 1876 a rather shaky parity of influence had been established, but mutual suspicion remained undiminished. In Tunis France had kept the upper hand. Italy replaced England as her chief rival there in the 1870s. It was perfectly clear that the two African regimes were heading for disaster: the only question was who would benefit from it.

I

The motives for stimulating the western powers' interest in the Mediterranean area are fairly complex. Because of the failure to see this aspect of Bismarck's foreign policy in proper relation to his views on Russia, the usual explanations are inadequate in some respects. Most authors understate his desire to encourage colonial rivalry, and exaggerate his interest in an Anglo-French *entente* at this time.[1]

After the war in 1870–1 the chancellor had discouraged French expansionism in North Africa. In 1875 he began to think it could be advantageous if France became active in north Africa and the Turkish Orient; the absorption of French power in that area would drain aggressive tendencies, and it would be a liability in war. During the Franco-Prussian War amateurish intrigues in Morocco had succeeded in tying down some French troops in Algeria. Bismarck understood that this line was worth pursuing. Throughout the seventies and for years afterwards he kept several thousand rifles and ammunition ready for shipment to Algerian rebels in case an appropriate opportunity should arise, but it never did.[2]

At the Congress Bismarck encouraged a French occupation of Tunis as compensation for the British advance in Cyprus.[3] This was an important step towards a period of better relations with France and the first example since 1870 of official encouragement for French expansionism.

From the Congress until the end of 1878 Waddington prepared the ground diplomatically for an eventual advance in Tunis, but his inborn caution and the veto of Gambetta kept him from immediate action. In no particular hurry, he was mainly concerned with keeping others out. Italy was his chief worry; she had been warned at the Congress and later that France would not permit another power to become established

[1] Especially Windelband, pp. 61–5; also Langer, pp. 221, 261; but not Medlicott, *Bismarck, Gladstone*, pp. 115ff.

[2] Bismarck to Roon, 17 May 1872, secret; Bismarck to Kameke, January 1875, secret; Holstein to Bronsart, 22 April 1886, secret, GFO, Frankreich 70 secreta; *GP*, no. 114; Kent, p. 94; Guillen, pp. 17, 19, 27f, 32, 67.

[3] Mechler, Berlin, 2 September 1917, memorandum, GFO, IB 17; *GP*, no. 657; *DDF*, ii, nos. 367–9; Ganiage, pp. 509–17.

there. Towards the end of 1878 there was a trial of strength
with the Bey. France feared an Italian intrigue and was
determined to win. In fact, the English representative in Tunis
seems, as usual, to have been more actively encouraging
defiance of the French, but this time he was without the backing
of his government.[4] Waddington decided to deliver the Bey an
ultimatum and was prepared, if necessary, to occupy parts of
the coast, but first he wanted to discover if he could expect
diplomatic support from Bismarck.

On 2 January 1879 Bülow assured St. Vallier, the French
ambassador in Berlin, that Tunis was in the French orbit. On
the following day St. Vallier journeyed to Friedrichsruh with
instructions to ascertain whether Prince Bismarck would agree
to the establishment of a protectorate and whether he was still
prepared to discourage Italian ambitions. The alacrity with
which Bismarck expressed approval of both propositions left
nothing to be desired except, perhaps, a little less enthusiasm.[5]

St. Vallier's report of his conversation is noteworthy because
it emphasizes Bismarck's initiative. The chancellor is reported
to have advised plucking the 'Tunisian pear'. After a lengthy
justification he went on to say that he had already spoken to
those governments—in Vienna, Rome, and London—whose
agents had more or less supported the Bey, but there is no
trace of any communications immediately prior to this and it is
unlikely that he had anticipated the French. During the Russo-
Turkish war the Italians had been urged to snatch Tunis or
Albania as compensation for the territorial expansion of other
powers, but at the Congress Bismarck told them that Tunis
was for the French; Italy should take her share of the spoils in
Tripolitania.[6] In April 1878 the English had been encouraged
to be conciliatory on Tunis in exchange for consideration on
Egypt; and after speaking with St. Vallier the chancellor

[4] Wesdehlen to GFO, Paris, 25 July 1878, no. 109 confid., GFO, IABc 79;
Hohenlohe to Bismarck, Paris, 20 December, no. 186, GFO, IB 17; *DDF*, II, nos.
352, 368; *GP*, no. 655; Ganiage, pp. 533, 538; Medlicott, *Bismarck, Gladstone*, p. 66.
[5] Russell to Salisbury, 4 January, no. 9 secret, FO 64/931; *DDF*, ii, no. 368; *GP*,
no. 657; Ganiage, p. 523; Langer, p. 221.
[6] Bucher to Keudell, 19 July 1877, no. 507 secret, GFO, IABe 61; St. Vallier to
Freycinet, 17 March 1880, no. 50 very confid., FFM, Allemagne 33; Palamenghi-
Crispi, p. 32.

informed London of the role inimical to the French played by
the English agent, Wood,[7] in Tunis; he argued that some sort
of satisfaction for France would improve relations with that
country and consolidate the peace. Waddington had also
repeatedly complained to Salisbury about Wood. Subsequently
he moderated his conduct and was recalled in April.[8]

On the main points St. Vallier's lengthy report was certainly
accurate. Conceivably he exaggerated Bismarck's enthusiasm;
he also favoured vigorous action in Tunis. And it was no
accident that in his reports Bismarck and Bülow waxed most
eloquently on St. Vallier's own favourite causes.[9] Yet there
can be no denying that Bismarck was keen to see the French
tied up in Tunis. Most likely the chancellor was in an expansive
mood and, again, generous with promises and expressions of
goodwill.

Bismarck's eagerness leads to the question of his motives
for encouraging the plucking of the 'Tunisian pear'. He said
frankly that he wanted peace and realized that the wise and
moderate republic, represented by Waddington and St. Vallier,
also stood for peace. He was, therefore, prepared to aid France
in the Mediterranean basin, her 'sphere of natural expansion',
because the more success she had there, the less she would be
tempted to seek revenge from Germany. Essentially, these
were the motives Waddington attributed to him.[10] But Bismarck's impatience made St. Vallier uneasy; he feared that the
chancellor might be trying to assume the role of arbiter of the
European peace or that he might be attempting to tease
England with Franco-German intimacy. In fact, Odo Russell
thought that Bismarck was bidding for an alliance with France.

These fears were unfounded. Bismarck's ostensible motivation
was certainly correct as far as it went. What he did not specify,
however, was the kind of satisfaction he had in mind. In 1875

[7] SIR R. WOOD (1806–1902). Consul-general in Tunis, 1855–1 April 1879.

[8] See correspondence in GFO, Tunis 1; Russell to Salisbury, 6 January, no. 12
confid., FO 64/931; Salisbury to Russell, 12 April 1878, FO 64/899; Russell to
Derby, 8 December 1877, no. 449 secret, FO 64/881; Russell to Salisbury, 4
January 1879, secret, SP, A/9; GP, nos. 401 and 656; Ganiage, pp. 530f.

[9] Rogge, Holstein und Hohenlohe, p. 147; Ganiage, pp. 543f; St. Vallier to
Waddington, 7 & 12 January, private, FFM, Allemagne M & D 166 bis.

[10] Russell to Salisbury, 2 March, no. 140 secret, FO 64/932; DDF, ii, no. 368;
Taffs, pp. 251f.

he had stated that if France was to become involved in north African quarrels her attention would be drawn from Germany. There is no reason to think that such 'quarrels' were less welcome in 1879. These 'quarrels' were to be not only with 'savage potentates'; a certain amount of tension with Italy and England would have been welcome. In the next three months Bismarck's approach became quite clear: in order to continue his contest with Gorchakov on the narrowed terrain left by his squabble with the Rumanians, he attempted to increase and preserve Russian isolation partly by encouraging the western powers and Italy to busy themselves with the Mediterranean. It is in this sense that Bülow's 'whispered' hint to Odo Russell can best be understood. Russell wrote that Bülow 'thinks that Russia will renew her attempts again and again to make an ally of France and that England alone can prevent it, so that Germany has the greatest interest in a strong and lasting Anglo-French alliance, which excludes, while it lasts, the possibility of a Franco-Russian alliance'.[11]

Bismarck's expressions of contempt for Italy were certainly partly a genuine reflection of his exasperation with her un-steadiness regarding Rumania. Just as certainly, however, he wanted the French to minimize the very real danger from this quarter.[12] His views on Anglo-French relations were more involved. Both Russell and St. Vallier were told that good relations were a guarantee of peace. Yet Bismarck knew that the activity of both in the Mediterranean could easily involve them in quarrels, and there is good evidence that he wished to see France at odds with Britain early in 1879.

Since the Bey gave in to the French demands, Waddington took no further steps against him. Thereafter the Tunisian question remained dormant for some time. Of course, rivalry on a local level between French and Italian interests continued, flaring up a year later and pushing France to the brink of occupation, but this decisive step was not taken until the spring of 1881, with the explicit approval of Bismarck.

. . .

[11] Russell to Salisbury, 13 January, private, SP, A/9; Medlicott, *Congress*, pp. 205f.

[12] Ganiage, p. 517, writes that Bismarck did not encourage Franco-Italian rivalry over Tunis.

In March 1879 a short episode occurred which is important for the interpretation of Bismarck's attitude towards French Mediterranean activity. Berlin heard that the French ambassador in Constantinople was desperately trying to acquire Rhodes or Crete. The British embassy was supposed to be seriously upset about this. The story was far-fetched, but the German ambassador in Constantinople was telegraphed not to interfere: since German interests would not be touched, any designs on Rhodes or Crete would not be in the least unwelcome; the greater her involvement in the East, the less there would be to fear from internal developments in France; the seizure of Turkish territory would not only upset the English, but also impede Franco-Russian cooperation.

Again, it is interesting to note the keenness with which Bismarck sought if not to further French interests in the Mediterranean, then at least not to hinder them. At the time he was troubled by French intrigues in Eastern Rumelia.[13] The seizure of a Mediterranean island would have been less dangerous for Germany; and Anglo-French tension was not undesirable. This is a good hint that what Bismarck wanted was a 'quarrelling friendship' between England and France. The incident closed when Hatzfeldt reported that it was merely a Turkish intrigue.[14] So the episode proved to be of no further consequence, but it adds colouring to our picture of Bismarck's foreign policy.

It is remarkable how rapidly Bismarck's attitude towards French ambitions in the Mediterranean area was altered. In November 1878 he had wanted the French to find some satisfaction there for their self-esteem; two months later he had ardently encouraged an active role. The possibility of French involvement in quarrels was now viewed favourably. The Franco-Russian rivalry which might develop was emphasized. We must assume that the crisis with Russia made the prospect of French entanglements in the Mediterranean more inviting. By repeatedly expressing goodwill he also found a currency in

[13] See above, p. 124.
[14] See correspondence in GFO, Türkei 135. Cf. Bülow to German missions, 21 February, GFO, IABq 110.

which he could repay the French for support in the Rumanian question.

II

In the first half of 1879 Bismarck displayed remarkable tenacity in reminding the French of the attractions of Egypt as well as Tunis. It is worthwhile examining this more deeply because after Disraeli's purchase of a large block of shares in the Suez Canal company in November 1875 Münster, the German ambassador in London, was confident that Disraeli would not let Egypt slip through his fingers; and Bismarck favoured the English in Egypt and would have been pleased if they had 'taken it'.[15] As long as France under Decazes was openly hostile to Germany, the purpose was obviously to create tension between the western powers and so, indirectly, weaken France.

Since December 1877 the international situation had changed, and so had Bismarck's Egyptian policy, but not so much as one might think. He began to advertise sympathy for cooperation between France and England, but he secretly continued to hope that they would not get on very well. The republicans were in power in France and consistently strove for better relations with Germany. But at the beginning of 1879 Waddington's new cabinet was shaky, and there were signs of a possible reorientation in foreign policy. Meanwhile, the Russo-German crisis had grown more acute. It was logical for Bismarck to advocate, ostensibly, an Anglo-French *entente* in Egypt as the internal situation in that country deteriorated.

The *entente* espoused by the chancellor was seemingly all to the advantage of the French. In January 1879 he encouraged Anglo-French friendship in the Tunisian question and in March in the Greek dispute.[16] In both cases the English had been awkward and were encouraged to make concessions for the sake of an *entente*.

German policy in Egypt had been one of attentive reserve in all political matters; collective action on the part of the great

[15] Bülow to German ambassadors, 8 December 1875, GFO, IABq 115 (see also Münster's reports in this file); Salisbury to Russell, 12 April 1878, no. 207 secret, FO 64/899; *GP*, nos. 227, 289, 290, 294, 396, 401; Lyons, ii, 104f, 150f; Knaplund, 'Salisbury Korrespondenz', pp. 123f.

[16] For Greece see above, pp. 60–2, and below, pp. 162ff.

powers was clearly preferred to joint Anglo-French steps. Where
France and England were united, however, the German representative was instructed to collaborate, avoiding initiatives.
In differences between the western powers German sympathy
was on the British side, but he was not to express this in any
way which might arouse French suspicions. In those questions
in which the rights and interests of German nationals were
involved, or on which the German government was especially
committed, as in judicial reform, he was to cooperate with his
Austrian colleague.[17]

France was more willing than England to follow a bond-
holders policy. This difference caused a certain amount of
tension, but Paris and London affirmed their mutual accord
wherever possible. Towards the end of February 1879 it was
reported that the English were very suspicious of the French,
believing they were behind the dismissal of Nubar Pasha, the
prime minister of the Khedive, who was greatly admired in
London.[18]

Going by the German press, one would think that a split
between the two would be propitious, but this was hardly so.
In accordance with his previous policy Bismarck praised an
Anglo-French alliance as the best guarantee of peace and
repeatedly urged on Russell and St. Vallier the necessity of
cooperation over Egypt. At the same time he told Russell on 2
March that if complications with France arose in Egypt he
would support England.[19] This was a display of sympathy he
could well afford to give. He had pressed the English to
cooperate with France in the Greek and Tunisian questions,
and it was wise to find them a sop. The point was that these

[17] Saurma to Bülow, Cairo, 11 March 1878, no. 26; Bülow to Münster, 7
March 1878, no. 145 confid.; Bülow to Stolberg, 14 March 1878, no. 198; Bülow to
Saurma, 2 January & 25 November 1878, nos. 1 and 12; 4 March 1879, no. 1,
GFO, IABq 115; St. Vallier to Waddington, 3 April 1878, no. 38 confid., FFM,
Allemagne 23.

[18] NUBAR PASHA (1825–99). Premier, August 1878–February 1879. Cecil, ii,
333, 348f, 352. No reference will be made to the routine correspondence on
Egypt in file GFO, IABq 115.

[19] Bülow, 12 April, note, GFO, IABq 115; Russell to Salisbury, 28 February & 2
March, nos. 131 secret and 137 secret, FO 64/931–2; Walsham to Salisbury, 5
July, no. 340 confid., FO 64/934; DDF, ii, nos. 390, 408, 440; Lyall, i, 306;
Medlicott, Bismarck, Gladstone, p. 118. It seems to have been no real change of
policy as M. Kleine maintains, p. 47.

accommodating remarks were not calculated to stimulate English interest in the *entente* Bismarck ostensibly praised. He clearly wanted to suggest a more active line and show himself in the light of a benefactor. In this way English and French policy could be influenced to a certain degree and directed to an area of less critical importance for Germany.[20]

Bismarck was no advocate of exclusive Anglo-French control in Egypt, yet he was an outspoken opponent of Italian participation there. In talks with St. Vallier he repeatedly abused the Italians and criticized the Russians. He was genuinely irritated with both, but he also wanted to keep France well away from them.[21] The success that Bismarck wished the Waddington government did not include the improvement of its international position.

Meanwhile, the situation in Egypt grew more tangled. In an attempt to straighten out the financial chaos, an inquiry commission had been forced on the Viceroy and its recommendations reluctantly accepted. A responsible ministry—containing a Frenchman and an Englishman, and led initially by Nubar—had been established in August 1878. Early in April it was replaced by a submissive ministry of native elements; finally, on 22 April, the financial plan of the inquiry commission was superseded by one of the Khedive's own making. According to German reports France and England were agreed on the necessity for joint action, but not as to the form; neither wanted to use force. After some irresolution, notes were sent to the Khedive at the end of April stating their views. They were still undecided what else to do when on 8 May Berlin vigorously protested against the Khedivial decree of 22 April.[22] Therewith the Egyptian question, previously a concern primarily of England and France, was brought into the arena of European diplomacy.

What could have been Bismarck's motives for this surprising step? Ostensibly, he wanted to protest about the injury

[20] St. Vallier to Waddington, 11 April, no. 76 confid., FFM, Allemagne 28; Kleine, pp. 47ff.
[21] St. Vallier to Waddington, 20 May, no. 120, FFM, Allemagne 28; *DDF*, ii, nos. 398, 403, 406, 408, 411, 414, 437, 440.
[22] Bülow to German ambassadors, 8 May, GFO, IABq 115; Langer, pp. 258-62.

to German capital and international law. True, Bismarck was still campaigning for a tariff and was soon to renew his complaints about British mistreatment of German interests in the Fiji islands, but such a protest—although a similar one had been suggested fourteen months previously—against formal violations of international agreements which only slightly affected Germany, can hardly be taken at face value. Germany had in Egypt about 32,000,000 marks; but this was merely a small fraction of the French and English commitment. Hitherto Bismarck had maintained his reserve, entrusting, as it were, German interests to the care of the western powers.[23]

To these two minor motives one might add another. At the time Bismarck was in a crusading mood against what he considered 'savage' or 'barbarian potentates'—such as the Khedive, the 'Chief of Nicaragua', the President of Peru, Prince Charles of Rumania and, perhaps, the Californian filibusterers in Samoa—who were impinging on the rights of German nationals.[24] No doubt, he was genuinely indignant at the Khedive's disregard for the great powers and banks.

The chancellor explicitly denied having any political aims in Egypt, yet they weighed more heavily than any of the motives mentioned. He clearly thought a joint rejection of the Khedivial decree would be the most successful procedure although he hinted that, if necessary, Germany would act alone. At first, an internationalization of the question was intended to make France and England compete for Bismarck's favour,[25] then by reserving his right to interfere, but allowing them to do much as they liked, he would be in a position to demand concessions elsewhere. The Anglo-Russian agreements in April on the evacuation of the Balkans lessened the tension in the Eastern Question. A Franco-Russian or Anglo-Russian *rapprochement* was not impossible. It was expedient to have England

[23] Bülow to Münster, 7 & 27 March 1878, nos. 145 confid., 194–5; Saurma to Bülow, Cairo, 14 October 1878, no. 94A; H. Bismarck to Bülow, Varzin, 4 June 1879; Bülow to Reuss, 8 June 1879, no. 414 confid.; Bülow to German ambassadors, 12 February & 7 March 1878, GFO, IABq 115; Derby to Russell, London, 9 March 1878, no. 132, FO 64/899; Townsend, p. 71; Freycinet, pp. 176f.

[24] Salisbury to Russell, 20 May, no. 269, FO 64/929; *DDF*, ii, nos. 418, 440.

[25] Bülow to German ambassadors, 19 May, GFO, IABq 115. Salisbury's guess that Bismarck's sudden interest in Egypt was due to the fact that Bleichroeder possessed Egyptian bonds seems unfounded. Windelband, pp. 62f; Radowitz, ii, 85.

and France occupied in Egypt where Russia was powerless. Still, he had no intention of letting the French and English become intimate or gain exclusive ascendency in Egypt.

There was another motive behind the *démarche*: the desire to use the Egyptian question as a further means of intensifying cooperation with Austria in such a way as to increase the friction between her and the western powers.[26] Andrássy was told that the German protest conformed with the previous policy of Austro-German cooperation which ought to be continued in Egyptian affairs; he was asked to instruct his agent to make a simultaneous and identic *démarche* with his German colleague. Austria was, in fact, the first to support the German protest, and she did so in very similar terms. Until the end of the year the *entente* with Austria may very well have been the most important element in the affair for Bismarck.

Some historians argue that the purpose of Bismarck's protest was to unite the two western powers. If so, one might well ask if it was necessary. Serious conflict between the two was less likely than resentment of intervention. Indeed, Bismarck followed an active policy, supporting the Austrians longer than was comfortable for France and England, yielding only when they obviously intended to act separately. Clearly he wanted the two powers bogged down on the Egyptian sands and friendship with Vienna strengthened as relations with Russia went from bad to worse.

Until Ismail[27] was deposed at the end of June Bismarck took Egypt seriously. He urged the powers to be firm, but till 27 May their response was disappointing. Faced with the possibility of having to act alone, Bismarck asked Moltke the next day how the screw could be tightened on the Khedive. He replied that the appearance of warships in the Mediterranean would add weight to the protest; but if more than a simple demonstration was intended, it would be difficult to indicate measures which would affect the Khedive personally. A bombardment of Alexandria would most likely injure European interests and provoke animated recriminations. A landing would be feasible, but it would necessitate measures out of proportion

[26] Windelband, p. 64.
[27] ISMAIL PASHA (1830–95). Khedive, 1863–June 1879.

to the results that were intended. Moltke felt that serious coercion should only be contemplated in connection with, or at least with the approval of, the more interested sea powers. Bismarck agreed with these reservations, but still thought such action desirable; he asked the German agent in Alexandria to make suggestions.

Vienna had hitherto confined itself to backing Berlin, but argued now that if the others did not follow their example, Berlin and Vienna ought to consult on subsequent moves; it would be intolerable if the Khedive tried to reach a direct understanding with France and England. In reply to a query by Andrássy as to his next step Bismarck explained that a simultaneous *démarche* by all the powers in Alexandria would be the most desirable move; failing this, joint representations in Constantinople could be made. If Paris and London were unable to agree, Germany could attempt an understanding with one of them, probably Paris, which would be more inclined to coercive measures. But first everything else should be attempted to obtain compliance and, if headway could not be made, no opportunity should be neglected to injure the Khedive.[28]

By now Germany had become more involved in the Egyptian question than a mere mediator would have been. Berlin assumed an indignant stance in the semi-official press and inquired what impression the hint about independent action had made. The powers began to view more favourably the German proposal of a joint rejection of the Khedivial decree and by 12 June all except Italy had protested; but their action was hardly concerted. Bismarck then made a last attempt to urge joint action in Constantinople. The proposal was not well received.[29]

Part of the French press had interpreted Bismarck's protest against the decree as an attempt to set England and France at variance. This was a warning that his initiative had gone far enough. In Paris the German *démarche* was justified with the argument that it had served to reunite these two powers who

[28] Moltke to Bülow, 29 May; H. Bismarck to Bülow, Varzin, 1 June, GFO, IABq 115.
[29] Bülow to German ambassadors, 27 May & 12 June, GFO, IABq 115; St. Vallier to Waddington, 29 May, private, FFM, Allemagne M & D 166 bis.

together provided the most effective guarantee for the future of Egypt. When the German consul personally encouraged the Khedive to follow the advice of his British colleague to abdicate, Bismarck immediately disavowed him, claiming he had no intention of interfering so deeply in Egyptian internal affairs.[30]

In the meantime France and England had decided on a more serious step. They wanted to demand Ismail's deposition. Germany and Austria were invited to join the *démarche*. The German agent was instructed to cooperate with his Austrian colleague. Although unhappy, Andrássy offered support to avoid separation from Germany. He thought it risky to allow the two powers to act alone. On 23 June Berlin learned about Andrássy's plan envisaging further internationalization of the Egyptian question. Essentially it involved changing the debt commission into an international board of control and the appointment of a German member.

This move gave Bismarck an excellent opportunity to withdraw into the wings: he encouraged the Austrians to pursue their initiative and emphasized his desire to cooperate all the more since ten months previously Berlin had toyed with a similar scheme. In this way the *entente* with Austria could be strengthened and German interests receive all possible protection without alienating the western powers. Vienna was informed that Bismarck also perceived the mutual advantages of not yielding the terrain solely to the western powers who could become dangerously intimate; because a rupture was equally undesirable, Germany had attempted, when a break was threatening, to promote rather than to disrupt Anglo-French cooperation. So long as Austro-German interests in Egypt remained identical, the weight of their cooperation would prevent a western monopoly. Bismarck added that solidarity with Austria was more precious than cooperation with England and France; since Austrian interests were greater, Germany would follow her lead.[31]

Early in July Bismarck asked Andrássy to present his plan;

[30] Radowitz to German ambassadors, 17 June, most confid.; Bülow to Hohenlohe, 16 June, no. 399, GFO, IABq 115; *DDF*, ii, no. 440; Windelband, pp. 63f.

[31] Radowitz to Frederick William, 30 August 1878; Jasmund to Bülow, Karlsruhe, 1 September 1878; Radowitz to Reuss, 26 June 1879, no. 461, GFO, IABq 115; Windelband, p. 64.

he also volunteered to advocate it. At the beginning of August
the idea was mooted in Paris, but the French remained cool; they
preferred to have a larger voice in Egyptian affairs than an international commission with extensive powers would allow them.

Meanwhile, the Egyptian government had negotiated a loan
from the Rothschilds and France backed the idea. Andrássy
would not accept it unless a liquidation and control commission were quickly summoned. He restressed the danger of
permitting the western powers to dispose of the country's
resources at will. After a moment of uncertainty Germany fell
in line with Austria. Then, in mid-September, the English
proposed as a compromise to subject the new loan to multi-
national control, and the Austrians, grown tired of resisting,
agreed. This time the Germans were hesitant; they had wanted
the loan to be assigned completely to the redemption of the
floating debt (in which their interests were relatively a little
larger than the western powers) and had relied on Austrian
leadership to secure this. Much persuasion was needed before
their neighbours finally agreed to cooperate on 30 September.[32]

Joint explanations in London sufficed to obtain Salisbury's
approval of the German objections; the French gave way
likewise. So Germany and Austria gained their point, but any
further ambitions they may have had were frustrated. England
and France passed over Andrássy's financial project, re-
established their 'condominium' by the appointment of their
own controllers, and, as a concession, suggested a liquidation
commission composed of all five powers. Haymerle,[33] Andrássy's
successor, wanted more: he suggested a scheme similar to
Andrássy's, but England and France had agreed not to permit
further interference. Bismarck replied that his views were
unchanged; aside from protecting the rights of German
nationals he had no intention of interfering. The chancellor
admitted that he had habitually followed the lead of Vienna,
but disapproved of Austrian quibbling over details.[34] Reassur-

[32] Radowitz to Jasmund, 19 September; Radowitz to Reuss, 19 & 28 September,
nos. 691 and 711, GFO, IABq 115.

[33] HENRY BARON VON HAYMERLE (1828–81). Envoy in Athens, 1870; in The
Hague, 1872–6; ambassador in Rome, 1877–9; foreign minister, October 1879–81.

[34] Russell to Salisbury, 26 November, no. 566 secret, FO 64/936; DDF, ii, nos.
475 and 477.

ing as this must have been for the French, it was not completely correct, for Germany's role had been more conspicuous. Not only had Berlin wanted to protect German capital; it had also been very concerned with the political implications of the Egyptian dispute. Bismarck was now in a position to 'make a concession to Waddington'. By November there could be no doubt that the Anglo-French *entente* in Egypt was strong enough to thwart any attempt to share controlling power, but not solid enough to threaten others. In addition, the *entente* with the Danube monarchy during the summer had paved the way for the alliance concluded in October.[35] Subsequently, to avoid offending others, support for Austria's Egyptian policy had less priority. So Bismarck wanted to tell Vienna that he recognized the Anglo-French claim to a privileged position in Egypt; the western powers could therefore be granted a mandate for the protection of Austro-German interests on the condition that they should be treated without discrimination. He emphasized that his main aim was to secure France some small satisfaction so as to help prevent the fall of Waddington.[36]

Haymerle agreed, but wanted to have at least an international liquidation commission. On 6 December Radowitz suggested that since the French and English also favoured the commission, Germany could accept whatever Austria and France agreed upon. Bismarck consented. Throughout the winter the Germans continued to talk affably to the western powers about Egypt, offering to help convince the others of the righteousness of their line. In the spring of 1880 the commission began its work. The German delegate repeatedly protested about the arbitrary behaviour of the western representatives and claimed much of the credit for the successful outcome, but in Berlin no one seemed to notice. By July the commission had elaborated the Law of Liquidation which for many years regulated the servicing of the Egyptian debt.[37]

Dual control in Egypt could then be firmly re-established. Although the French and English governments stood behind

[35] See below, Chapter viii.
[36] Széchényi to Haymerle, 6 December, private, WS, PA III 119; *GP*, nos. 660–1; Windelband, p. 99.
[37] H. Bismarck to Radowitz, Varzin, 14 December, GFO, IABq 115; Freycinet, pp. 186–92.

their two mighty controllers, the other powers had contested their right to monopolize the Egyptian question; and it was obvious that only a fairly close *entente* between the western powers could ensure their priority. It was Bismarck's action which had internationalized the Egyptian question. He used the ensuing negotiations as an instrument of his own general European policy. Because Germany had no overriding material interests in Egypt and Bismarck was not greatly concerned with protecting them, he was in a position to retreat at a propitious moment, and Italy and Austria, not Germany, were regarded by the western powers as the intruders.[38]

[38] See for instance Salisbury to Russell, 23 & 31 December, private, SP, A/27; Salisbury to Lyons, 13 December, private, SP, A/26; Adams to Salisbury, Paris, 3 November, private, SP, A/8; Waddington to St. Vallier, Paris, 24 November, no. 196, FFM, Allemagne 31.

CHAPTER VII

Germany and Rumania at Sword Point

By the end of April 1879 the worst disputes over the execution of the Berlin Treaty had been resolved. While Russo-German tension rapidly mounted, a short period of *détente* between the other powers followed in which two of the remaining problems, the Greek border dispute and the question of Rumanian independence, attracted the attention of the cabinets. Owing primarily to lack of urgency, the solution of both was more tedious than the main problem of the foregoing winter—the Russian evacuation. The most interesting aspect of both is the way in which the rapidly changing position of Germany affected them. The handling of the Greek frontier was made entirely subordinate to the Rumanian struggle. The increasing friction with Russia stimulated Bismarck's interest in coming to terms with Bucharest, but the importance of the railway dispute is amply illustrated by his stubborn refusal to make sacrifices for the sake of better relations with the powers.

On the question of the Greek border the Treaty was vague, the Porte determined to resist, and the powers divided. The frontier was finally regulated only after three years of negotiation. The Treaty was a little less vague on Rumanian independence, but the powers were just as divided, and the stubborn resistance of Rumania held them in check until the material interests of the Germans had been satisfied. Then, after having made little more than formal concessions, Rumania busied herself with neutralizing in practice any liberalizing effect these concessions might have had.[1]

During the winter the powers had pressed for the recognition

---

[1] For this chapter consult Medlicott, 'Recognition', Meisl, pp. 44–73 and *Aus dem Leben*, iv, 176–243. The daily German correspondence on Rumania is in the following files: Rumänien 1, IABq 104 and IABq 133 ix.

of Rumania, and Bismarck had been obliged to make some small concessions to them so as to prevent his isolation. But on 18 May the powers were warned once again that a default in this matter would correspondingly diminish his interest in the execution of other treaty stipulations. As in so many other things, Bismarck continued to expect the assistance of Andrássy.[2]

At the beginning of April 1879 Bismarck also encouraged Bleichroeder to come to terms with the Rumanians as quickly as possible in the railway dispute.[3] But he was not yet inclined to present his case unambiguously to the Rumanians. Although Germany had pressed them to resolve the railway question and Austria had hinted at the connection between this issue and independence, the Rumanians could not accurately know whether concessions to the company would remove the main stumbling block to the attainment of independence. Since the rail negotiations came to nought, Bismarck hinted again that the essential reason for his attitude towards the Rumanian government was its systematic abuse of German capital: Rumania would not find Germany among her friends until she had changed her ways.[4]

Not only had Bismarck retreated before the powers in the Jewish emancipation question, his attitude towards the Rumanians was also slightly modified and the approach to the railway dispute had become more direct.

The Italian and Austrian attitudes had caused some worry, but the relatively cool reception of a renewed French initiative in the Greek border quarrel made France all the more dependent on Berlin. By aiding Paris on Greece, Bismarck secured approval for his tough Rumanian policy. This enabled him to keep the other powers from bolting.

At the end of February the French inquired whether Germany would be prepared jointly to press the Porte for concessions in the negotiations on the Greek border which had ostensibly started towards the beginning of the month.[5] Russia

---

[2] Bülow to German ambassadors, 18 May, GFO, Rumänien 1.
[3] See above, p. 116.
[4] Bülow to Hatzfeldt, 25 April, no. 191, GFO, Rumänien 1.
[5] This discussion is continued from above, p. 62.

and Italy would cooperate, it was thought, but perhaps not England or Austria. Because of disturbing reports from the Balkans Bismarck was more willing to help than previously. It seemed abundantly clear that the shock which had paralysed French foreign policy since the war was subsiding. The problem for Berlin was where to channel the recovering and traditional French vitality in foreign affairs. Pro-Greek activity would lead to a desirable tension between Paris and Petersburg since in the long run the aspirations of Slavs and Greeks were incompatible; also a reward to the French for services rendered over Rumania was indicated; and since the Emperor sympathized with the Hellenic cause, the frontier dispute was convenient for these purposes.[6]

Bismarck had good reason to urge London and Vienna to cooperate. The British were told they should be glad to find a currency in which the French could be repaid for numerous favours, especially in Egypt. And the Austrians learned that Bismarck wished to 'walk the same path' as Andrássy; he was discreetly told that the negotiations with the Porte on Novi-Bazar[7] should be no hindrance, because Bismarck thought oriental monarchs did not appreciate obliging sacrifices; pressure in the Greek question would induce concessions elsewhere. In fact, the Austrian foreign minister did shrink from pressing the Porte for this very reason, but when he learned that the other powers were prepared to join the French, he consented.[8] Here, also, Bismarck stressed his desire to keep in step with the Austrians and successfully persuaded Andrássy to readjust his policy. He was understandably glad when Austria agreed to lend a hand, although Andrássy's hesitation to initiate the necessary action grated on his nerves. Realizing that the reason was simply Andrássy's fear of an unsatisfactory issue of his own negotiations with the Porte, Bismarck

---

[6] Bülow to Reuss, 20 March, no. 176, GFO, IABq 133 viii (the daily correspondence on Greece is in this file); Bülow to H. Bismarck, 7 January, FA, B–25; St. Vallier to Waddington, 27 February, no. 40, FFM, Allemagne 27. The remarks in Lhéritier, iv, 24, are misleading.

[7] For these negotiations see Medlicott, *Congress*, pp. 265–80.

[8] Bülow to Reuss, 28 February, no. 113; Bülow, 2 March, memorandum, GFO, IABq 133 viii; St. Vallier to Waddington, 29 March, no. 64 confid., FFM, Allemagne 27; Lhéritier, iv, 27.

persuaded France to help. The Austro-Turkish convention was then signed on 21 April.[9] Since by this time the Turkish-Greek negotiations had broken down, more energetic action was necessary. At the end of April Waddington suggested a simultaneous *démarche* demanding the renewal of negotiations as well as mediation by a conference of the powers in Constantinople.

Berlin welcomed this initiative. Hatzfeldt was authorized by telegraph to take part in the planned conference and St. Vallier was told that Bismarck was trying to talk every one (particularly the awkward Italians) into cooperation.[10] There was a special reason for the cordial reception of the French step. In the south-eastern Balkans the French and Russian agents had continued their independent line.[11] The danger of a Franco-Russian *rapprochement* still existed and might have continued unless French ambition could be attracted to other areas. This private diplomacy culminated at the very moment when the Russian government unambiguously displayed its determination to withdraw from the peninsula. At a dinner party given in his honour towards the end of April the Russian governor general of Eastern Rumelia brought out a toast to a Franco-Russian alliance. This toast must be regarded as the last desperate protest of these agents disavowed by their own governments.[12]

In Berlin the news of these attestations of mutual sympathy was received more philosophically than the reports of Franco-Russian intrigues in March. Nevertheless, Bismarck saw an additional reason for caution, and informed Petersburg that such occurrences were not likely to instil confidence in Russian diplomacy. A report of the incident was also inserted in the press and, following the pattern with the news of Russian armaments, the information was relayed to London and Vienna.[13]

[9] Bülow to Hohenlohe, 8 April, no. 227 confid., GFO, IABq 131; Russell to Salisbury, Berlin, 8 April, no. 201 secret, FO 64/932; St. Vallier to Waddington, 1 & 11 April, tel. and no. 78 confid.; Waddington to St. Vallier, Paris, 22 April, tel., FFM, Allemagne 28.

[10] St. Vallier to Waddington, 1 May, no. 99, FFM, Allemagne 28; *DDF*, ii, nos. 412–13.   [11] See above, p. 127f.

[12] The British were also concerned about Franco-Russian cooperation. Medlicott, *Congress*, p. 206.

[13] Bülow to Reuss and Münster, 8 May, nos. 340 and 309, GFO, IABq 133 iv; Müller, no. 35.

With the exception of Russia the other powers had reservations about Waddington's proposal, so Bismarck told Waddington that he feared a formal conference might just as easily emphasize the differences between the powers as force the Porte to give way. Then, as an afterthought, he suggested the transfer of the conference to Paris. He would have gladly given the Greek question a more French flavour. But Waddington was not tempted.[14] In the next few weeks Bismarck continued this line: he seemed only willing to go beyond moral support when it would require minimal effort, involve France more deeply, and improve his own diplomatic position.

Waddington was forced to drop the notion of a formal conference, but he was unwilling to abandon the idea of united action. The powers agreed to summon Greece and Turkey to start negotiations; but for any effective concerted action, a more complete agreement would be necessary. The main obstacle was the difference of opinion on Janina, a strategically placed, predominantly Greek city surrounded by Moslem Albanians. In view of British and Italian reluctance to advocate cession to Greece, Waddington was in an uncomfortable position. Virtually without support until the end of May, he may have been willing to accept defeat, but at the beginning of June Andrássy sided with him,[15] and this enabled Waddington to continue his attempt to convert England.

The dispute over Janina had led to perceptible discord between the western powers. Berlin apparently believed the French were more disturbed by Britain's attitude on Janina than by her Egyptian policy; yet Bismarck made no real attempt to harmonize the French and English views.[16] The way French pretensions were supported in June shows clearly that Berlin was not very fond of a close Anglo-French *entente*.

In May the favourable German reception of the French initiative did not imply much concrete support. In June

[14] Bülow to Hohenlohe, 3 May, nos. 296–7, GFO, IABq 133 viii; *DDF*, ii, nos. 419, 421–2.

[15] Russell to Salisbury, Berlin, 15 May, no. 244, FO 64/933; *DDF*, ii, no. 423; Lhéritier, iv, 31.

[16] Münster to Bülow, London, 21 May, private, GFO, England 69; Russell to Salisbury, 23 May, private, SP, A/9; Lyons to Salisbury, Paris, 29 May, private, SP, A/8; Lyons, ii, 177–80.

Bismarck became more active, but the reason for his sudden interest is to be found not in the Greek border dispute itself, but rather in the latest development of the Rumanian question.

News from Bucharest was not promising and on 2 June reports from Paris showed that Waddington feared isolation in the Rumanian question if a solution could not soon be found; he also seemed ready to give way to England on Janina. If to reach agreement with England, Waddington was prepared to concede this point so dear to him, the value of German support would correspondingly diminish. It was not at all unlikely that France would then abandon Bismarck in the Rumanian dispute.[17]

The time for action had come and Bismarck decided to combat the Rumanians 'with full diplomatic force'. What he had in mind was an ambassadorial conference in Constantinople, or at least multilateral consultation on the means to assure the execution of the Treaty. Bismarck wanted to point out to the powers, especially France, that henceforth Germany would link the Greek and Rumanian questions. He argued that the Porte had merely been advised to make concessions to Greece, whereas Rumania's obligations were clear; none of the stipulations of the Berlin Treaty was more binding for Germany than that concerning Rumania. His ambassadors in Vienna and Petersburg were to emphasize that as long as Rumania had not fulfilled her obligations Berlin would remain indifferent to the execution of the rest of the Treaty. In consideration for Andrássy, who had already given support in Bucharest, Bismarck wished to hear his views before formally suggesting a conference. At the same time, however, the chancellor thought Vienna should be lectured that respect for the decisions of the Congress had not been encouraged by the conduct of those who had prematurely recognized Rumania.[18]

The fact that the German view on the Greek frontier was loudly advertised as a reward to France for support against

[17] St. Vallier to Waddington, 30 June, tel., FFM, Allemagne 29; Bleichroeder to Bismarck, Berlin, 1 June, FA, B–15.
[18] H. Bismarck to Bülow, Varzin, 8 June, GFO, Rumänien 1; 4 June, GFO, IABq 133 ix; St. Vallier to Waddington, 10 June, tel., FFM, Allemagne 29.

Rumania was a broad hint that other cabinets could obtain similar rewards by offering equal support. But it is not clear that they valued Bismarck's problematical services enough to make the necessary sacrifices. Russia, at any rate, seems to have regarded Bismarck's reference to Rumania as an excuse to refrain from lending a hand in those questions which interested her. And the Austrian foreign minister showed plainly that he wanted the matter shelved for the present. On 21 June he proposed to give the Rumanians some more time, but if this were without effect, the powers should act. Austria had a unique means of pressure, he said, because she could threaten the rupture of diplomatic relations, and if need be, actually break them off. But first of all he would hint to the Rumanians that European action was imminent. It seems obvious that Andrássy would eventually play his part, but he wanted to postpone the matter until the Russians were out of the country. He feared they might utilize the convenient pretext of acting as the mandatory of Europe to remain there.

Bismarck was not at all pleased with this reaction. He accepted the offer to warn Bucharest, but complained about Austria's early recognition. He also grumbled that if the powers neglected to uphold their own decisions, Germany might start negotiations with the Porte on measures to be applied against Rumania. Bismarck thought that Europe should be spurred on to maintain the dignity of the Congress in relation to Rumania; joint pressure would be just as effective then as later; so far, no attempt had been made, and if it were further postponed, other powers would establish—as Italy was about to do—the *fait accompli* of independence in spite of the decisions of the Congress. Bismarck thought that Andrássy's fears about the suspension of the Russian evacuation were groundless since a *démarche* by the powers would hardly have such a sudden effect.[19]

The main reason for Bismarck's irritation was certainly the well-founded suspicion that the other powers were anxious to recognize Rumania. If Italy could not be restrained, the French and English might quickly follow suit. The chancellor was thoroughly disgusted with Italian tergiversation, so he

[19] Radowitz to Reuss, 26 June, no. 463, GFO, Rumänien 1.

told the ambassador in Rome to seek no conversations with the Italian ministers and to take all communications *ad referendum*. When they noticed this coolness, he was to mention mainly the Rumanian affair and irredentist activity.[20] Characteristically, tension with Italy bound Bismarck more closely to Austria. In this case, the link was forged more by the process of negative selection than by sympathy. Bismarck hesitated to make a formal display of vexation in Rome, but he gave free vent to his spleen in conversations with St. Vallier,[21] hoping perhaps that the Italian cabinet would get wind of it. In addition, his words were calculated to restrain the French by convincing them of the despicable company they would keep if they made concessions to Rumania.

The chancellor's anger was increased when the Italian ambassador announced on 10 July that Rome had heard that some of the powers might use force if the collective *démarche* failed. He added that his government could not go so far. Bismarck responded indignantly that such eventualities were not being discussed, and he would prefer to dispense with their cooperation in joint representations if the Italians wished to declare that they were not in earnest. Now this rebuke was certainly undeserved. As will be seen shortly, the rumours of coercion were actually set afoot by the German government itself. Italy had every right to refuse participation, but Bismarck had been worked up over the conduct of the Italians for some weeks and took advantage of the opportunity to reprimand them. Fortunately for Germany, a change of government in Rome led to a more cooperative spirit, which lasted until December when public opinion apparently forced an independent recognition.[22]

Salisbury was also growing uneasy, fearing that non-recognition would diminish English influence in Rumania if France and Italy became more lenient. Berlin decided to waste no further time, and on 23 June the suggestion for a collective summons to the Rumanian government to fulfil its obligations

[20] Bucher to Keudell, 19 June, no. 383, GFO, Rumänien 1; Bülow to Reuss, 17 May, no. 371, GFO, Österreich 70; Windelband, p. 101.
[21] St. Vallier to Waddington, 12 July, no. 167, FFM, Allemagne 29; *DDF*, ii, no. 440.
[22] Radowitz to Keudell, 11 July, no. 425, GFO, Rumänien 1.

was made to France and Britain; in case of failure a conference in Constantinople was proposed. The British agreed and, as a morale booster, Germany said that their cooperation had increased the pleasure of supporting them in Egypt.[23]

Meanwhile, Berlin tried to lure Andrássy from his reserve and dispel his suspicions of intended military coercion. He was told that Bismarck wanted nothing more than the proposed collective *démarche* and, perhaps, the rupture of Austrian diplomatic relations; this should suffice. If not, Turkey could allow the passage through the Dardanelles of German warships alone, or together with those of France and England to blockade the Rumanian coast. Such measures, it was said, would certainly be effective.[24] This programme of action could console Andrássy only inasmuch as it did not imply the despatch of a corps of troops to Rumania, which he had especially feared. Nevertheless, the blockade plan was bad enough, and he definitely opposed any kind of forceful intervention. It is, however, unlikely that Bismarck actually intended to go to such extremities which surely would have met with much resistance. He probably intended to demonstrate dramatically the importance of the matter, and so induce Andrássy to grant the needed assistance. Bismarck thought the news of this plan would have a similar impact on the other powers—and an intimidating effect on Rumania—when it leaked out, as it quickly did.[25]

From the Austrian point of view the new turn of events was anything but encouraging. Andrássy wished to escape from the predicament into which the Germans had pushed him, and asked Berlin to try to obtain Russian participation in the European action, or at least abstention from encouraging resistance to the execution of article XLIV (Jewish emancipation). A tactful suggestion in Petersburg might have worked, but none was made. Bismarck was quite prepared to say academically that support for other countries would depend on their assistance in the execution of article XLIV, but he refused to

---

[23] Radowitz to Reuss, 23 June, no. 449, GFO, IABq 133 ix; Salisbury to Walsham, 18 June, no. 318, FO 64/929; Walsham to Salisbury, Berlin, 28 June, no. 322 confid., FO 64/933; DDF, ii, nos. 440 and 442.

[24] Radowitz to Reuss, 2 July, no. 481, GFO, IABq 133 ix.

[25] Cf. Winckler, 'Bismarcks Rumänienpolitik', pp. 77ff on this point.

enter into negotiations on this issue. Turning the tables on the Russians, Bismarck expected support in specific instances on the basis of general policy statements, and then when this was not forthcoming, he showed irritation and increased coolness.

In the meantime the work of the Bulgarian delimitation commission had progressed rapidly since its resumption in April. Friction was at a minimum and the delegates' task was nearing completion. The time would then come to reconsider the Silistria border,[26] so Petersburg proposed either a direct *entente* amongst the cabinets, or the nomination of a new commission with conciliatory instructions; its decision, if unanimous, would be final, otherwise the powers would decide the matter.

On 12 July the Russian *chargé* made this communication, described as urgent, and asked for an early answer, but Radowitz replied that before responding, he wanted to learn the position of those cabinets with a greater interest in the question. In addition, he pointed out that his government's concern for the execution of the Treaty had cooled because of the indifference some powers had shown for the emancipation of the Rumanian Jews.[27]

Russia had never insisted on the execution of article XLIV, and Bismarck had never really tried to obtain her help. Germany and Russia had not clashed on this question before. Henceforth, the emancipation question was to serve as just one more, needless, source of friction. Bismarck's temporizing is in itself no matter of great importance, but for the Russians it was additional proof that support was being gratuitously withheld. Consequently, they continued, and perhaps increased, their agitation in Moldavia, hoping to improve their own poor relations with Rumania by a demonstration of sympathy with a popular cause. Organs of the Tsarist government reputedly

---

[26] See above, pp. 112–14.

[27] Radowitz to Schweinitz, 13 July, no. 430, GFO, IABq 133 i; St. Vallier to Waddington, 17 July, no. 173, FFM, Allemagne 29. Radowitz repeated this reference to Rumania when explaining the cool reception of further Russian requests for support on 14 August. Radowitz to Schweinitz, 14 August, no. 502 confid., GFO, Russland 65 secreta.

went so far as to state that Rumania could only count on Russian friendship if the demands for emancipation were resisted.[28] Bucharest pretended to enjoy this newly won popularity, but it is questionable whether such subterfuge was in fact well calculated to ingratiate the Russians with Rumania. What is certain is that it drove Austria and Germany closer together.[29]

Bismarck's insistence on the execution of article XLIV had caused difficulties with every great power. Since at the moment the others were more or less with him, he had yet another cause for anger with Russia. And here, too, he stressed cooperation with Vienna although he did not always try to hide his annoyance at Austrian hesitation.

Parallel with this diplomatic activity, Bleichroeder was encouraged to be reasonable in his conversations on the transfer of the railway. The fact that the banker had by this time recovered the money personally advanced to the company was an added inducement for him to cooperate. Hints were dropped to the Rumanians that if these negotiations bore fruit, Bismarck would hasten the recognition of independence. The Rumanians appear to have guessed which way the wind was blowing, but remained suspicious. They believed it would be foolish to make apparently far-reaching concessions merely on the basis of a hint; they chose to yield gradually as the Germans modified their attitude towards Jewish emancipation. So the minister of finance, Sturdza,[30] journeyed to Berlin with compromise proposals. By this time, mid-July, the previous German position had become well nigh untenable, and as soon as Sturdza had demonstrated goodwill in both the railway and Jewish questions the German cabinet proved conciliatory, but still did not want

[28] Radowitz to H. Bismarck, 26 July, GFO, IABq 133 ix; Bleichroeder to H. Bismarck, Berlin, 25 July, FA, B–16; St. Vallier to Waddington, 25 July, no. 182, FFM, Allemagne 29; Walsham to Salisbury, Berlin, 22 July, nos. 368–9 confid., FO 64/934.

[29] On 24 September it was reported that Russian agents were working against the acceptance of the railway convention. Rotenhan to Bülow, Bucharest, no. 74 confid.; *Norddeutsche Allgemeine Zeitung*, 1 October. But this was a passing phase because by December there were no longer signs of Russian interference. Rotenhan to Bismarck, 17 December, no. 100, GFO, IABq 104.

[30] D. STURDZA (1833–1914). Minister of finance, 1877–end 1879.

to inform the western powers of the connection between the two matters.[31]

In negotiations with Sturdza Radowitz insisted on both a clear acceptance of the principle of religious equality and the enactment of a law emancipating a limited number of Jews. Only then could one make further allowance for local difficulties.[32] This was an important concession, but no abrupt turning point.[33] Some months earlier the Germans had agreed to accept a limited emancipation, but they had no intention of giving in completely until the railway dispute had been satisfactorily resolved.

Bismarck was taking the waters at Kissingen. Before departing from Berlin he had left instructions to bide time in the emancipation question and to decide either for or against Rumania in the details according to the state of the discussions on the railway. Now he thought his assistant had gone too far, and argued that Germany could not show indulgence on article XLIV until her material interests had been satisfied.[34]

This is the clearest statement so far made of the connection between the two questions. But before signing the rail convention Sturdza wanted to see Bismarck who condescended to grant a single interview and, with characteristic candour, told him that although the Treaty demanded grave sacrifices, Rumania would have to make them because it was bad for a small nation to stand outside the bounds of international law. He mentioned the danger of Rumania's geographical position between two powerful and menacing neighbours; she needed disinterested friends such as Germany and France; he wished to be on good terms with Rumania and did not expect the Jewish problem to be solved overnight, but in stages. However, Germany had recently been cavalierly treated, and in order to improve relations the railway question had to be solved once and for all.[35]

---

[31] Radowitz to H. Bismarck, 24 & 27 July, FA, B–90; Salisbury to Walsham, 14 July, no. 354, FO 64/930.

[32] Radowitz to Reuss, 19 July, no. 520, GFO, IABq 133 ix; Leven, pp. 314f.

[33] Cf. Winckler, 'Rumänienpolitik', p. 80; also Leven, p. 312.

[34] Radowitz to H. Bismarck, 26 July, no. 4; H. Bismarck to Radowitz, Kissingen, 28 July, GFO, IABq 133 ix.

[35] Winckler, 'Rumänienpolitik', p. 81. The British *chargé* still strangely thought that the rail convention would not influence the granting of independence. Walsham to Salisbury, Berlin, 19 July, no. 360, FO 64/934.

Now Sturdza had it on supreme authority that the rail convention had priority over Jewish emancipation. He returned to Berlin, signed the convention and departed for Bucharest.

If the Rumanian assembly had passed the convention on the spot, Germany would not have stood in the way of recognition. The crisis with Russia had reached its peak and Bismarck could hardly have welcomed further friction with the western powers or Austria. Also the Emperor took a renewed interest in an accelerated recognition. Prince Charles Anthony of Hohenzollern, the father of Prince Charles, took it upon himself to plead his son's case with the Emperor on 27 July. William, not *au courant*, believed that the English were the driving force behind the pressure for emancipation. Charles Anthony sought to disprove this and compared the rough and inconsiderate attitude of Germany with the increasingly more moderate English approach. He believed he had succeeded in opening William's eyes. He was confirmed in this belief by a communication from William on 6 August which stated that Berlin would be easily satisfied. This communication could only have encouraged Rumanian resistance to the ostensibly stiffer line of his government.

Radowitz claimed that William would not cause further trouble, but confessed that he had been 'enormously scared'. The Emperor's influence in favour of Rumania was obviously a factor to be reckoned with.[36] It meant that in the end Berlin would have to be satisfied with the minimum in the Jewish question, although, as events were to show, William was willing to lend full support to the railway negotiations.

The powers (Russia excluded) approved the approach to the emancipation question worked out by Radowitz and Sturdza, but it was too liberal for the Bucharest government. The draft convention also met with opposition, so Boerescu, the new foreign minister,[37] decided to tour the various European capitals and whittle away as much as possible from Sturdza's concessions. When he arrived in Berlin Radowitz categorically refused to consider any postponement of the enactment of the

---

[36] O. Bülow to Radowitz, Gastein, 5 August, no. 43, GFO, IABq 133 ix; Radowitz to H. Bismarck, 7 August, FA B–90.

[37] B. BOERESCU. Rumanian foreign minister, July 1879–81.

convention, but was less intransigent on Jewish emancipation. Bismarck felt that Radowitz had not been sufficiently firm and instructed him to say that unless the railway convention was quickly passed, Germany would insist on strict execution of the Treaty and join the other powers in serious action.[38] The Rumanians nevertheless would not be hurried. Since for the next two months the attention of the German cabinet was absorbed first by the crisis with Russia, and then by the ensuing negotiations for the Austrian alliance, they could assume with apparent justification that the moment had come for the most advantageous solution.

The powers were certainly very tired of the question by now and quite willing to accept a minimum; indeed, with the exception of Germany, they would have been prepared, though reluctantly, to recognize Rumania in the spring. Although for many reasons it was desirable to bring the matter to a close, the Germans were not prepared to make a single significant concession until the railway question had been finally solved.

[38] H. Bismarck to Radowitz, Kissingen, 11 August, GFO, IABq 133 ix.

CHAPTER VIII

The Austro-German Alliance

By mid-1879 cooperation between Austria and Germany had developed to such an extent that none of the major problems troubling the powers remained unaffected by it. Both powers wanted the *entente* and profited by it, but the driving force came from Berlin and the Germans hoped to gain the most from it.

Germany was in a unique position. She wished neither to join the western powers in pressing Russia to execute promptly the terms of the Berlin Treaty, nor to second the Russians in their resistance to such pressure. Thus Bismarck might easily have acted as impartial mediator between the powers. But the chancellor was not willing to play such an insignificant role in international politics for which neither his temperament nor ambition suited him. True, he did want to maintain a position between the rival powers which would enable him to preserve good relations with all of them. His stake in the Eastern Question was a minor one and so long as it remained acute he had sufficient ground for manœuvring to maintain this ideal position between the powers. However, his interest in the Rumanian railway necessitated giving at least a semblance of assistance to the western powers on whose support he depended to force an adequate settlement of the German claims. Throughout the winter of 1878–9 he was able to follow this line, avoiding conflict with Russia; but the longer the matter was dragged out the greater was the likelihood of friction.

This is exactly what happened in July 1879. The Rumanian question in itself was not sufficiently significant to create excessive embarrassment, but at the same time the chancellor was following a vigorous campaign against Gorchakov and what he was supposed to represent. These two factors taken together proved decisive and measurably diminished Bismarck's freedom of action. Austria alone could offer material

assistance in his squabbles with Rumania and Gorchakov. If
Russia would not turn over a new leaf, he could always make
Austria his ally, who would be all the more valuable because
of her connections with England. Bismarck may very well
have been prepared to resort to an alliance with both of these
powers if Russia had refused an understanding with Germany
and Austria on his own terms.

It is often held that by June Bismarck was aiming at the dual
alliance to force Russia to her knees; but it is not necessary to
assume this. If Russia had shown a sincere desire for an understanding, Bismarck probably would not have taken the last
step to an alliance. After all he had avoided this kind of commitment throughout the seventies. There had of course been
moments in the previous three years when he had considered a
formal link with another power. Soundings for an alliance had
been taken in Petersburg, Rome, and London as well as in
Vienna; but nothing had come of them. And one cannot say
that he had shown any particular sympathy for Vienna before
the Congress. However, by mid-1879 he was seriously considering the advantages of an Austrian alliance and was prepared, if
necessary, to go this far. He was also fairly confident of Austria's
readiness to ally with him if need be. In January 1877 he had
proposed an alliance which Vienna immediately accepted but
Bismarck did not further pursue. In the autumn of 1876
Andrássy had suggested an alliance; he repeated the offer in
March 1878. Bismarck rejected both proposals although he
admitted sympathy for an alliance. In 1878 he took just the
opposite line from that which he had followed in the autumn
of 1876; he held that to be effective, an alliance would have to
emerge from a serious threat; since at that time there was no
such danger, he believed that an alliance would merely provoke
Russia.[1]

His treatment of Andrássy in 1879 does not give the im-

---

[1] Bülow, 27 January 1877, memorandum; Bülow to Stolberg, 31 January 1877,
no. 105 secret; Stolberg to GFO, Vienna, 29 January 1877, tel. 17, GFO, IABi 57
secretissima; Bülow to Stolberg, 6 March & 6 April 1878, nos. 170 secret and 272
secret, GFO, IAAl 41; Münch, reports, Vienna, 8 October 1876, WS, PA rot
453 Liasse I; Schweinitz, i, 383, ii, 60, *Briefwechsel*, pp. 125f; Frauendienst,
passim; Brauer, p. 60; Scharff, 'Bismarck, Andrássy und die Haltung Österreichs',
pp. 234-40.

pression that he was actively preparing for an alliance, nor does his handling of Haymerle immediately after the alliance indicate that he was particularly pleased with his achievement. He was neither suitor nor bridegroom in the conventional meaning of the words: he was merely growing more dependent on Austrian support. Although he was willing to pay for this support, he did not at all like the feeling of dependency.

Bismarck's treatment of the Russians is anything but clear. It is unlikely that he wished to provoke them in order to have an excuse for the alliance with Austria. This would have been a hazardous policy, inconsistent with the past, which could have led to a general conflagration. And he had failed to take advantage of some good opportunities for provocation. One could of course argue that continued consideration for the Russian position was required by his Emperor's proclivities, and that it was necessary therefore to resort to rather devious means to irritate Russia, while at the same time maintaining little more than the appearance of formal support in the commissions. Then from June until August Bismarck did actually progressively abandon Russia. But this was the closest he came in this period to a break with Russia and his talks with Saburov, the Russian envoy to Greece,[2] as well as subsequent events indicate that his heart was not in it.

In June Bismarck's instructions to the German agents in the Serbian and Montenegrin commissions, where Austrian and Russian policy was similar, to cooperate especially with their Austrian colleagues must be considered as an important shift of emphasis even though damage to the Russian line did not immediately result. In the Eastern Rumelia commission, however, the German agent was instructed to vote with the Austrian and against the Russian delegate. All in all, the tendency to stress cooperation with Austria under the cover of imperial solidarity became increasingly apparent. Still, this is no conclusive evidence that Bismarck wished to provoke the Russians.

On 30 May the Serbian premier asked the powers to give his country a more easily defensible frontier. The Austrian reaction was cool; the Russians seemed indifferent, although they

[2] See below, pp. 183f.

showed more sympathy for the Serbs later. But beforehand the German delegate was instructed to work together with his Austrian colleague; Berlin apparently believed that Russia would follow an analogous line. After the German government learned that this was not so, no change was made in the instructions.[3] Apart from this rather minor point the work in the Serbian commission progressed rapidly without further incident until completion in late August.

The German attitude on the Montenegro commission was similarly altered. In May the work of the commission, barely begun, was interrupted by Turkish objections which the powers all opposed. Radowitz argued on 17 June that Germany would like to go hand in hand with Austria, the most interested power.[4] At that time, because of the consensus of Russian and Austrian views, cooperation with Austria could not trouble Russia, but after a month differences arose between the two. When the border at Mrković was discussed at the end of July and the beginning of August the Russians noticed the preference given by the Germans to their neighbour.

In the commissions for the delimitation of the Bulgarian and Eastern Rumelian frontiers work progressed apace in June and early July but was subsequently held up by Russian obstruction. Nevertheless, the latter commission functioned fairly well and the original instructions to cooperate with both the Russian and Austrian delegates were not altered. In the former the first symptom of a revised attitude appeared on 19 July when the German delegate was instructed to vote with his Austrian colleague for the *thalweg* of the Danube as the northern border of Bulgaria. There was no real controversy on the point although the Treaty prescribed the right bank, a less favourable frontier for Bulgaria. Until the question of the military road became acute in mid-August there was a minimum of friction in this commission between Germany and Russia.[5]

[3] Radowitz to Bray, 22 June, no. 4 confid.; 2 July, no. 5 confid., GFO, IABq 133 ii.

[4] Bülow to Reuss, 22 May, no. 387; Radowitz to Reuss, 17 & 22 June, nos. 439 and 446, GFO, IABq 133 iii.

[5] Bülow to Alvensleben, 4 April, no. 191, GFO, IABq 133 i. The significance of Müller's no. 36 can be exaggerated. See also Müller, p. 69 and Medlicott, *Congress*, p. 380.

The Austro-German *entente* was most apparent in the Eastern
Rumelia organization commission. Towards the end of May
the question of the future competence of the commission was
being discussed. France and Russia wanted the advice of the
commission to bind the governor general. All the other powers
were against this. The German delegate refused to take a stand,
but since a decision within the commission was not forthcoming
he asked for instruction.

On 14 June he was telegraphed to support the Austrian
view,[6] that is, to oppose a Russian proposal. This instruction
was meant as a general guide line. Two weeks later the question
was raised whether the governor general was authorized to
appoint officials in the postal service; France and Russia refused
to enter discussion until it was decided whether the proposals
of the commission would bind the governor or not. Bismarck
prescribed *sicut Austria* and tried to persuade France to leave
Russia in the lurch. Shortly thereafter it was reported that the
vast majority of the commission had held earlier that the
governor and not the Porte was authorized to appoint the
postal officials. Now, however, the Austrian delegate was
siding with the Porte; but except the Turkish delegate, the
others supported the pretensions of the governor general.
The German delegate was explicitly instructed to support
Vienna. A few days later it was learned that the Austrian
delegate was following an independent line in various matters
and that the German commissioner hesitated to change his
position on the appointment of postal officials. Thereupon
his instructions were defined. He was told to support those
views of his Austrian colleague which were based on instructions from Vienna, but not his or anybody else's personal
initiatives.[7]

In spite of this reservation, by mid-July the tendency to
support Austria, even against Russia, in the Eastern Rumelia
commission was quite obvious. Bismarck thought he was in a
sufficiently strong position to force the Tsar to come to terms

---

[6] Hatzfeldt to GFO, Pera, 12 June, tel. no. 46, GFO, Türkei 136.

[7] Hatzfeldt to GFO, Buyukdere, 3 July, no. 291; Radowitz to Hatzfeldt, 26
June, tel. no. 68; 13 & 17 July, nos. 315 and 318, GFO, Türkei 136; St. Vallier to
Waddington, 19 July, no. 177, FFM, Allemagne 29; Müller, no. 36.

and abandon Prince Gorchakov.[8] The Russians, however, were provoked by Bismarck's behaviour. His distinction between Gorchakov's irresponsible diplomacy and justified Russian policy was unclear. The Russians surely expected support in the eastern Balkans, and if Bismarck were to remain true to his scheme for the division of the Balkans in two spheres, he should have afforded it, but Russia's utter isolation hindered this because he also wanted healthy relations with the western powers whose support he needed in the Rumanian question. Also, since Bismarck felt that Russian policy there came under the category of Gorchakovian subterfuge, he had no intention of exposing himself. But not only did he withhold support, he also failed to observe a consistent policy of neutrality by often siding with Austria.

In Berlin the reported reinstatement of Ignatiev and the realization that Shuvalov's sun was definitely setting[9] must have seemed like fairly conclusive evidence that the otherwise peaceful, but weak, Tsar was again losing his grip on the situation and drifting off in an adventurous direction. So at this stage one of the hitherto most important reasons for supporting Russia—to pave the way for Shuvalov—had become invalid. Bismarck as a result did not immediately adopt a hostile attitude in the commissions, although he occasionally backed Vienna and emphasized cooperation with her where Austria and Russia were agreed. He waited until the Russians joined requests for further support with disregard for German policy on Rumania and continued subterfuge on the lower Danube which increased the resistance of Bucharest to German demands. Then he openly displayed his displeasure, and cooperation with Austria became more pronounced and detrimental to Russian intentions. Petersburg could hardly miss this change in attitude, and when an attempt was made to put the heat on the Germans, the pot quickly boiled over.

[8] Cf. however, Medlicott, *Congress*, pp. 370f, and A. J. P. Taylor, pp. 259f, who believe that Bismarck wished to provoke the Russians. Renouvin, pp. 100f, states that Bismarck adopted an anti-Russian line to keep Austria from joining Russia or the western powers. On the other hand, most German historians regard Bismarck's policy as the reaction to a real danger from Russia.

[9] Münster to Bismarck, London, 20 June, no. 71 most confid., GFO, Russland 61; 24 June, no. 72, GFO, England 69; Schweinitz, ii, 63.

But even before the Russians asked for aid in July Bismarck vented his spleen on them and showed irritation in other ways.[10]

The deposition of the Khedive by the Sultan[11] gave Bismarck an opportunity to air the subject of Russian diplomacy. He invited St. Vallier to visit him on 27 June, ostensibly to talk about the Egyptian question, but in fact it merely provided the framework for a frank discussion touching on the whole range of international difficulties. Most of the conversation appears to have been devoted to the disturbing internal evolution of Russia. According to Bismarck, the sensible Shuvalov had been cast aside and Gorchakov was again ascendant. He had succeeded in strengthening his position by coming to terms with Katkov,[12] Ignatiev, and Miliutin. Bismarck then went on to paint a very gloomy picture of Russian conditions. New adventures were likely, and as symptoms of the turn of events, he stated that Gorchakov had thwarted the visit of Tsar Alexander for William's golden wedding anniversary, and was encouraging Turkish opposition to France.[13] The Russians liked neither the Anglo-French *entente*, the good relations between France and Germany, nor Austro-German intimacy. But, Bismarck asserted, in spite of the ill humour of the men on the Neva, this last point was and would remain

[10] For instance, by refusing to provide Gorchakov with the customary rail coach when he travelled through Germany on leave. Hohenlohe, ii, 271.

[11] See above, p. 157.

[12] M. KATKOV (1818–87). Russian conservative publicist, editor of *Moskovskiia Vedomosti* and *Russkii Vestnik*.

[13] A recent report stated that Alexander had been kept from attending William's golden wedding anniversary by Gorchakov who might have hinted that the German government feared the danger of assassination. Münster to Bismarck, London, 20 June, no. 71 most confid.; Hohenlohe to Bismarck, Paris, 20 June, private. Bismarck lost no time in bringing this to the attention of William. Bismarck to William, 23 June, GFO, Russland 61. Langenau to Andrássy, Petersburg, 13 June, no. 27–C, WS, PA X 73. St. Vallier to Waddington, 6 June, FFM, Allemagne M & D 166 bis.; Tatishchev, however, believes that Alexander wished to avoid the reunion with William, ii, 539. Miliutin writes that the trip was abandoned for non-political reasons (entries for 17, 23 May 1879). For Russian activity in Constantinople at the time, see Medlicott, *Congress*, pp. 314f. There is no evidence substantiating Fournier's suspicion that Hatzfeldt was instructed to inform the Porte that Germany and England were its best friends. On the contrary, Germany was pressing the Porte for concessions. *DDF*, ii, no. 433; Russell to Salisbury, Berlin, 9 & 17 May, nos. 241 secret and 247 secret, FO 64/933.

more and more the basis of his diplomacy. He stressed co-operation with Austria in the Egyptian, Greek, Rumanian, Serbian, and Montenegrin questions which resulted from his desire to avoid any discord between the central European empires. He added that he attached such great value to this *entente* that he was prepared to make real sacrifices—as proof he mentioned the Austro-German Treaty of Commerce.[14] The existence and the integrity of the Habsburg dominions were for Germany the primary condition of security; he could not permit a Russian siege of Vienna. He went on to say that the *Dreikaiserbund* had ceased to exist and unfortunately could not be revived. For the last two years constant vigilance had been necessary to prevent the hostility between Petersburg and Vienna from leading to a rupture. But he was not certain whether he could prevent conflict for long.[15]

Bismarck's remarks were much too carefully worded to be discarded as a mere outpouring of irritation with Russia and others. His interest in seeing France and England engaged in Egypt clearly emerges; he did his best to encourage their activity in this area because it would lessen the likelihood of complications with these powers, further his community of interests with Austria, and strengthen his position in relation to Russia. His remarks were also calculated to arouse suspicion of Russian and Italian subterfuge. Thus French pre-occupation with Egypt should not lead to the improvement of relations with Petersburg or Rome. Bismarck clearly exaggerated his readiness to make sacrifices for the Habsburg monarchy. His probable aim was to prepare the ground for a further *rapprochement* with Austria by conveying the impression that it was the reaction to, rather than the cause of, Russian aggressiveness and that there-fore a peacefully inclined France would have nothing to fear unless she were so imprudent as to cultivate closer relations with Germany's eastern neighbour. Although the chancellor may not have definitely counted on it, he must have reckoned with the possibility that France would pass on the substance of his conversation to the Russians. Still, in spite of all this de-famation, Bismarck's tirade was aimed primarily at Gorchakov

[14] See below, pp. 196-8.
[15] *DDF*, ii, no. 440.

and his concern with the internal development of Russia did
not lead him to turn his back on her.

Bismarck exaggerated the danger from Russia. Although it
is clear from the Russian sources at our disposal that no
aggression was planned in the near future, her internal and
external policy was hardly calculated to promote confidence
in her goodwill or ability to subdue extremist elements. Bismarck's fears, as expressed in his conversation with St. Vallier,
were neither wholly unfounded nor completely feigned. He
was more troubled than he should have been, but less than he
seemed to be. He was not panicked by his fears; the contrary
indeed was the case. But he was obviously moving away from
his eastern neighbour. By spreading alarm he increased Russia's
isolation and Gorchakov's embarrassment.

Bismarck's conversations with the Russian diplomatist,
Saburov,[16] one month later went essentially in the same vein.
This time, however, it was not necessary to provide any
extraneous framework for the discussions and the tone appears
to have been more complaining than irritated. Saburov,
previously envoy to Greece, intended the coming autumn to
assume his duties as ambassador to Turkey. Apparently on his
own initiative, he went to Kissingen and asked for an interview. The chancellor had no particularly favourable opinion
of the young Russian diplomat—a nephew of Gorchakov
and follower of Ignatiev, he thought—but he hesitated to
refuse an interview and asked for Radowitz's views of his
colleague in Athens. Radowitz was acquainted with Saburov's
ideas on Russo-German relations as well as with his harsh
opinion of Gorchakov; he regarded the Russian diplomat as a
reasonable man and warmly recommended him.[17]

Bismarck subsequently granted Saburov two interviews in
which he complained of Gorchakov, reiterated his own services
to Russia, and emphasized that he would gladly have done
more, had the Russians requested it and treated him properly.
Saburov expressed agreement with much of what Bismarck

[16] P. A. SABUROV (1835–1918). Envoy in Athens, 1870–9; ambassador in Berlin,
January 1880–4.

[17] DDF, ii, no. 406; Radowitz, ii, 97. Cf. Münster to Bülow, London, 31 May,
no. 60 confid., GFO, England 69.

had to say; he was nevertheless considerably disturbed. In recording his impressions of the interview he wrote, 'Bismarck seemed a *prey to some secret irritation*—indeed, something slightly more definite than a mere cooling of relations with Prince Gorchakov'. After taking leave of Bismarck, Saburov journeyed to Berlin and spoke to Radowitz in the middle of August. Russo-German tension had mounted rapidly since the end of July and the chancellor's assistant apparently spoke more plainly to his old colleague than had Bismarck whose remarks had more of an historical slant. Saburov found his first impression verified: he assumed that Bismarck felt the Russians wished to abandon their traditional dual *entente* with Germany in favour of new combinations. He believed that if the Germans were to become firmly convinced of this they themselves would seek new alliances. Saburov's suspicions on the whole were justified. Considering Bismarck's frank conversation with St. Vallier one month earlier, Radowitz, and perhaps Bismarck, must have hinted at the possibility that Germany could look elsewhere for an alliance.[18]

After talking with Radowitz Saburov journeyed to Petersburg to tell the Tsar his impressions and plead the case for a *rapprochement* with Germany. On arrival in the Russian capital he drew up a memorandum on his ideas at Giers's request and presented it on 17 August, two days after Alexander had sent his famous 'box on the ear letter' to William.[19] Although containing nothing new, Saburov's memorandum made a deep impression: one can only understand its profound effect if one assumes that hitherto the Tsar had not actually realized the consequences of Russia's utter isolation. It was most likely the shock of this realization and the regret of having written to William as he had which made Alexander suddenly perceive the advantages of a *rapprochement*. Giers had neglected to assume the initiative with the Tsar, but he welcomed and supported Saburov's move. The news of Andrássy's visit to Gastein at the end of August[20] must have served as added proof for the

[18] Simpson, pp. 50–8; Schweinitz, *Briefwechsel*, pp. 146–8. Radowitz to H. Bismarck, 15 August, no. 14 most confid., GFO, Russland 65 i secreta; *GP*, no. 461; Miliutin, iii, entry for 11 August.

[19] See below, pp. 191f.

[20] See below, p. 192.

authenticity of Saburov's conjectures.[21] What part the failure of alliance feelers to France and Italy played in inducing Alexander to view an understanding with Germany more favourably it is difficult to say. Apparently some vague attempts were made at least on the authority of the minister of war; their failure documented Russia's complete isolation, thus further suggesting the necessity of an agreement with Germany.[22]

Tsar Alexander had waited too long. Meanwhile another series of events had both convinced Bismarck of the necessity of joining Austria in an alliance and created the opportunity.

In June Bismarck had begun siding with Austria in the commissions. Perhaps because the delegates were generally working well with one another, this Austro-German accord did not become manifest until well into July. By this time Bismarck openly supported Austria against Russia. His stiffer attitude was due not only to the greater opportunity for expressing it, offered in the form of Austro-Russian conflict in the commissions, but also due to continued Russian coolness in the Rumanian question. The Russians were told as much, but they ignored the warning. Though no truly important matters were at stake, Petersburg was quite upset by this concerted Austro-German opposition and probably interpreted it as the latest in a whole series of unfriendly gestures. The Russian press renewed its attacks, encouraged by an article on 2 August in *The Times* which asserted that whenever 'a distinct contest has arisen between the claims of the Western Powers and of Russia in the East, Germany, under Prince Bismarck's influence, has, in the end, inclined the balance in favour of the West'. In Russian eyes this seemed an indisputable truth.

[21] Simpson, pp. 63–5; Radowitz, ii, 97f; Schweinitz, ii, 72. Schweinitz to Bismarck, Petersburg, 15 & 28 August, nos. 281 most confid., and 291 secret; Schweinitz to GFO, 27 August, tel. 104; Radowitz, 27 August, memorandum, GFO, Russland 65 secreta; Goldschmidt, no. 9; see discussion in Schüssler, pp. 18–22; Windelband, p. 71; Skazkin, pp. 106f.

[22] For the Russian alliance feelers see, for instance, Medlicott, *Congress*, p. 377; Becker, p. 29; Skazkin, pp. 107f. Manteuffel to Bismarck, Bromberg, 4 September, GFO, Russland 65 i secreta; Windelband, p. 76 and footnote 98. Radowitz to O. Bülow, 11 September, private, GFO, Russland 65 Handakten secreta. Miliutin's diary contains nothing.

Not only did Petersburg refuse to check the outbursts of the press, it also abstained from publishing an article in the official journal which dissociated the government from this activity, although the article had been approved by the council of ministers. In fact the semi-official press took part in the campaign against Germany. The *Agence Russe*, organ of the Russian foreign ministry, was a major offender. Giers admitted having close links with the paper, but said he did not see the editor for weeks on end and was dissatisfied with him.[23] Official Russian spokesmen claimed to lack the means which other governments possessed to check the press. This view was received in Berlin with suspicious contempt. Bismarck took steps to have the threats parried by the German press. He attributed them to panslavs and nihilists who wished to destroy the links with the powerful, conservative German empire; the contentions of the *Times* article were refuted and German policy portrayed as pro-Russian.[24]

The press campaign gained added significance by simultaneous Russian demands for support in the Balkan commissions and, finally, complaints about German opposition in them. During the summer manœuvres the Tsar could not have been nicer to the French representatives and was pleasant enough with the British ambassador, stressing the desirability of a cordial understanding on all matters pending. But with Schweinitz the story was different; he assumed a rather menacing attitude in repeating the familiar complaints which culminated in the barely veiled threats: 'If you want to preserve the friendship which has united us for a hundred years, you should change this' [partisanship for Austria]; and, 'Il est tout naturel que le contre-coup se produise ici; ... cela finira

[23] Schweinitz to Bismarck, Petersburg, 5 & 15 August, nos. 268 and 281 most confid.; Schweinitz to GFO, 5 & 10 August, no. 272 and tel. 103, GFO, Russland 65 secreta; Kálnoky to Andrássy, Petersburg, 26 August & 10 September, nos. 38 and 42–C confid., WS, PA X 73; Grüning, pp. 67–73; Miliutin, iii, entries for 18 & 26 July, 1 August; Vogüé, entry for 11 July. It appears that the articles in the German press were written in reply to attacks by Russian newspapers. Cf. however Schweinitz, ii, 64.
[24] Radowitz to H. Bismarck, 15 August, no. 14 most confid., GFO, Russland 65 i secreta; H. Bismarck to Radowitz, Kissingen, 8 & 18 August, GFO, Russland 65 secreta; see also Radowitz to Stumm, 13 October, no. 625, GFO, IABi 60; Miliutin, iii, entry for 24 August.

d'une manière très sérieuse'.[25] The Russian government believed that the Germans were coaching the opposing team.[26]
Schweinitz did not know what to make of all this. He
admitted that the tone of the Tsar's speech was 'mild, not at
all threatening', but added that he reported Alexander's
remarks 'in the mildest form' and that he believed the Tsar
wanted his philippic to be telegraphed straight away to Bismarck and William. This made the matter seem ominous.

The two most serious criticisms were of German conduct in
the question of the Eastern Rumelian postal service and the
delimitation of the Montenegrin frontier at Mrković. In both
instances it was thought that the German delegate had originally
shared the views of his Russian colleague, but was later instructed to abandon him and vote with the Austrian commissioner. Radowitz asserted that the German delegates had
been given no such special directions; they were merely following their general instructions to vote with Austria and Russia,
and to remain in the background where these were divided,
but finally to join the majority, if it included the Austrian
delegate.[27]

In the question of the Eastern Rumelian postal service the
German delegate had been explicitly instructed to join his
Austrian colleague and abandon his previous point of view
shared by the Russian as well as most of the other delegates.[28]

According to the Berlin Treaty Mrković went to Montenegro. When the commission arrived there, it discovered that the
name referred both to a village and a district. Towards the

[25] Bismarck saw Schweinitz's report (*GP*, no. 443) on 12 August.

[26] Radowitz to H. Bismarck, 15 August, no. 14 most confid., GFO, Russland 65 i
secreta; Schweinitz to Bismarck, Krasnoe Selo, 12 August, no. 278 most confid.,
GFO, Russland 65 secreta; Dufferin to Salisbury, Petersburg, 13 August, no. 387
secret, FO 65/1046; 14 & 26 August, SP, A/14; Chanzy to Waddington, Petersburg, 14 August, no. 37, FFM, Russie 259; Schweinitz, ii, 65–7.

[27] For Russian complaints see: Schweinitz to Bismarck, Petersburg, 22 July,
no. 261 confid., GFO, Türkei 136; tels. from Giers, Petersburg, 30 July, 5 & 15
August, copies, GFO, IABq 133 iii; Schweinitz to Bismarck, 5 August, no. 271;
Giers to Arapov, 5 & 9 August, copies, GFO, IABq 133 i; *GP*, no. 443. For
Radowitz's defence see: Radowitz to H. Bismarck, 11 August, no. 11, GFO,
Russland 65 i secreta; Radowitz to Schweinitz, 13 & 18 August, nos. 494 & 513,
GFO, IABq 133 iii; 14 August, no. 497, GFO, IABq 133 i; Radowitz, 24 August,
memorandum, GFO, Russland 65 secreta; Müller, no. 40.

[28] See above, p. 179.

end of July the Russian, Austrian, German and Montenegrin delegates voted to give the whole district to Montenegro, whereas the other commissioners wished only to hand over the village. Subsequently, the Austrian was instructed to change sides, so the German delegate joined him in accordance with his general instructions which were repeated on 1 August, before the second vote. It should be pointed out, however, that the phlegmatic German delegate had failed to keep Berlin abreast of the commission's activity. Between the beginning of June and 2 August no report had arrived from him and the next came on 16 August. In the latter Mrković was mentioned for the first time more than a week after the final vote. Beforehand Germany was apparently not informed as to the Austro-Russian differences. Therefore, the shift in the German vote must be regarded as a vote for Austria rather than against Russia.[29]

In both cases the Germans did shift their vote from one originally in agreement with Russia to one against her. But Berlin did not take the initiative in either case, and in the dispute over the postal service the German delegate was warned to beware of his Austrian colleague's whims.

The German attitude on the Silistria question also upset the Russians. On 12 July they had proposed to reconsider the Bulgarian border at this point.[30] By the beginning of August, no one had favourably answered the Russian suggestion. Petersburg scented a German intrigue, but the other powers neither needed nor received encouragement from Berlin to resist the Russian proposition. On the other hand the Germans did not advocate the Russian view, although this might have served as a suitable means of indirectly pressing Rumania in the railway question.

One issue had already been satisfactorily solved before Russia requested assistance.[31] In two minor matters the Ger-

---

[29] Radowitz to Reuss, 1 & 15 August, nos. 557 and 595; Radowitz to Schweinitz, 16 August, tel. 83, GFO, IABq 133 iii.

[30] See above, p. 170.

[31] The memorandum presented by the *chargé* on 6 August (Russland 65 i secreta) argued that Turkish troops could be called to Eastern Rumelia only if the commission so desired. The commission had already resolved this issue and Turkey had accepted its decision. Correspondence in GFO, Türkei 136.

mans seemed prepared to accept the Russian proposals; but in order to keep in step with Austria, they could only partially consent to one, and could not consider the other. Russia had suggested that in case the Montenegrin commission could not agree on a definitive border, a provisional line should be adopted until finally decided by the powers. Radowitz accepted the proposal. Vienna agreed to the drafting of a provisional frontier, but wanted the commission to have the final decision. The German delegate was therefore instructed to vote with his Austrian colleague. Secondly, Russia had proposed to transfer the task of reconsidering the border at Silistria to the Serbian commission. Austria balked, so the suggestion came to nothing.[32]

In two other questions the German delegates were instructed to join their Austrian colleagues. In one of these—whether the *thalweg* of the Danube was to form Bulgaria's northern frontier or not[33]—the Russians and Austrians held similar views. In the other they were diametrically opposed. This was the dispute over the Turkish military road through Bulgaria. The Congress had conceded Turkey this road through the south-western tip of Bulgaria as the best land route from Constantinople to Albania and Novi-Bazar. The Russians rejected it because they had discovered an alternative route avoiding Bulgarian territory. They also held that the Bulgarian delimitation commission was unauthorized to resolve the issue. By this time, 12 August, the Russian requests for support and their criticism of German policy had become quite insistent. Bismarck did not want them to think he would bend under pressure, so the German delegate was directed to vote with Austria in this matter; and all other German votes cast together with Austria were to stand. But, the chancellor instructed, in the future the German delegates in the various commissions were not to attempt mediation, and to take everything *ad referendum*.[34] This general instruction marks the end of the brief period of exclusive Austro-German cooperation in the commissions. Contrary to

[32] See correspondence in GFO, IABq 133 i and iii; Müller, no. 42.

[33] See above, p. 178.

[34] Radowitz to Schweinitz, 14 August, no. 498, GFO, IABq 133 i; Müller, nos. 43 and 44; Medlicott, *Congress*, p. 350.

Bismarck's assertions he had yielded slightly to Russian demands and threats, and in the following weeks the Russian
position received more consideration.

On the same day (12 August) that the delegates were instructed to discontinue their somewhat one-sided support of
Austria, it was learned that Andrássy was determined to resign.
This news altered the situation. Bismarck immediately attempted to arrange an interview with the Austrian foreign
minister.[35] In retrospect, he claimed that at this stage he had
feared Russia's firmness might have been induced by the
assurance of an agreement with Austria. Andrássy's retirement
would then open the door to a change of course which seemed
all the more likely since it was rumoured that Waddington's
position was also threatened and that he could be replaced by
Freycinet,[36] a close friend of Gambetta. Assurances that no
reorientation in Vienna was contemplated did not absolutely
convince Bismarck because on previous occasions Andrássy
had referred to the possibility of seeking support elsewhere as an
alternative to a closer understanding with Germany.[37] Nevertheless it is odd that the chancellor should have been troubled
by the nightmare of an Austro-Russian agreement at just this
moment. But he consistently argued that this was so and if we
recall that he often suffered from similarly far-fetched, passing
nightmares, one can accept his testimony. Thus, what he
probably expected from Andrássy was, first of all, some sort of
assurance that no agreement with Russia existed or was in the
offing. What else he wanted at this stage it is difficult to say.
Before the arrival of Alexander's letter the Russian threats
were not sufficiently clear. The Austrian reaction was also uncertain, so he could hardly persuade William to agree to an
alliance. He did, however, advocate closer cooperation with

[35] Radowitz to H. Bismarck, 12 August, tel. 1, GFO, Österreich 70; Bismarck
to Reuss, Kissingen, 13 August, tel. 1, GFO, Russland 65 i secreta; see also
Windelband, p. 66.

[36] C. DE FREYCINET (1828–1923). Minister of public works, December 1877–
December 1879; prime minister, December 1879–September 1880, 1882, 1886,
1890–2; minister of war, 1888–93, 1898–9.

[37] Frauendienst, p. 361. See the discussion of this point in Schünemann, p.
560; Windelband, p. 66.

Austria and England as the alternative to the then unreliable eastern orientation.

For some time he had been considering the advantages and disadvantages of an alliance with Austria; his campaign against Gorchakov presupposed a close accord; and Austro-German cooperation in the commissions from June to August against Russia necessitated the willingness of both parties to develop this *entente* in case their behaviour should cause annoyance— which it did. If Bismarck had really wanted to provoke the Russians, this was the opportunity. Their threatening attitude delivered a splendid excuse to use with William who would otherwise have been reluctant to follow such a line. But the chancellor wished to avoid excessive provocation and instructed his delegates to discontinue one-sided cooperation with Austria.

On the 19th he wrote a plaintive letter to his old friend Orlov, Russian ambassador in Paris, asking for a meeting. Bismarck portrayed his policy as pro-Russian, complained about the conduct of Gorchakov and the Russian press, and dropped a hint that Russia might lose her link with Germany. At this point he did not want to cut off any avenues of retreat, and so wished to continue talking with Russian statesmen, but the tone of the letter is more sad than angry and certainly does not betray a man who was happily nearing a cherished goal.[38] All this was changed by the Tsar's letter of 15 August which Bismarck saw on the 21st. In it Alexander complained to his uncle, William, that the German delegates in the various commissions supervising the execution of the Treaty were gratuitously becoming more hostile; such behaviour could, by poisoning the relations of Russia and Germany, have calamitous consequences. He ended with the fateful flourish:

Est-ce digne d'un véritable homme d'Etat de faire entrer dans la balance une brouille personnelle, quand il s'agit de l'intérêt de deux grands Etats faits pour vivre en bonne intelligence et dont l'une a rendu à l'autre, en 1870, *un service que d'après Vos propres expressions Vous disiez n'oublier jamais.* Je ne me serais pas permis de Vous les rappeler, mais les circonstances deviennent trop grâves

---

[38] Orloff, pp. 165f. PRINCE N. ORLOV (1827–85). Envoy in Brussels, 1860–70; ambassador in Paris, 1872–84; in Berlin, 1884–5.

pour que je puisse Vous cacher les craintes qui me préoccupent et dont les conséquences pourraient devenir désastreuses pour nos deux Pays. Que Dieu nous en préserve et Vous inspire!

This may have been a personal outpouring, but the disparaging reference to Bismarck and the twice repeated threat about disastrous consequences touched the match to the powder keg. The chancellor termed it an 'effusion of gall' which, he feared, was calculation rather than mere nervousness.[39] The masterful language of the Tsar's letter encouraged him to take the step he had hoped to avoid but which his own policy had made more likely. The letter also greatly diminished the German Emperor's power to resist and helped convince others close to him of the necessity for an Austrian alliance. Thus in the end William was fairly well isolated as a result of his pro-Russian attitude.

When Bismarck saw Andrássy in Gastein on 27–8 August he could readily convince himself that apprehension about an Austro-Russian plot was unjustified. He immediately offered an alliance and Andrássy accepted. The subsequent negotiations with Austria and Bismarck's struggle with his Emperor for the approval of the alliance are sufficiently known to obviate a detailed treatment of this material here. The treaty, drafted by Andrássy and Bismarck on 24 September 1879 in Vienna, was signed on 7 October and was to last for five years. It provided for mutual defence against Russian attack, but only benevolent neutrality in case of defensive war with another power unless Russia joined the fray.[40]

Bismarck and Andrássy were immediately agreed on the basic character of the alliance—a defensive treaty directed

[39] Radowitz to Bismarck, 5 September, tel. no. 35, GFO, Russland 65 i secreta; *GP*, no. 446; Medlicott, *Congress*, p. 381.

[40] Despite minor oversights and a tendency to minimize the asperity of the struggle between William and Bismarck the whole issue is well documented in the *GP*. Goldschmidt and Windelband correct this and add interesting detail. Radowitz gives the best eye-witness account. Busch gives Bismarck's official version. Schüssler adds to it. Heller interprets the then available material. Schünemann discusses Heller and adds scraps. Rothfels treats the feeler to England, adding a little. Wertheimer is the most valuable for the Austrian side; for many years his was the only reliable account of the more interesting German events. Pribram is disappointing. Medlicott discusses the whole problem. The best account is in Windelband, pp. 66–89.

against Russia. Bismarck proved so amenable to Andrássy's
views that one can only assume he regarded the details as
unimportant. The chancellor's suggestion to subject the treaty
to the approval of parliament was designed to impress Andrássy
with his fervour for the dual monarchy and cannot be taken
seriously. He had flourished the proposal of an 'organic
alliance' as early as 1867 and had repeated it occasionally
since then, but it would have alienated Russia and given
parliament a weighty voice in foreign affairs. Bismarck consistently sought to avoid both, and there is little reason to
suppose that at this juncture he desired otherwise. Another,
more important, point where the German and Austrian views
were at variance concerned the scope of the treaty. Bismarck
argued at the insistence of the Emperor that it should also be
directed against France. Andrássy refused to contemplate this
extension and Bismarck readily gave way. The same conciliatory attitude was conspicuously absent from the struggle
with William to obtain his signature for what was in reality
the Austrian version of the treaty. All the chancellor was
willing to concede to the Emperor were formal points designed
to spare Russian susceptibilities, but nothing of real substance.
William was finally overcome not by Bismarck's eloquent and
forceful arguments but rather by his flanking manœuvre which
created a conflict of loyalties. The chancellor wisely remained
in the background, confined himself to the writing of a series of
superb memoranda, and organized the offensive. He succeeded
in uniting the ministry, the general staff, the Crown Prince
and public opinion, but his agents successfully fought the
battle for him. The Emperor, in virtually complete isolation,
submitted, but remained unconverted. Nothing can better
reflect his utter despair than the note penned at the moment of
submission: 'those who have induced me to take this step shall
answer for it one day up above'.[41] This was the last of the
titanic struggles with the Emperor and Bismarck carried off
the laurels, but one wonders whether the domestic and foreign
consequences of this victory were worthwhile, even from the
chancellor's personal point of view.

[41] Stolberg to William, Baden-Baden, 3 October, GFO, Russland 65 secreta;
Windelband, pp. 80, 575f.

Bismarck's motives for seeking the alliance remain unclear. His own testimony, while illuminating, cannot be taken at face value. Much of it is neither consistent with past and future policy nor with his diplomacy. In his memoirs, for instance, he carefully elaborated the drawbacks of the alliance and the value of the link with Russia. When Andrássy had offered an alliance just before the Congress, he had taken a similar line. However, in his contemporary despatches to William Austria was painted in glowing and Russia in gloomy colours but the Tsar was spared; in the press the distinction between the Tsar and his advisers was blurred, the national argument underlined and William portrayed as virtually treacherous. To the Russians he argued that the alliance was meant to keep Austria in harness; the French were told that it was aimed solely against Russia as long as the radicals were not in power in Paris; and the British were informed that the alliance had brought Russia round and that everything was fine again.[42] Bismarck's own explanations merely add to the mystery and the inconsistencies can only be accounted for by considering the purpose of each. Surely none reveals the whole truth and nothing but the truth.

A definitive answer to the riddle may never be found; but it would appear that Bismarck did not actively strive for the alliance. He kept it in mind as an eventuality (a last resort)[43] which gave him reassurance in the struggle with Gorchakov. As Russo-German relations worsened, the *entente* with Austria grew closer. If Bismarck's main aim was to bring Russia round on his own terms, it seems unlikely that, had a more conciliatory line been adopted at the last minute instead of the attempt to force Germany's hand, he would still have urged the alliance with Austria. At best this would have necessitated considerable effort, prejudiced relations with Russia and given Austria the diplomatic advantage.

In fact, the decisive reasons for concluding the alliance were

[42] Széchényi to Haymerle, 31 October, private, WS, PA rot 454 Liasse II; Russell to Salisbury, 24 October, no. 517 secret, FO 64/935; St. Vallier to Waddington, Varzin, 14 November, no. 1 confid., FFM, Waddington papers, vol vi; *DDF*, ii, no. 476; *GP*, nos. 447, 455, 458, 461, 477, 482; *Kölnische Zeitung*, 7 & 8 October; Busch, ii, 404–16; Lyall, i, 303–6; Simpson, p. 74.

[43] For the opposite view see Oncken, i, 225–30; and, more recently, the conclusion of Böhme's book.

of a negative sort; Bismarck had no particular sympathy for the Habsburg monarchy. To justify the alliance he often referred to historical and racial ties; but this must be considered more an effective argument than a primary motive. The rumours of Russian alliance feelers in France and Italy during the summer appeared after the decision for the alliance had already been taken; so they, too, must be eliminated.

There was, to Bismarck's way of thinking, one essential motive for the alliance. It would, he thought, strengthen his position in relation to Russia in order to bring her to terms—to the return to the *Dreikaiserbund* under his leadership and the less erratic policy this implied. The miscarriage of his previous efforts at intimidation had been dramatically demonstrated by the events of the summer, but also by the increasing Russian wariness of Germany, documented by the re-establishment of the abnormal cavalry dispositions on the German border. Bismarck probably did not fear an imminent attack, but he believed that anti-German feeling was waxing and that Russia was becoming less reliable. Schweinitz's efforts to explain away Alexander's aggressiveness as a temporary mood from which he would soon recover had the opposite of the intended effect on Bismarck, who feared just this instability of the Tsar. At an unfavourable juncture, Russia might very well abandon Germany and even join a hostile coalition. Such considerations did not lead Bismarck to revise his tactics, but rather to continue in the same vein by improving his own ability to harm Russia so as to force the logic of an agreement on her. Austria, therefore, had to be restrained from eventually joining either the western powers or Russia by binding her closely to Germany.[44] Since Austria was weaker, there was relatively little danger that the obligations assumed would necessarily involve Germany in disastrous complications as long as her diplomacy was carefully conceived. And from the military point of view, the alliance did considerably strengthen the defensive position of Germany.

Bismarck's concerted attempt to combat the economic and

[44] Taylor, pp. 259, 266, holds that Bismarck's 'real fear was of Austro-Hungarian restlessness, not of Russian aggressiveness'; and 'Russian aggressiveness was his excuse, not his motive'.

social effects of the Great Depression by means of state intervention and control led to a rather different approach to
domestic politics. Clearly the dual alliance fits into this picture
of a more cautious Bismarck interested in protection and
insurance. But the Three Emperors' League or an alliance with
Russia would have served this purpose equally as well. The
readiness for a more formal approach to foreign policy, and
in consequence an alliance, was surely prepared by the new
course in domestic policy; but the Austro-German alliance
was the product of the power struggle between Russia and
Germany and not of any real sympathy for central Europe.

It has sometimes been argued that Bismarck intended to
create just such an economically united central Europe, or at
least a customs union with Austria. Böhme is a recent advocate
of this view, but there is little evidence to support it. He
mentions in this context the plea of the French economist and
journalist, Molinari,[45] for a central European customs union.
The project was widely discussed in public, but Bismarck's
reaction was clearly unfavourable. He seems occasionally to
have toyed with such ideas and early in 1880 he publicly acclaimed the virtues of a customs union. Privately he advocated
treating Austria more favourably than others, but the Austrians
could perceive no tangible signs of this love. Bismarck claimed
that some minor quarrels would have to be patched and the
honeymoon would come later—it never did.[46] At this stage of
his career he was interested in other, more practical matters.
The effect and certainly the purpose of his policy was diametrically opposed to schemes like Molinari's and his isolated
references to them only make sense if regarded as tactics, not
strategy.

There is some indication that in autumn 1879 Bismarck was
willing to make commercial concessions to Austria, but they
failed to materialize and in fact the treatment of his newly
won ally was hardly very generous. In previous years, but

---

[45] G. DE MOLINARI (1819–1911) was a prominent liberal economist associated
with the *Journal des Debats*. Although Belgian born, he worked mainly in Paris.

[46] Böhme, pp. 597–9, 603f; Bülow to Hobrecht, 6 October 1878; Bülow to Wes-
dehlen, 16 November 1878, DZA, AA 7556; Reuss to Bismarck, Vienna, 15
February 1880, confid; Philipsborn, Berlin, 19 February 1880, note; Bismarck to
G. von Baussnern, 5 March 1880, DZA, AA 9952; Matlekovits, pp. 71, 101, 826–33.

especially since the Congress, he had spoken of the political necessity of economic concessions to Austria whenever Russia seemed particularly unreliable or threatening. But amicable assurances were never followed by significant concessions. The beginning of November 1878 was such a period. The Austro-German commercial treaty of 1868 had conceded Austria higher tariffs. Since then Germany had lowered her rates, and when the treaty came up for discussion in mid-1877, the Germans decided to insist on concessions from Austria. Discussion started, but the treaty expired on 31 December 1877; it was subsequently extended until June and then December 1878 because no real settlement could be reached. Late in 1878 Bismarck wanted a further extension for one year so as to gain time for his planned tariff reform. But Austria was keen to resume discussions for a new treaty. The chancellor made no substantial concessions, but he wisely wished to sweeten the bitter pill he was asking his neighbours to swallow. They were informed that as soon as he was finished with his reform project, he would gladly grant Austria more favourable commercial terms than any other country. After much haggling a compromise was agreed which pleased no one—the old treaty was replaced with one granting most favoured nation treatment for one year. By the autumn of 1879 the German tariff reform was completed and the alliance signed. Vienna expected the promised commercial concessions. The chancellor reiterated his belief in their necessity on political grounds but was not in fact prepared to give way on essential points. He offered not to raise the duty on Austrian goods if Vienna proved cooperative. Haymerle, Andrássy's successor, had hoped for more and was determined to drive a hard bargain. Bismarck was beside himself and grumbled that good political relations with Austria could not be purchased at the expense of German producers; 'in the political field the mutual services of both the friendly neighbours balance'.

In the commercial sphere Austria's new ally was no easier to deal with than hitherto and the provisional treaty was pared down further and prolonged until mid-1880. If anything, commercial relations were worse than before. And they did not quickly improve. The treaty was again prolonged for a further year and a definitive agreement not signed until May 1881. But the atmosphere remained cloudy as long as Bismarck was in office; afterwards it rapidly cleared. Yet there was never any really sunny weather. The inherent logic of German economic expansion before 1914 was towards the development of world-wide trade and not towards the creation of an economic central Europe.[47]

It might be gathered from this[48] that Bismarck did not intend to sacrifice much for Austrian support. Holstein's belief that he had been waiting thirteen years for this moment could hardly be farther from the truth.[49] As far as he was concerned no 'era of good feelings' ensued. In fact, he was determined to concede only a minimum, and to use the alliance mainly for his own purposes. Whether it could be maintained for long on this basis is open to question. It emerges fairly clearly from the negotiations that Bismarck hoped the alliance would continue for some time after its conclusion. He was, however, sufficiently pessimistic about the permanence of alliances to allow one to assume that he would not have hesitated long to drop his partner, if ever German interests made this desirable. To gain support for the alliance he of course used, but was little influenced by, arguments based on national sentiments, and he was very successful in this. There were some who were uneasy about Austrian Catholicism or aggressiveness, others feared the set-back to conservative solidarity which a close alignment with Austria signified, and still others wanted a connection with England rather than Austria, but, on the whole, Bismarck had widely based public

[47] See above, p. 103; Bülow to Reuss, 6 November 1878, DZA, AA 9942; Bismarck to GFO, Gastein, 11 September 1879; Bismarck to Hofmann, 26 September 1879; H. Bismarck to Philipsborn, Varzin, 10 November 1879, DZA, AA 9949; Berchem to GFO, Vienna, 28 November 1879; Philipsborn to H. Bismarck, 17 December 1879; H. Bismarck to Philipsborn, 19 December 1879, DZA, AA 9950; Scholz to Hohenlohe, 7 June 1880, no. 79; Bismarck to Scholz, 16 June 1880, DZA, AA 6966; Austrian draft treaty, copy, BA, R 2/1511; Russell to Salisbury, 8 November 1879, private, SP, A/9; St. Vallier to Courcel, 23 November 1880, private, FFM, Allemagne M & D 167; Poschinger, *Aktenstücke*, i, nos. 141, 144, 171, 172; Bazant, pp. 25–55; Matlekovits, pp. 70–82; Benedikt, p. 139; Böhme, pp. 9, 525–9, 587–604. Böhme's account of the negotiations is misleading. For some of the wider issues see H. C. Meyer's article.

[48] See also below, pp. 205f.

[49] Holstein, *Lebensbekentnis*, p. 126.

support for a seemingly nationally inspired and therefore rather permanent policy.

Some aspects of Bismarck's political thought, particularly the alliance with Austria, wrongly cast a harsh nationalistic light on him. His attitude towards the Slavs lends validity to this view. For Bismarck they were an effeminate race, sensitive, emotional, and without the solid core which makes statesmen; the seriousness and efficiency of the Baltic Germans were the true foundation of the Russian empire. In this respect Bismarck shared the prejudices of his countrymen. It would be tempting to regard him simply as a nationalist and he certainly was proud of his Prussian background and German blood, but his thought was essentially oriented on the state and the struggle for power rather than on the nation.

In October 1879 Bismarck did not intend to 'opt' for Austria, or even to give his ally marked preference over Russia. As long as the German foreign office interpreted the alliance in this manner, it would not 'inevitably' lead to conflict with Russia, who, after all, had other rivals against whom German support, mediation, or even neutrality would be useful.[50] On the one side, the treaty gave Germany the support she needed to force Russia to come to terms; on the other, if it were to be maintained at all, it did give Austria certain advantages which even Bismarck's reserved approach to the dual monarchy could not easily prevent and which in Russian eyes would loom larger than life. Hence, in the long run the alliance complicated the re-establishment of congenial relations with Russia, but skilful diplomacy might well have mastered this difficulty.[51] The alliance could give Bismarck added security only if he followed a more indulgent line towards Russia and this he intended to do once she had come round, but the legacy of struggle and his combative approach to politics were troublesome

[50] On the question of Bismarck's 'option' for Austria—that is, whether the alliance was intended to be fundamentally enduring, or merely a tactical instrument —there has been much discussion. Those like Heller who believe that Bismarck 'opted' usually admit an element of inevitability in a Franco-Russian alliance, whereas their opponents deny this. For purposes of illustration, see Heller, pp. 55–7; and Schünemann, pp. 549–94. For a recent statement of the inevitability theory see Taylor, pp. 265f.

[51] But cf. Medlicott, 'Three Emperors' Alliance', p. 64.

obstacles to his ingenuity on which he heavily relied. To adapt his own expression: now that he had secured his pistol after having observed the disturbing symptoms of his partner on a long walk through the woods, he should have continued with greater composure than before. If he did not do this, the fault lay more in his own inability to adjust completely to the new situation than in the 'pistol'. The justification for the alliance must be sought in the manner of its application and not in its design. Bismarck was only partly successful; but does this mean that lesser men who had the qualities he lacked were doomed to failure?

The alliance was meant to bring the Russians to terms, but also to form the basis of a new orientation in case they remained hostile. For this reason Bismarck heartily welcomed the fact that the alliance indirectly brought closer relations with England. As long as he was not fairly certain that Petersburg would be willing to reach a triple understanding, it was in his interest to discover how far he could, if need be, rely on England.[52] When troubled by similar apprehensions in January 1877 he had followed much the same line.[53] This is probably the significance of the feeler to England in 1879. In this sense the English reaction was not at all unfavourable. On 16 September Münster was instructed to ask what the position of England would be if Germany clashed with Russia by refusing to submit to unreasonable demands in questions of no concern to her. Without further ado Disraeli answered that England would 'keep France quiet'. Subsequently, he and the Queen were pleased that nothing came of the feeler, although Salisbury seems to have had regrets. Odo Russell certainly did, but his views on Germany at the end of the year were too sanguine for Salisbury's liking. Completely misreading the situation, Russell thought that Bismarck had always preferred an English to an Austrian alliance, but since Derby had so

[52] Renouvin, p. 103, suggests that Bismarck may have hoped the Russians would get wind of his feeler in London in order to put added pressure on them. Schüssler analyses the extensive literature on the subject. See also Medlicott, *Congress*, pp. 385–9.

[53] See correspondence in GFO, IABi 57 secretissima and Türkei 124; Windelband, p. 47; Medlicott, 'Bismarck and Beaconsfield', pp. 241f.

coolly received his advances, he had approached Austria and was bidding for a French alliance; the British ambassador held that if London were to remain cool, he would gradually drift back to the already open arms of Russia.[54]

Münster, the German ambassador in London, was another adherent of a link with Great Britain. He argued that both English parties would be prepared to give assistance should Germany quarrel with Russia over the Eastern Question, but in Berlin neither his judgment nor his behaviour was appreciated. Bismarck would have wanted more than Disraeli offered in case of war with Russia; but his was certainly a generous offer in answer to a casual feeler and an excellent starting point for further negotiations. Although in March 1880 Bismarck expressed regrets to Russell that England had not formed a triple alliance with Austria and Germany,[55] the fact remains that in September 1879 he had refused to consider the matter further, mainly for two reasons. First, the Russians had in the meantime made an initial display of sincere goodwill[56] which, although vague, was sufficient to allow Bismarck to drop any idea he may have had of an eventual pro-British orientation. Secondly, the English reaction proved his thesis that the Austrian alliance would 'fetch England'; although it may not have been adequate cover for war with Russia, it could serve as insurance if negotiations with the Tsar were to fail. In this case at least limited cooperation with England would be possible.

This English insurance afforded important security in the following months before Bismarck could obtain greater certainty about Russian intentions. His diplomatic activity in this period shows that while striving to avoid a break between the powers over eastern affairs, he supported both England and Russia in such a way as to perpetuate their rivalry. Thus, the Russians and English would be interested in assurance against

---

[54] Salisbury to Russell, London, 14 January & 25 February 1880, private, SP, A/27; Russell to Salisbury, 27 December 1879, 4 January 1880, private, SP, A/9; 28 February 1880, SP (correspondence with O. Russell); Knaplund, *Letters*, pp. 144f, 154; Nostitz, pp. 123ff; Cecil, ii, 373; *GP*, nos. 709–15.

[55] Skazkin, p. 132; Russell to Salisbury, 30 March 1880, private, SP, A/9; Limburg-Stirum to H. Bismarck, 27 October 1879, FA, B–70.

[56] See below, pp. 215ff.

one another and German relations would be good enough with both to enable Bismarck, if absolutely necessary, to elect for either without being drawn into a war. There were two difficulties in this policy. The first was achieving the correct balance. It was necessary to support Russia just enough to convince her of the advantages of German goodwill, but not enough to make her believe this could be got for nothing, and not enough to estrange England or to irritate Austria. On the other hand he had to support England and Austria enough to maintain good relations—which, by the way, were still necessary in the Rumanian question—as well as to preserve the atmosphere of suspicion between England and Russia. Too much support here, or the appearance of it, might, however, antagonize the Russians. The second difficulty lay in the fact that while avoiding excessive generosity and the pitfalls accompanying such a policy, he also forfeited the advantages which more intimate friendships implied. The other powers remained sceptical of his sincerity.[57]

In addition to this another, perhaps less pressing, consideration had to be borne in mind. The main problem with Austria was to get her to see the advantages of an agreement with Russia. But after Andrássy's resignation it would be unwise to push Vienna too far in this direction because, although it was relatively small, the danger still existed that Austria might treat separately with Russia, or, questioning German dependability, abandon her new ally for the sake of English friendship. It was, therefore, wise to apply but slight pressure at first, and to lay greater emphasis on the desire for an alliance with Austria, and so to increase confidence in Bismarck's good intentions.

[57] See Medlicott, *Congress*, p. 393, 'Three Emperors' Alliance', pp. 67, 77f, 81f.

CHAPTER IX

The Dual Alliance and the Submission of Rumania

During the summer the Berlin and Bucharest governments had sketched a solution to the Jewish and railway questions. Berlin expected the Rumanian chambers to pass some emancipation legislation and accept the railway convention. Both things were very unpopular amongst Rumanians and they hoped to prise further concessions from Germany. Since from the middle of August for about two months German statesmen had more important problems on their hands, the Rumanians probably felt that time was working for them. In fact, the conclusion of the dual alliance robbed them of all hope and after a brief fight they agreed to a favourable compromise on the Jewish question and they accepted the terms of the railway convention. They even began to look to Berlin and Vienna for political leadership.[1]

Until the enactment of the laws on Jewish emancipation at the end of October the German cabinet abstained from pressing the Rumanians, limiting itself to warding off attempts to bargain over the convention. This passive attitude was easy enough to understand in view of the international situation; but, seizing the opportunity thus given them, the Rumanians continued their obstructive policy in the railway negotiations. Further pressure was necessary to regain lost ground and force adoption of the unaltered convention.

In September Radowitz made it abundantly clear that the railway convention was of extreme importance and hinted broadly that adjustments could be made in Berlin's attitude

[1] For this chapter consult Meisl, pp. 70–88; *Aus dem Leben*, iv, 240–98. See above, p. 161, n. 1.

on Jewish emancipation. So on 7 October the council of ministers in Bucharest accepted the convention. Berlin thought it would be enacted in a few days, and let matters slide until the beginning of November when it seemed as if Rumania wanted to force recognition without having passed the convention.[2]

By this time the constitutional revision adopting the principle of article XLIV of the Berlin Treaty had passed both Rumanian houses and nine hundred individuals of Hebrew faith were emancipated. None of the powers was satisfied, but the Rumanian government could rest assured that in the end they would acquiesce. On 21 October, William had virtually told Princess Elizabeth of Rumania[3] that she could count on him. Hoping to avoid further concessions, Rumania pressed for recognition; she warned the powers that, if they should refuse, the precarious emancipation settlement could be frustrated by Russian subterfuge in Moldavia.[4]

Radowitz suspected that the railway convention would be forgotten if the Rumanians obtained their independence before it became law. Therefore he reassured himself that England and France would not formally recognize the country. He pressed for immediate enactment of the convention, intimating that German support could not be expected for the definitive delineation of the Silistria border until the convention had been adopted.[5]

This was no idle threat. In July Russia had proposed the reconsideration of the border to the east of Silistria.[6] The powers had agreed, but Austria and England wanted a majority decision to be final. After much haggling in which Germany played a passive role Russia finally accepted the principle of a majority vote, but proposed that the final decision should be taken by the ambassadors in Berlin. Bismarck rejected the idea,

---

[2] Winckler, 'Rumänienpolitik', p. 87.

[3] ELIZABETH (1843–1916), daughter of Prince of Neuwied.

[4] Radowitz, 17 October, memorandum; note, 24 October, GFO, IABq 133 ix; Reuss to GFO, Vienna, 6 November, no. 449, GFO, Rumänien 1; Bleichroeder to Bismarck, Berlin, 28 October, FA, B–15.

[5] Radowitz to William, 10 November, GFO, IABq 133 ix; Salisbury to Russell, 5 November, SP, A/27; DDF, ii, no. 475.

[6] See above, p. 170.

believing that in view of recent experiences he ought to dodge responsibility for a decision which would clash with Russia's views. The Emperor reluctantly approved, stating that since an anti-Russian policy had been forced upon him, it was indifferent whether this relatively unimportant matter was regulated contrary to Russia's wishes. Subsequently, the new commission began its deliberations and, since Russia was conciliatory, it was advisable—after she had been outvoted six to one—to offer some minimal compensation to facilitate an honourable retreat. Haymerle suggested an insignificant border rectification at Silistria in favour of Bulgaria. Bismarck doubted whether the concession would satisfy Russia; he certainly would have agreed to more generous compensation. Strengthened by German support, Russia fought tenaciously for a favourable agreement. The dispute was finally settled on the basis of Haymerle's proposal, but not until the following summer.[7]

It was urgent for the German government to force acceptance of the convention. The Emperor disliked the idea of pressing the powers to withhold recognition until the railway interests had been satisfied. Because of the serious conflict between Bismarck and William during the previous two months over the Austrian alliance, it was advisable to avoid unnecessarily frustrating the aged sovereign. The powers were restive. Germany's new ally also wanted to come to terms with the Rumanians.[8]

Since Bismarck had so readily availed himself of Austrian support against Rumania in the past months, his attitude towards Austro-Rumanian relations in the autumn gives an indication of his interpretation of the alliance, and what he expected from it. When Bismarck learned of the Rumanian machinations, he asked Vienna for the continuation of pressure in Bucharest. Suspicious of Haymerle, the new Austro-Hungarian foreign minister, he remarked that if Austria should press for recognition

[7] See the correspondence in GFO, IABq 133 i; Windelband, pp. 80f; Medlicott, *Congress*, pp. 350f, 400f.

[8] Limburg-Stirum to Holstein, 28 October, no. 6, GFO, IABq 104; Windelband, pp. 131f.

we must answer coolly and indignantly that *we* are demanding support and assistance from Austria and will not give in. We must not think that friendship with Vienna obliges *us* now to accommodate every Austrian wish, just the opposite! Until now Austria has had much more from our alliance, because *we* could just as easily have come to terms with Russia, but Austria could not. The ground on which we could accommodate either Russia or Austria is still very large.[9]

Fortunately for Austro-German relations, Haymerle took the wind out of Bismarck's sails and readily agreed to make vigorous representations in Bucharest.

Bismarck was preoccupied with the idea that Vienna could 'mint five mark pieces from the taler of the alliance'.[10] He was clearly determined to use the alliance as an instrument of his own policy; the establishment of better relations with Rumania would have to wait until after the railway convention had been adopted. But he felt the constraint of his situation and warned Bleichroeder not to overreach himself: later Germany might not be able to afford a political quarrel over the protection of the rail interests no matter how many Germans were involved. But Bleichroeder remained firm in what he considered the major issues and the German cabinet fully supported him.

Bismarck, less sanguine and conciliatory than Radowitz, was thoroughly roused against the Rumanians. When St. Vallier visited him on 14 November in Varzin, he was surprised to see the chancellor so worked up. Bismarck believed the moment had not come to abandon his reserve, wishing to wait until they had poured some wine into the pure water they had served him. Even though he had no illusions about the importance of the obtainable concessions, he felt that the dignity of the powers required insistence on a minimum of formal satisfactions.[11] This display of real irritability was certainly calculated to strengthen the French will to resist recognition. In order to demonstrate more clearly that they had profited from their previous attitude, he promised to advocate anything they

[9] H. Bismarck to Radowitz, Varzin, 11 November, GFO, IABq 104.

[10] Limburg-Stirum to [Rantzau], 1 October 1880, FA B–70.

[11] Russell to Salisbury, 26 November, no. 566 secret, FO 64/936; St. Vallier to Waddington, 16 October, no. 197, FFM, Allemagne 30; *DDF*, ii, no. 477.

proposed in the Greek question. St. Vallier then asked him to seek support in Vienna. Bismarck balked at the thought of dealing with Haymerle; he emphasized the Austrian reservations but promised finally to come out in favour of the French views.

At this point the Italians decided to recognize Rumania. This news annoyed Bismarck who in December was suffering from nervous exhaustion as well as from bouts of neuralgia and indigestion; in this condition he was always especially touchy. He wished to notify Rome in an icy manner that this was a breach of the Treaty: although Italy had blandly promised to accredit her envoy simultaneously with the other powers, no general understanding had been attempted. Rome had been under severe pressure from public opinion to recognize Rumania, and, probably believing that the others were about to take this step, decided to anticipate them by a few days. The Italian envoy, Tornielli, was accredited on 18 December.[12] The desire to use genuine feelings of racial affinity with the Rumanians as a springboard to influence in the Balkans or at least greater security against Austria outweighed the counsels of humanity and the wrath of Bismarck.

On 9 December the Rumanian chamber passed an amended form of the convention which was unacceptable in Berlin. Radowitz suspected an attempt to sabotage the convention and immediately asked Vienna for support. He labelled the vote of the chamber a premeditated infraction of all previous obligations. Bismarck was furious. He argued that since the Rumanians had resorted to chicanery Russia should be supported in the Silistria dispute: a faithless government could not be assisted. Radowitz was to talk firmly to Haymerle who should have given greater and more persistent support. He unfairly claimed that Andrássy's help had been more effective. In fact, Andrássy had not given particularly spontaneous aid: he had often stalled and then supported Berlin in such a way

[12] COUNT G. TORNIELLI (1836–1908). General secretary in ministry for foreign affairs, 1876–June 1878; December 1878–July 1879; envoy in Belgrade, September 1879; in Bucharest, December 1879–88. Radowitz to Keudell, 17 December, no. 670 confid., GFO, Rumänien 1; Radowitz to H. Bismarck, 10 December, no. 24; Radowitz to Keudell, 13 December, tel. 74, GFO, IABq 104; Windelband, p. 101; Radowitz, ii, 112.

as to deflect Rumanian irritation from Austria. Bismarck had
not always attempted to conceal his dissatisfaction. On the
other hand Haymerle readily responded to pressure. The
Rumanians had given him misleading assurances, and he was
genuinely offended.[13]

The fact that the Rumanians felt themselves favourably
placed was partly due to the failings of German policy. While
busy negotiating the Austrian alliance, Bismarck had neglected
the railway dispute. Bucharest was able to shelve it until the
emancipation laws had been passed. This put the Germans in a
delicate position: they had to lay their cards on the table and
admit that they could not grant recognition until the convention had been adopted unchanged. In mid-December
Germany asked for and obtained outright support from the
powers, including Italy. The German imperial family also
jostled the Rumanians. Prince Charles was told that unless the
unchanged convention was adopted, he would lose the favour
of the Emperor. The Empress underlined the dangers in a
letter to Charles's father.[14] This colossal pressure from all sides
broke the resistance of the Rumanians and the convention was
passed on 28 January 1880. Everyone had been waiting for this
moment, especially the Emperor who, still believing that
England opposed recognition, remarked that the moment had
come to speak an earnest word with the English. But neither
France nor England needed coaxing. Radowitz stated on 2
February that the railway question had been satisfactorily
solved and Germany was prepared for recognition.[15]

There had been recent reports that partially Russian-
inspired separatist activity in Moldavia was increasing. The
Austrians were therefore elated when Rumania asked for their

[13] H. Bismarck to GFO, Varzin, 12 December, tel. 10, GFO, IABq 104; H.
Bismarck to Radowitz, 13 December, GFO, IABq 133 i; Radowitz to H. Bismarck,
10 December, FA, B–90; Russell to Salisbury, 15 December, no. 610 confid., FO
64/936; St. Vallier to Waddington, 16 December, FFM, Allemagne M & D 166
bis.

[14] Radowitz to Hohenlohe and Münster, 13 December, tels. 79 and 93;
Radowitz to Reuss, 15 December, tel. 190, GFO, IABq 104; Russell to Salisbury,
9 & 25 December, nos. 594 confid. and 631 secret, FO 64/936; St. Vallier to
Waddington, 11 & 15 December, nos. 232 and 233, FFM, Allemagne 31.

[15] Bismarck to William, 31 January, GFO, Rumänien 1; Salisbury to Russell,
23 December, private, SP, A/27.

good offices to obtain recognition. This allowed Bismarck to give Austro-German relations a fillip and clear the way for a *rapprochement* of both countries with Rumania. Hitherto he had consistently stressed cooperation with Austria on Rumania, but often awkwardly demanded concessions. Since the difficulties with Bucharest had been surmounted, Bismarck could devote more attention to his neighbour's point of view.

On political, economic and military grounds Haymerle advised binding Rumania more closely to Austria. He, and also Andrássy, were really after the extension of the dual alliance to include Rumania. Andrássy wrote as much to Prince Charles and Kálnoky was instructed to broach the subject when visiting Bismarck in February, but he apparently thought it unwise to talk about it then, and in the following year Haymerle contented himself with more or less veiled references to this objective.[16] For the time being, however, Bismarck had no knowledge of this and could readily agree with Haymerle's innocuous desire for better relations. So he recommended Austria's good offices to the western powers as a means of strengthening her position in Rumania, which, he argued, would help to secure the peace. France could not accept this line of reasoning, so the chancellor dropped the matter, but not before emphasizing in Bucharest that Austria's friendly intervention had induced the powers to overlook the in-adequate execution of article XLIV. Finally, the three powers simultaneously recognized Rumanian independence on 20 February.

It is unlikely that the outburst of anti-semitic feeling in Germany towards the end of 1879 had any effect on German policy, although it strengthened the hand of the Rumanians. The Russian intrigues in Moldavia were more important. Their influence on the actual course of negotiations was small, but they did help to cement Austro-German friendship. After the railway problem had been solved it was just one more reason for Rumania to incline towards the two central European

[16] COUNT G. KALNOKY (1832–98). Envoy in Copenhagen, 1874–9; ambassador in Petersburg, 1880–1; foreign minister, 1881–95. Haymerle to Francis Joseph, Stift Neuberg, 9 September 1880; Andrássy to Prince Charles, undated, private, WS, PA 454 rot.

powers rather than the empire to the east. Another was the fear of being crushed between the millstones of Russia and Bulgaria.

For economic and political reasons Rumania's suspicion of Austria remained for some time, but in the spring Russia seemed more dangerous. With the Bratiano[17] mission to Berlin in March 1880 and a continued conciliatory attitude in commercial questions an attempt was made to improve relations with Berlin and Vienna, if possible, on a contractual basis. In view of the tension with Russia German policy became warmer, but Bismarck was reluctant at this stage to go much further than non-committal assurances of friendship and reminders of the wisdom of good relations with Austria—and even Russia. Initially, Vienna could not have been happier about this development, but by the summer the honeymoon was over and Bismarck began complaining about imperious Austrian manners.[18] Further alarming phases of Russian behaviour were necessary before he was willing to ally with Rumania, but he clearly appreciated the value of that country as a friend or ally in any subsequent contest with Russia.

In the long and arduous Rumanian dispute the alliance with the bankers Hansemann and Bleichroeder had also proved its value in the struggle for the protection of German capital abroad. The next, Samoan, episode had already begun and in the course of the 1880s many others were to follow.

Meanwhile in the Greek frontier dispute little progress had been made since June 1879. This was the result partly of strong English and Italian resistance to the transfer of Janina. Just as important, however, was Waddington's decision to postpone further action until the difficulties over Egypt had been mastered. The powers agreed to urge Greece and Turkey to renew negotiations, and in the middle of June they presented notes in Athens and Constantinople. But with this their co-

---

[17] J. BRATIANO (1821–91). Rumanian premier, 1876–88 (except for April–June 1881).

[18] Reuss to Bismarck, Vienna, 7 March 1880, no. 113; Radowitz to Reuss, 12 March, no. 172; Bucher, 16 March, memorandum; Rantzau to Limburg-Stirum, Friedrichsruh, 26 September; Limburg-Stirum to Reuss, 8 October, no. 783, GFO, Rumänien 1; *Aus dem Leben*, iv, 342f, 349.

operation ceased. Since a united front was not maintained, the
Turks continued to stall. Although at the end of July a change
of government in Italy brought a more favourable approach
on Greece, the British view was unchanged and Waddington
remained passive.

This was the situation when in the first week of August
Berlin learned that the agitation on the Greek-Turkish frontier
was much more serious than during the previous winter. Bismarck had been encouraging the French to move rapidly
ahead, but for his part wanted to maintain his reserve. He
argued that since the Greek dispute was of no particular interest,
he did not care what happened—in fact, complications might
be convenient.[19] This was the moment when Schweinitz's
first report on his conversations with Alexander had arrived
and the Russo-German crisis was at its peak.[20] It is interesting
to note that Bismarck welcomed the possibility of complications
which could draw the attention of the French to the Mediterranean, where they might clash with the English. This is the line
he had followed in March when he feared the possibility of
Franco-Russian cooperation in the Balkans. He also had the
news relayed to Vienna so that the Austrians would see the
danger and place a premium on cooperation with Germany.

The negotiations between Greece and Turkey were finally
resumed towards the end of August. Since after a month's
discussion no progress at all had been made, France asked
Berlin to help get things moving. At this difficult juncture
Bismarck's earlier enthusiasm for supporting France had
dwindled. He had not been looking forward to this initiative,
but felt that his promise of aid would have to be kept.[21] So
Germany consented to the proposal and, in order to maintain
cooperation with the Hapsburg monarchy, she successfully
persuaded the Austrians to do likewise.

The negotiations had developed no further than this when
St. Vallier visited Bismarck on 14 November. The French
ambassador asked for diplomatic support in Constantinople

[19] Radowitz to Hatzfeldt, 15 August, tel. 91 confid., GFO, IABq 133 viii; St.
Vallier to Waddington, 25 July, no. 181 confid., FFM, Allemagne 29.
[20] See above, pp. 186f.
[21] Bülow to Hatzfeldt, 26 August, tel. 96, GFO, IABq 133 viii.

and Vienna. Bismarck agreed to assist in Constantinople, but told St. Vallier that the Austrians feared an uprising in the western Balkans if Epirus went to the Greeks. He added that he valued the security of Austria too highly to assume responsibility for such an eventuality, but finally agreed to recommend the French views to Vienna. Although Haymerle wished to avoid irritating the Porte, Bismarck's doubts about the extent of his assistance were exaggerated, for he was ready enough to back the French. Quite naturally, he wanted to stay in the background. In addition to the need to repay France for services in the Rumanian dispute, Bismarck still wanted some sort of satisfaction for her in the Mediterranean area. His desire to aid the moderate Waddington must have been stimulated by a report from Constantinople that the French ambassador was continuing his pro-Russian intrigues.[22] So concessions in the Egyptian[23] and Greek questions were understandable. So also was the rather showy and unfair way he did this at Haymerle's expense.

Bismarck's frank statement on Austria's reluctance to admit the cession of Epirus to Greece seems to have impressed Waddington, who had been vainly struggling for several months to soften the English on this point. On 9 December 1879—just before he fell from power—the French premier suggested that Turkey should retain most of Epirus (including Janina), and as compensation for Greece a correspondingly greater portion of Thessaly could be ceded. With the exception of Britain all the powers accepted this proposal. London suspected Franco-Russian designs in the east and probably also ambitious schemes by Freycinet's new philhellene cabinet (formed on 28 December). Not wanting to betray distrust of a French cabinet led by such a close friend of Gambetta as Freycinet, Bismarck wished to support France as previously in a cautious, but honest, manner. When it was reported that Salisbury wanted Turkey to retain all of Epirus, he commented that this was 'rather foolish; they ought to leave the French whale this buoy to

play with'. Finally, the English suggested a commission to fix
the line before recommending it to Greece and Turkey. When
England and France had at last agreed on the details and
presented the plan in March 1880, the Porte objected.[24] So no
real progress had been made till Gladstone took office in April
1880. He held the Greeks in higher esteem. This removed one
of the main stumbling blocks to an agreement. In June the
powers easily agreed on a line even more favourable to the
Greeks than that suggested at the Congress. Athens accepted
it, but Constantinople, of course, remained adamant. It was
not until March 1881, after much unfriendly negotiation, that
the Turks agreed to a compromise solution which allowed
them to retain the coveted city of Janina.

[24] Radowitz, 21 January 1880, memorandum; H. Bismarck to GFO, Varzin,
13 December 1879, tel. no. 13; Schweinitz to Bismarck, Petersburg, 9 January
1880, no. 12; Reuss to Bismarck, Vienna, 18 January, no. 27, GFO, IABq 133
viii; Windelband, p. 107; Medlicott, *Congress*, pp. 354f, 395; Lhéritier, iv, 42ff.
For subsequent negotiations see Medlicott, *Bismarck, Gladstone*.

CHAPTER X

The Russo-German Armistice: Steps towards a Revived *Dreikaiserbund*

In early summer 1879 Russo-German relations had become increasingly strained. Berlin gave Vienna mounting support in the current Balkan squabbles, the intrinsic value of which was minimal. During the Russian manœuvres early in August the Tsar complained bitterly about this; he used language which in the nineteenth century was regarded as very ominous. At the same time Bismarck heard that Andrássy had decided to retire. The chancellor feared that these two developments might be related and decided to make a slight concession in the instructions to the German delegates in the international commissions. This marks a turning point to a less consistently pro-Austrian line. It is interesting to note that at almost the same moment the Russians also began to see the advantages of a more conciliatory attitude. Thus by the use of demonstrated antipathy both empires had achieved a small initial success. Both soon realized the futility of continuing the same policy and were prepared to come to a limited mutual understanding, a *modus vivendi*, which would permit them to benefit from cooperation without abandoning positions of force in relation to each other.

At first neither was conscious of the changed attitude of the other; but both the Russian statesmen and Bismarck, who was not yet sure of Austria, felt isolated and dared not further provoke the other. Bismarck drafted a rather moderate answer to Alexander's letter which made it easier for the Russians to make the conciliatory gestures they had apparently already planned. They attempted to explain away the letter as a personal effusion written by a nephew to his uncle. A meeting of the two sovereigns on 4 September on Russian territory brought about a full personal reconciliation, but the distrust of the statesmen for one another remained. Both sides tried by a show of conciliation, but without a corresponding abandonment of their positions of strength, to induce the other to come to terms. Bismarck's situation was delicate, because he was attempting to strengthen his position by means of the Austrian alliance. First he had to overcome the formidable resistance of William. The Russian show of conciliation was welcome as an indication that his tactics were successful, but it was untimely and complicated his attempt to convince William of the necessity of the alliance.

The Russian situation was more precarious. The interior condition of the country was anything but encouraging and Russian military strength was inferior to that of the Austro-German block then forming. So the Russians continued their efforts to increase their military power. Lignitz, the German military *attaché* in Petersburg, thought that the ranks of the new twenty-four reserve divisions would be virtually complete by the following spring.[1] The disposition of the Russian troops could leave no doubt that the army was supposed to exert pressure on Germany and Austria rather than Turkey.

In this chapter the initial and, for German policy, decisive steps towards a renewed Three Emperors' League are traced. Bismarck's use of conciliation and diplomacy to reach this goal is discussed in the first section; his more threatening devices are dealt with in the second part.

I

The Russians had decided to seek an arrangement with Berlin before the Austro-German negotiations had actually begun; the news of these negotiations made them more determined to reach this understanding. Towards the end of August the newspapers were admonished by the Tsar and their activity was damped down for several days. This warning might not have been solely motivated by the wish to placate the Germans, but at least it did clear the air. In return William agreed to

[1] Lignitz, Petersburg, 21 August, report, GFO, Russland 65 i secreta.

have the German government press cautioned.[2] So for a few days, the newspaper war subsided. Meanwhile Field Marshal Manteuffel[3] had been sent to Warsaw where he arranged a meeting of the two Emperors at the Russian frontier station of Alexandrovo which took place on 4 September. Directly afterwards Saburov made a short visit to Berlin. Together these events formed the first stage in the coming Russo-German *rapprochement*, but they also indicated the limitations of any future agreement.

The two Emperors readily convinced one another of their unchanged friendship. The Russians did their best to convince William and his *entourage* of their sincere desire to come to terms. Hints were even made that they would be ready for an offensive and defensive alliance. On the other hand, Manteuffel obtained from the Russians themselves his information about their unsuccessful alliance feelers in France and Italy. Although Alexander denied having anything to do with it, authentic French sources offered indignant confirmation. This, considered together with rumours (which Bismarck may have heard) of an attempted *rapprochement* with Sweden aimed against Germany, seemed very ominous indeed. Miliutin's explanation for the armaments increases and the stationing of troops along the German border was that Russia feared an offensive alliance between England, France and Austria; there was no hint that a change in the troop disposition could be contemplated as a concession for an understanding.[4] In addition, despite repeated

[2] Goldschmidt, no. 9; Radowitz, 31 August, note, GFO, Russland 65 i secreta; Radowitz, 7 September, note; William, 3 September, note; Radowitz to Eulenburg, 3 September, GFO, Russland 65 secreta; Walsham to Salisbury, 30 August, no. 429, FO 64/934; Plunkett to Salisbury, Petersburg, 30 August, no. 415, FO 65/1046; but cf. Széchényi to Andrássy, 13 September, no. 26–B, WS, PA III 119; Kálnoky to Andrássy, Petersburg, 10 September, no. 42–C confid., WS, PA X 73; Medlicott, *Congress*, p. 385; Windelband, p. 71; Skazkin, p. 114; Vogüé, entry for 28 August.

[3] BARON E. VON MANTEUFFEL (1809–85). Commander-in-chief of army of occupation in France, 1871–3; viceroy in Alsace-Lorraine, 1879–85.

[4] Dufferin to Salisbury, Petersburg, 26 August, no. 401 confid., FO 65/1046; Kálnoky to Andrássy, Petersburg, 29 August, no. 39–B confid., WS, PA X 73; Hohenlohe to GFO, Paris, 10 September, tel. 88 secret; Wesdehlen to Bülow, Paris, 17 September, no. 196 confid., GFO, Russland 65 secreta; Manteuffel to [Bismarck], Warsaw, 1 September, tel.; Bromberg, 4 September; Radowitz to Bismarck, 5 September, tel. 37, GFO, Russland 65 i secreta; cf. however Miliutin, iii, entries for 25 & 26 September; Vogüé, entry for 30 September.

assertions that the pro-German party was 'on top' and Gorchakov was designated *un homme mort*, Alexander renewed his
accusation that Bismarck permitted the quarrel with Gorchakov to distort his foreign policy. It emerges fairly clearly
from this that the Russians wanted Germany to realize the
disadvantages of an independent line; they had little sympathy
for the policy of friendship which they knew was necessary.
Saburov's reassurances were balanced by observations on the
extent of anti-German feeling in Petersburg. The impression
they created was essentially the same as that resulting from the
interview in Alexandrovo.[5]

Bismarck initially opposed the meeting at Alexandrovo,
realizing it would re-cement imperial friendship, thus com-
plicating his efforts to bring about an Austrian alliance. The
symptoms of a more amenable Russian attitude were of course
welcome in so far as it would serve as a point of departure for a
rapprochement after he had concluded the dual alliance.[6] Otherwise he found the information coming from Alexandrovo and
Berlin anything but comforting. He wished to make further
concessions dependent both on imperial approval of the
alliance with Austria, and on an unambiguous demonstration
of Russian conciliation. Bismarck was not at all pleased that
William had requested the press to tread softly, although he
saw the advantage in this and suggested articles asserting that
the press war had been one-sided, the German newspapers
having remained relatively passive. The purpose of this, he
informed Radowitz, was to prepare public opinion for the
fact that Germany was being forced against her will to 'opt'
for Austria. The press was also to deny that personal discord
existed between himself and Gorchakov: there were sufficient
other reasons for coolness towards Russia. The *chargé* in Petersburg was instructed to take the same line.[7] In view of the

[5] Goldschmidt, no. 9; Miliutin, iii, entry for 23 August; Medlicott, 'Three
Emperors' Alliance', pp. 64–7; Skazkin, p. 119.

[6] W. Bismarck to [Bülow], Gastein, 5 September, GFO, Russland 65 secreta;
Schüssler, pp. 16f.

[7] Bismarck to GFO, Gastein, 7 September, tel. no. 49, GFO, Russland 65 i
secreta; 8 September, tel. no. 55; 11 September, tel. no. 59; Radowitz to Bismarck,
9 September; Bismarck to Radowitz, 11 September, tel. 58; GFO, Russland 65
secreta; Radowitz to Stumm, 4 October, no. 600, GFO, Russland 61; Windelband,
pp. 74f; see also Waldersee, i, 194f.

Tsar's repeated criticism of Bismarck on this account as well as the reports that Gorchakov was finished, it would have been well to drop this point. Bismarck, however, did not want the press to abandon the battle against Gorchakov's ideas.

Bismarck's unbending attitude towards Russia throughout September is further illustrated by his reception of a memorandum prepared by Giers and given to Manteuffel at Alexandrovo. It concerned three questions pertaining to the execution of the Treaty. The Russian point of view on all three had previously been brought to the attention of Berlin, and support was now requested. Bismarck was furious that the Russians had taken advantage of the meeting of the two Emperors to press for further aid in the work of the commissions. By this time he was sure of Austria and telegraphed categorically that in view of the events of the preceding three weeks the instructions were not to be changed; he was prepared to make a cabinet question of the incident.[8] Bülow immediately interpreted this in terms of *sicut Austria*, which was not quite correct, but in practice there was little difference. One of the Russian suggestions, concerning the Montenegrin commission, evaporated because of its adjournment. Another, on the appointment of a technical commission to reconsider the Silistria issue, was helped along by a Russian concession accepting the principle of majority decision. The third suggestion concerned the military route through Eastern Rumelia and Bulgaria which the Tsar was determined to defeat. The German delegate had been instructed to vote with Austria in this as in the question concerning the *thalweg* as the northern border of Bulgaria. Both were still being discussed, but the German delegate had hesitated to vote as instructed because of clashes between the Austrian and Russian commissioners. With the exception of these two instances he had been told to withhold his vote in such a case. The instructions were repeated and in both questions he voted with his Austrian colleague. As far as the Danube frontier was concerned, the principle of the *status quo ante* was agreed for the islands, otherwise the *thalweg*. This was better for Bulgaria than the Congress decision, but not

[8] Radowitz to Bismarck, 5 September, no. 26, GFO, Russland 65 i secreta; Müller, no. 48.

quite as favourable as the *thalweg* pure and simple as suggested by Russia. Until the last moment there was much confusion over the military route, but Germany was prepared to accept any Austrian proposal which attained a majority. Finally, with majority backing, the Austrian delegate proposed to grant the Turks the principle of the road, but leave the regulation of the details to negotiations between the Turkish and Bulgarian governments. The Russian commissioner showed little enthusiasm for the motion, although in fact it effectively shelved the question.[9]

It was not until after his talks with Saburov at the end of September—when the Russian offers had become more precise and he was more certain that the Austrian alliance would be approved by the Kaiser—that Bismarck deemed it opportune to continue the more conciliatory line broken off after Alexandrovo.

In their first meeting Bismarck assured Saburov of his sincere desire for an understanding on the basis of the *Dreikaiserbund*. He explained that the Austrian alliance would separate her from the western powers and so facilitate the re-establishment of the *Dreikaiserbund*. Saburov was not won over to the revival of the League, but agreed to consider it, if it would benefit Russia. He said that at the moment the Tsar's main preoccupation was the danger of a Turkish occupation of Eastern Rumelia. This was, for a change, a significant issue. If Russia could keep Ottoman forces out of Eastern Rumelia, the future unification of this province with Bulgaria would be greatly facilitated and so the chief British gain at the Congress undermined. Bismarck thought the time had come for a concession and agreed to recommend the Russian view in Vienna.

Saburov was evidently so pleasantly surprised with this display of goodwill that in the next conversation his proposals were much farther reaching. Initially, he had intended merely to give assurances of good intentions, leaving specific arrangements till later, but he immediately hinted at an offensive and defensive alliance. Bismarck rejected the idea, saying he could

[9] Radowitz to Hatzfeldt, 8 September, tel. 102; Hatzfeldt to GFO, Buyukdere, 21 September, tel. 94; Radowitz to Reuss, 20 September, no. 694, GFO, IABq 133 i; Medlicott, *Congress*, p. 350.

only consider a defensive alliance. Still, he agreed to consider a Russian attempt to take Constantinople as legitimate self-defence in case Turkey was on the point of dissolution. He made it abundantly clear that if Russian expansionism led to a conflict with Austria, the Tsar would have to reckon with the possibility of German resistance; the most that could be hoped from Austria was observance of the *status quo*. Saburov understood Bismarck's rather roundabout statements on this point. However, as a demonstration of goodwill, Bismarck drafted with him a Russo-German alliance, which conceivably would oblige Germany to join Russia in an Austro-Russian conflict. But the chancellor had already announced that it was a triple agreement which interested him. Bismarck was certainly in an expansive mood and just as the Russian diplomatist had apparently surpassed his instructions, so he himself made promises he presumably did not intend to keep. The perhaps incidental concession on Constantinople was the only one not contradicted by other declarations and reservations. It was to become the key to the further negotiations. Saburov, surprisingly, was not interested in the Straits then, but Giers and Miliutin very much were because of their concern with the English threat. After lengthy discussion in Petersburg a compromise was reached whereby Saburov was to accept the proposal for a triple agreement and push for, but not insist on, support in the Straits question.[10]

Well chosen from the German vantage point, it concerned one of the primary goals of Russian foreign policy, but was not likely to lead to any early involvements. It touched no German interests, could be reconciled with the Austro-German treaty, and was also compatible with fairly healthy Anglo-German relations, although it excluded a now unlikely Anglo-German offensive alliance. Aside from this, however, it was advisable for Bismarck to play down his good relations with England the more Russia showed willingness to come to an understanding. Henceforth, he demonstrated a certain anxiety lest Anglo-German relations should become too close or appear too anti-Russian. Although he still did not trust the Russians, he

[10] Simpson, pp. 69–92; Radowitz, ii, 97–102; Medlicott, *Congress*, pp. 390–92; Miliutin, iii, entry for 3 October; Skazkin, pp. 114–19, 132.

wrote immediately to Andrássy hinting at their offers; but the Austrians stood fast in their pro-English inclinations.[11]

Bismarck was not a little upset by Salisbury's reference to the Austro-German alliance in a public speech on 17 October as an anti-Russian pact and so as 'good tidings of great joy'. Partly because of this and partly to save William further annoyance, Bismarck decided not to share in any communication to England as to the Austro-German understanding, but merely to refer to that made by Austria.[12] Until the Russians had been informed he wanted England to learn as little as possible. Although Bismarck did not shy from applying various types of pressure to force the Tsar back to the *Dreikaiserbund*, he feared English indiscretions could create the impression of an opposing triple alliance. This would make the Russians less amenable. On the other hand Bismarck did his best to convince the Austrians of the necessity of communicating to Russia as much of the agreements as possible, but Andrássy and Haymerle were opposed. Bismarck was motivated partly by consideration for William's views. This explains the urgency with which he pleaded his case. Moreover, he wished to leave the Russians in no doubt as to the character of the alliance— that is, that Austria and Germany would jointly ward off an attack, but that the terms entailed no united front against tsarist Balkan policy. In this manner he desired to demonstrate clearly the power of the Austro-German block, but also the advantages of an understanding with it. Only concerning the form of the communication was consideration for Russia decisive.[13] Not until after the form and the substance of the communication to Russia had been decided did Bismarck begin to drop his resistance to a more complete communication to England. Haymerle wished to obtain the approval and support of London. He also thought it best to assist British

---

[11] Radowitz, ii, 102; *GW*, XIV, ii, no. 1619; Reuss to Bismarck, Vienna, 2 October, no. 399 most confid., GFO, Russland 65 secreta; Haymerle to Kálnoky, Vienna, 25 October, tel. no. 68, WS, PA rot 454 Liasse II.

[12] *GP*, nos. 507 and 511; Goldschmidt, no. 17; Medlicott, *Congress*, pp. 393f; Schüssler, pp. 40ff. Russell thought Salisbury's speech made a favourable impression in Berlin. Russell to Salisbury, 24 October, no. 517 secret, FO 64/935.

[13] Reuss to Bismarck, Vienna, 19 October, no. 421 secret; Bismarck to Radowitz, Varzin, 13 October, GFO, Russland 65 secreta; *GP*, nos. 488–9, 491.

policy in the East, fearing that the Anglo-French *entente* might otherwise grow too intimate. Bismarck remained cool, assuring his Austrian colleague that close cooperation between England and France was advantageous.[14]

The necessity for this attitude is all the more apparent since at the same time (the beginning of November) rumours of a British naval demonstration against the Porte aroused Russian suspicions of a move on Constantinople. Towards the end of the year the Russian press turned more against England and, for the most part, correspondingly spared Germany.[15]

A refusal to seek support for the dual alliance or to assist England in the east did not imply any wish to separate from her. On the contrary, in December 1879 and January 1880 Bismarck supported British policy at Constantinople when it was not directly opposed to Russia or when it was not ostensibly provocative. The English were even advised not to irritate the Turkish government on minor questions. The German *chargé* showed a cooperative attitude towards British policy especially in Armenia. He had previously been told to avoid the initiative, but on humanitarian grounds to help his colleagues support reasonable Armenian demands. At the beginning of 1880 these instructions were repeated. Even though his French and Italian colleagues remained passive, Radolinski, the *chargé*, backed Layard's efforts on behalf of the Armenians until he was cautioned by Bismarck in March 1880.[16] It seems difficult to

[14] Reuss to Bismarck, Vienna, 19 October, no. 421 secret, copy; 15 December, no. 526 most confid., GFO, Russland, 65 secreta; *GP*, nos. 510-11, 513. See also Windelband, pp. 98f. Bismarck spoke similarly to Dufferin and Odo Russell. Russell to Salisbury, 25 & 26 March 1880, nos. 147 confid., and 148 secret, FO 64/959; *GW*, viii, no. 257; and also to Hohenlohe, but his remarks to the latter on 22 February 1880 show that he probably still had in mind a 'quarrelling friendship' as his ideal, Hohenlohe, ii, 280, 291.

[15] Stumm to Bismarck, Petersburg, 8 and 18 November, nos. 333 and 342 confid., GFO, Russland 65 secreta; 23 November, no. 349, GFO, Russland 61; Plunkett to Salisbury, Petersburg, 8 & 22 October, nos. 511 and 543, FO 65/1047; Kálnoky to Haymerle, Petersburg, 8 October, no. 45–B; 8 November, no. 52; Langenau to Haymerle, Petersburg, 3 December, no. 58–C; 17 December, no. 60–C, WS, PA X 73; Chanzy to Waddington, Petersburg, 7 November, no. 54, FFM, Russie 259; Medlicott, *Congress*, p. 394; *DDF*, ii, no. 477.

[16] See correspondence in GFO, IABq 133 xiii and Türkei 137; Russell to Salisbury, 27 & 28 December, no. 637 and 642 secret, FO 64/936; 3 January 1880, private, SP, A/9; Goldschmidt, no. 19, pp. 27f; Medlicott, *Congress*, pp. 343–5, 395; Windelband, p. 128.

avoid the conclusion that, although Bismarck rejected much of what Haymerle suggested, in many points his own policy was similar, differing sometimes only in details and tactics. He wanted to accustom the Austrian horse to his bridle.

One reason for Bismarck's slightly greater consideration for British policy at the end of the year may be deduced from the fact that Gorchakov reinstalled himself as chancellor when he returned to Petersburg early in December. Before his return to Russia, Decazes, former French foreign minister, had arranged an interview with the diplomatic editor of the *Soleil*, the main organ of the Orleanist party. In it Gorchakov gave assurances of sympathy for the French, advising them to be strong and stating that Bismarck's enmity was due largely to his esteem for France. Subsequently, he told the French that he meant everything he had said, but to the Germans Gorchakov disavowed much of what the *Soleil* printed, absurdly saying that he had not known the man he had spoken to was a reporter. This was grist for Bismarck's mill, but he still kept on repeating that there was no friction between himself and the Russian chancellor; he wanted to combat the idea that the dual alliance was the result of a mere personal feud. When Gorchakov passed through Berlin on his way home he made on Radowitz the impression of a 'lampe qui s'éteint'. Hardly had he returned when the German ambassador wrote of the confusion reigning in the Russian foreign ministry. An energetic circular on behalf of the Montenegrins followed, thus suggesting that Gorchakov was again directing affairs.[17] This impression, however, was misleading. In the following months he was not consulted on many important matters. Nevertheless, Bismarck's distrust mounted although the Russians had shown signs of a more sincere desire to come to terms. The newspaper campaign was waning as a result of orders from the minister of the

---

[17] See correspondence in GFO, Russland 65 ii secreta; H. Bismarck to Limburg-Stirum, Varzin, 30 October; Schweinitz to Bismarck, Petersburg, 5 December, no. 361, GFO, Russland 65 secreta; Radowitz to Bismarck, 3 December; Schweinitz to Bismarck, 5 December, no. 362, GFO, Russland 61; Plunkett to Salisbury, Petersburg, 24 September, no. 463, FO 65/1047; St. Vallier to Waddington, 16 October, FFM, Allemagne M & D 166 bis; Viel Castel to Waddington, Petersburg, 23 September, no. 44, FFM, Russie 259; Vogüé, entry for 20 September; Radowitz, ii, 111f; Skazkin, p. 113.

interior. Oubril, the ambassador in Berlin, was replaced on 4 January 1880 by Saburov and the heir apparent made a fairly successful peace mission to Vienna and Berlin.

A further consideration induced Bismarck not to neglect the English entirely. He was beginning to prepare the public for the new German army bill by pointing out the dangerous Russian armaments increases and threatening troop disposition on the German border. Since his efforts in this direction were also intended to force military concessions from the Russians, it was advisable to have some insurance.

For the rest of the winter Bismarck's policy towards England remained essentially the same. To the Austrians he referred to British diplomacy as provocative, but to the Russians he hinted at the necessity of remaining on good terms with England.[18] He could not afford to allow Anglo-German relations to deteriorate further before the *rapprochement* of the three empires had made more progress.

From the Saburov-Bismarck talks at the end of September the Russo-German *rapprochement* slowly became a reality. At this time Bismarck had agreed to back Russia's most important immediate demand—the prevention of a Turkish occupation of Eastern Rumelia—and to grant a free hand in her most important long-range goal—the possession of the Straits. Yet Bismarck did not abandon his aloofness in other Balkan questions: his somewhat ambiguous support was confined to the eastern part of the peninsula. At the beginning of 1880 the liberal policy of Miliutin, the Russian minister of war, and the panslavs in Bulgaria aroused suspicion. Perhaps in order to embarrass Miliutin, who he thought was following a line contrary to the Tsar's, he drew the attention of London and Vienna to the dangers inherent in the Bulgarian situation, but by May he again began supporting the Russians, although still not without reservation.[19]

[18] Bismarck to Schweinitz, 4 March 1880, no. 115; Bismarck to Reuss, 26 March, no. 210, GFO, Russland 69 secreta; Schweinitz to Bismarck, Petersburg, 23 March, no. 100 secret, GFO, IABi 57 secretissima; Windelband, p. 121; Schüssler, pp. 52f.

[19] See correspondence in GFO, Bulgarien 1 and 2; Windelband, pp. 129–30, 133–6.

Bismarck lost no time in passing on to Vienna Russia's anxiety about an occupation of Eastern Rumelia. Fortunately, Andrássy also opposed a Turkish occupation, had already advised against it, and promised to repeat his warning. Hence Bismarck was spared the trouble of pressing Austria, but this did not mean that the danger of an occupation was completely eliminated. On 13 October Salisbury complained bitterly about Russian machinations in the east. He said the situation had become so critical that it would be necessary to send in Turkish soldiers. Berlin then advised the Porte against sending troops and hinted to the French and English that such hazardous action would be synonymous with the renewal of the war. Salisbury did not subscribe to this view, but decided not to pursue the matter further.[20] This rather cautious support proved sufficient. The problem never did become acute, partly because most of the powers recommended moderation, and partly because the Turks themselves were reluctant to risk an occupation.

It has already been seen in earlier references to the Rumanian question that the railway dispute encouraged Berlin to take a persistently strong line with Rumania. A further manifestation of this in November was a nearing of the Russian and German views on the Silistria question.[21] Whatever the motives, the German attitude in these two questions did help in a small way to clear the air between Russia and Germany.

In the western Balkans the story was somewhat different. Bismarck felt that this was Austria's legitimate sphere of influence, and in Serbia and Montenegro he supported her views unhesitatingly. Prince Nicholas of Montenegro was still not in possession of certain territories which the Treaty of Berlin granted him. His patience was wearing thin and the financial resources of the country were strained by the necessity of

[20] Münster to Bismarck, London, 14 October, no. 115 most confid., GFO, Russland 65 secreta; see correspondence in GFO, Türkei 136; Russell to Salisbury, 22 October, no. 512, FO 64/935; Salisbury to Russell, London, 22 October, no. 534, FO 64/930; Haymerle to Széchényi, Vienna, 11 November, WS, PA III 119; St. Vallier to Waddington, 16 October, no. 197, FFM, Allemagne 30; Windelband, p. 129.

[21] See above, p. 205.

keeping a large number of men under arms. Towards the end of October the Prince announced that he would take Gusinie (part of the territory promised him in the Treaty) by force, if the Porte failed to turn it over immediately. The Treaty had only required Turkey to evacuate the territory, not to present the Montenegrins with it. The evacuation had already taken place, but the Porte, seeking to gain time as usual, asked Germany to restrain the Montenegrins until the belligerent population in that area could be pacified. Since Haymerle had repeatedly advised Nicholas to bide his time, the German agent at Ragusa was instructed to support any further *démarches* his Austrian colleague might make in this direction. In December Haymerle also demanded sharply that the Turks immediately execute the Treaty and Bismarck used similar language. The French and Russian agents followed suit.[22]

The continued procrastination of the Porte, perhaps encouraged by the English, could have brought the three eastern powers closer together through their common opposition to Turkish manœuvres, but Russia and Austria were still too suspicious of one another.

In January 1880 the Italian government attempted to arrange a territorial exchange. Russia favoured it, but Haymerle was suspicious and remained on his guard: he saw the Italian initiative as an assault on outlying Austrian forts. Tension mounted sharply, but in time subsided and after much tedious negotiations an agreement was finally reached on 18 April. The role of the Berlin cabinet was that of a spectator. The only initiative it appears to have assumed was a roundabout attempt both to encourage Italian machinations in the Albanian area and to stimulate Austrian suspicion of them. Evidently it would have suited Bismarck's plans for imperial solidarity if the Italians had lived up to the reputation he had made for them, but they did not.

The powers having come to terms, the local population prevented implementation of the settlement and Bismarck, emerging from his reserve, began in May to argue in favour of Austro-Russian cooperation on Montenegro and other Balkan

---

[22] See the correspondence in GFO, IABq 133 and 133 iii; Windelband, pp. 128f and 133; Medlicott, *Congress*, pp. 352–4.

questions. Haymerle preferred London, but the policy of the new British government was throughout the summer, if anything, more anti-Turkish than the Russian line. The British seemed to be dangerously active, even belligerent, along the Austrian frontiers, so he slowly began to see the sense in Bismarck's reasoning. The dispute was finally satisfactorily solved in the autumn. Montenegro abandoned the mountainous Gusinie for the coastal town of Dulcigno. This was brought about under British leadership with the aid of a joint naval demonstration and the threat of further coercion against Turkey. Vienna was frightened only marginally less than Constantinople and the decision was taken to go ahead earnestly with the negotiations for the renewal of the Three Emperors' League.[23]

German support of Austrian policy in Serbia at the beginning of 1880 was straightforward enough. It showed, however, some of the difficulties involved in the ostensibly practical scheme for dividing the Balkans into two spheres of influence. Serbia was obliged by treaty to construct that part of the Vienna-Constantinople railway which went through her territory. Turkey and Bulgaria were in a similar position. Fearing Austrian domination and exploitation, all three attempted to postpone or prevent construction and received sporadic aid from Russia. It would have been senseless for Germany to endorse Austrian views in favour of the railway only in the western Balkans (Serbia) and not in the east (Bulgaria and Eastern Rumelia), but this gave Vienna a clear advantage in the Russian sphere. Germany was faced with a similar dilemma regarding the Danube, and supported her ally here as well.[24]

The reluctance of Austria and Russia to consider schemes of self-limitation, and the views of Germany on the future of the two great avenues to the eastern Balkans—the Danube and the Balkan railway—jeopardized the success of the plan to divide the peninsula into spheres of influence. Bismarck often repeated

---

[23] Hohenlohe to Hatzfeldt, Berlin, 2 May, tel. 27, GFO, IABq 133 (details in this file); Bismarck to Reuss, 8 February, no. 93 confid., GFO, Italien 70; Hohenlohe to Reuss, 2 May, no. 306, GFO, Russland 69 secreta; St. Vallier to Freycinet, 11 May, no. 120 confid., FFM, Allemagne 35; Medlicott, *Congress*, p. 353 and *Bismarck, Gladstone*, chapters iii and vi.

[24] See the correspondence in GFO, IABq 133 xx, xxii, xxiii; Türkei 121 and 144.

that consistency was no virtue in politics. Here one is tempted
to ask whether this was not a question of wrongly applied
consistency.

To understand fully Bismarck's hostility for Italy in the
western Balkans, it is necessary to glance briefly at the irredentist agitation. Before the outbreak of serious trouble in the
Balkans in 1875 the Italian irredentists had been few and
moderate. They quickly became more numerous, radical, and
aggressive. Their agitation reached a peak just before the
Congress of Berlin. It was hoped to obtain territorial concessions in return for any Hapsburg advance in Bosnia-
Herzegovina. Cairoli, premier then as well as throughout
1880, clearly sympathized with the irredentists. He was warned
by Vienna, London, and Berlin. Then after the Congress the
irredenta agitation reached new heights and plans for an assault
on Austria were well advanced. Cairoli, reluctantly, put a
damper on this and things rapidly returned to normal, but the
suspicion of his connection with irresponsible activity remained.[25]

From January to March 1880 Bismarck made several
attempts to encourage Austrian—and, incidentally, French
and English—suspicions of irredentism. He advised strong
measures and spoke sharply in Rome. This was partly the
natural expression of exasperation at Italian conduct in the
Rumanian dispute. He also thought that the Italian government had been rather too reluctant in refusing the alleged
Russian alliance proposals the previous summer. Promises of
support against irredentism had been and still were a method
of cementing friendship with Austria. At this point, however, Bismarck wished to demonstrate the advisability of
an understanding with Russia to forestall attack from two
sides. Austria sought to counter the danger by cooperating with
England whose navy could hold the Italians in check in time
of crisis. Bismarck insisted that English support would be forth-

[25] B. CAIROLI (1825–89). Premier, 23 March–9 December 1878; premier and
foreign minister, 12 July 1879–14 May 1881. Bülow to Keudell, 8 April 1878, no.
212, GFO, IABe 61; Gravenegg to Andrássy, Rome, 11 June 1878, private,
confid., WS, PA XI 87; Paget to Salisbury, Rome, 3 April, 20 May and 5 June
1878, private, SP, A/11; Haines, pp. 23–47.

coming in any case and that it was therefore unwise to give too much aid in the Near East. Such a policy, he said, would antagonize the Russians who at the moment appeared to be in a peaceful mood worth encouraging. Since Bismarck by no means intended to abandon, but merely to edge away from England, Haymerle, for his part, agreed to adopt a slightly more restrained attitude in London, and, apparently, to display more firmness in Rome.[26]

As if to offer compensation for this rather negative side of his Italian policy concerning the Balkans, Trentino, Egypt, and Tunis, Bismarck welcomed Rome's attempt at colonial expansion in the Red Sea area ostensibly for cultural and commercial reasons, but probably calculating that it would produce minor scrapes with Britain, resulting in a 'balance of tensions' favourable to Germany. Still, a generally less scornful attitude towards the Italians had to wait until the autumn of 1881.[27]

After the conclusion of the dual alliance in October 1879 good relations with France were mandatory if Russia was to remain isolated and amenable to Bismarck's plans for a triple agreement. Waddington, then French premier and foreign minister, was not apt to truck with the Russians. And St. Vallier warned him to disregard hints at an alliance. He argued that the Russians would merely use a favourable response to get better terms with Germany: Decazes had foolishly fallen for that trick and was left sitting between two stools.[28] Waddington hardly needed persuading, but one could never know who would succeed him in office.

The chancellor's first task was to reassure the French about the significance of the alliance. He went to great lengths to explain it with a mixture of spurious and correct information

[26] See correspondence in GFO, Italien 70; Österreich 70; and WS, PA rot 454 Liasse II; also Bismarck to Reuss, Varzin, 18 & 28 January, FA, B–93; St. Vallier to Freycinet, 8 & 11 March, nos. 37 confid., and 44, FFM, Allemagne 33; *GP*, no. 513; Krausnick, *Gespräche*, pp. 22ff; Windelband, pp. 101–4; Medlicott, *Bismarck, Gladstone*, p. 51; Taffs, pp. 265f.

[27] Keudell to Bismarck, Rome, 31 March, no. 22 confid.; Bismarck to Keudell, 9 April, no. 145, GFO, IABq 76; Windelband, pp. 105, 272ff.

[28] St. Vallier to Waddington, Coucy, 11 September, FFM, Allemagne M & D 166 bis.

as the result of Russian threats and his desire to re-establish a form of the innocuous German Confederation. Russia was unreliable, treacherous and belligerent, but Germany willing and able to assist France—England was too, up to a point, but Bismarck clearly wished some doubts to linger about the extent to which friendship with England should be developed. All in all, however, he praised the dual alliance and the Anglo-French *entente* as the best guarantees for peace. Forgetting himself, he said in the same breath that if Gambetta and his pack of adventurers came to power, he would have to revive the Holy Alliance.[29] This was meant as a psychological pick-me-up for the moderate republicans then in power. Fortunately, the faithful Waddington took the record of this with him when he cleared his desk in the foreign ministry.

Having fairly successfully reassured the French, Bismarck began to retreat into the background in Egyptian affairs and he continued to offer support in the Greek question and later on Morocco. Hitherto he had attempted to build up the minimal German influence in Morocco and had, more often than not, cooperated with England: accordingly support for France was a new departure. Henceforth, German foreign policy never lost sight of the value of Morocco as a pawn in international affairs.

The chancellor welcomed French activity in areas where no collision with German interests was likely, and he hoped it might prop up Waddington's moribund government, and then, when it fell in December 1879, encourage the next cabinet to follow in his footsteps. Freycinet, the new premier and foreign minister, was an old associate and supposedly the cat's paw of Gambetta. For years the chancellor had been vainly telling his emperor that Gambetta was preferable to Mac Mahon.[30] But neither Bismarck nor most other established diplomats were pleased with Freycinet's radical airs. He was in fact prepared to follow a somewhat more ambitious line than his predecessor, and Gambetta toyed for a moment with the idea of a triple

[29] St. Vallier to Waddington, Varzin, 14 November, no. 1 confid., FFM, Waddington papers, vol. vi; St. Vallier to Waddington, Berlin, 29 November, private, FFM, Allemagne M & D 166 bis.

[30] EDMOND PATRICE COMTE DE MAC MAHON (1808–93). Duc de Magenta; maréchal de France; French president, 1873–9.

entente with England and Russia, but both were convinced of the necessity for improved relations with Germany.

For the time being Germany's relations with her western neighbour remained on an even keel as French relations deteriorated with Italy and England over Tunis, Morocco and the Balkans. Friction between France and Russia was even worse because of the Hartmann affair. Hartmann had attempted to assassinate the Tsar and escaped to France where the government refused extradition.[31]

The Franco-German understanding suffered momentarily as a result of Gambetta's Cherbourg speech in August 1880. The speech was an odd mixture of bellicosity and resignation. William was quite troubled, but Bismarck and Radowitz, acting ambassador in Paris, were not. Relations quickly improved, and when Ferry formed a new cabinet in September there was smooth sailing once more.

Clearly, after the conclusion of the Austrian alliance, Bismarck strove to maintain the gulf between Russia and the west by active support of France, occasional cooperation with England and serious warnings to Italy. The attention of these powers was drawn away from Russia and their inclination for anti-German adventures paralyzed by the perpetuation of a 'healthy' state of mutual tension.

II

Bismarck intended to induce the Russians to come to an agreement not only by a show of some conciliation and by preparing the ground for a renewal of the *Dreikaiserbund*, but also by means of a display of force. First of all it was necessary to consolidate his position of power by concluding the alliance, preventing the Austrians from reducing their military forces,

---

[31] Bismarck to Schweinitz, 7 April, no. 185 secret; Bismarck to Hohenlohe, 8 April, no. 164; Hohenlohe to Radowitz, Berlin, 23 April, no. 195; 9 June, no. 298; Holstein, 2 July, note, GFO, Frankreich 87; Hohenlohe to Radowitz, 17 June, no. 311, GFO, Tunis 1; Hohenlohe to Radowitz, 10 June, tel. no. 43, GFO, IABq 133 vi; Bismarck to Weber, 9 April, no. A–1, GFO, Afrika generalia no. 2; *GP*, nos. 662–5; *DDF*, ii, nos. 476–7; iii, nos. 21–164; Windelband, pp. 99–188; Medlicott, *Bismarck, Gladstone*, pp. 67–134; Daudet, pp. 191ff; Guillen, pp. 98–106; Lyons, ii, 202, 204f; Vogüé, entry for 23 August 1880.

and making preparations for the expansion of the German army. On the economic front he also began to take a stiffer line. As a warning, he stood firm over a minor dispute about the navigation of the Memel and in the autumn of 1879 and following winter he repeatedly considered retaliatory and transit tariffs as well as increasing the duty on grain.[32] In proportion to his steadily increasing basis of power, Bismarck urged the dismissal of the Russian chancellor and pressed for military concessions. If he could succeed in obtaining the transfer of some troops from the border, the military bill would become less urgent, but more important still, this would be a welcome sign of a sincere desire to accept German leadership. Bismarck only reluctantly abandoned his campaign when the final passage of the military bill was assured[33] and the Russians had clearly shown that, although they wanted an understanding they would not permit interference in domestic affairs.

When Russo-German tension was at its height in August and September 1879 the military question did not figure prominently. In his attempt to convince William of the necessity for the Austrian alliance, Bismarck referred to the Russian army increases and the troop encampments in Poland, but his arguments were mainly political. After the ratification of the Treaty his attention was concentrated more on military matters. On 20 October Limburg-Stirum, acting secretary of state for foreign affairs,[34] and Moltke expressed astonishment at a newspaper report that Austria planned to dismiss 20,000 men from the army. Bismarck had been receiving disturbing private information on Russian preparations for war; in Vienna he affected amazement and hinted at the advantages of remaining strong. Haymerle sought to placate the Germans by saying that the troops were only sent on leave in order to assuage the financial susceptibilities of parliament. In this way he hoped to secure enough backing for the Austrian army bill (which subsequently passed unchanged in December). Bismarck

[32] Poschinger, *Aktenstücke*, i, nos. 171–4; *Volkswirt*, i, 269; details in DZA, AA 15844–7; Bismarck to Scholz, 16 June 1880, DZA, AA 6966; Philipsborn to Hofmann, 28 May 1880, DZA, AA 10475.

[33] On 9 February 1880 it passed the Bundesrat and on 10 April the Reichstag.

[34] F. W. COUNT ZU LIMBURG-STIRUM (1835–1912). *Chargé* in Constantinople, 1871; envoy in Weimar, 1875; temporary state secretary, 1880–1.

argued that this approach only suggested the possibility of getting by on less; the proper tactics were to demand more.[35]

Meanwhile reports arrived giving details of the Russian troop dispositions in Poland. The chancellor's reaction to this new development is instructive. He admitted that for the most part the deployment had existed before the war. At that time, he said, Russia could not decide whether to fight Austria or Turkey; it was significant that the same positions were being resumed. Bismarck attributed this to Miliutin, who, he conceded, had no specific plan. Indeed no one in Russia had, but the military force could be used by any adventurer who happened along. He wished to know what Moltke thought of the troop dispositions and added that perhaps the best way to avoid setting light to the piled-up kindling was to have the newspapers publish the exact material. This was the beginning of a concentrated effort to excite public sentiment against the Russian troop encampments and to induce the Tsar to make reductions. It is interesting to note that after Salisbury's Manchester speech (17 October)[36] the Russian press spared the Germans and attacked England. The continuation of the newspaper duel resulted probably less from the pugnacity of slav journalists than from the insistance of the Germans on the threat created by the Russian troops. One of Bismarck's motives for inspiring the press in this manner was to precipitate in Russia a discussion of the troop dispositions. Strangely enough, he expected the Russian press to blame its own government for military provocation. But, owing partly to government orders, the Russians at first remained reticent. This refusal to discuss the matter publicly irritated Bismarck perhaps as much as their earlier polemics.[37]

The Austrians, apparently, did not realize that since the recent war the tsarist army in Poland had not been appreciably strengthened. Moltke told practically everyone who would

---

[35] See correspondence in GFO, Österreich 70 and IABi 57 secretissima; GW, XIV, ii, no. 1626; Radowitz, ii, 107; Windelband, p. 119.

[36] See above, p. 221.

[37] H. Bismarck to Stolberg, Varzin, 29 October; Radowitz to Berchem, 2 December, no. 846, GFO, IABi 57 secretissima; Széchényi to Haymerle, Berlin, 11 December, private, WS, PA III 119; Egerton to Salisbury, Vienna, 7 November, no. 716 confid., FO 7/965.

listen that it had been, and he pretended to be very uneasy; but he privately reassured Bismarck and on 2 December reported that there had been no important shift of troops into Poland since late 1875 when a large number of newly formed cavalry units was sent to the German border. As a counter measure Bismarck had strengthened the garrisons in the west so as to thwart effective Franco-Russian cooperation.[38] Since then the increases in the Russian garrisons had corresponded to the expansion of the army as a whole. Although there were about one third more troops stationed near the German border than in 1867, in view of the strengthening of German military resources through unification, the effective Russian position was perhaps no stronger. Moltke's report contained the following table.[39]

The Deployment of the Russian Army West of the Line:
Riga–Kiev–Khotin

	1867	1875	1877 (Spring)	1879
(a) Active Army				
Infantry	114,855	123,200	125,440	131,492
Cavalry	10,676	26,528	26,528	27,466
Artillery	10,655	14,996	18,863	22,604
Total	136,186	164,724	170,831	181,562
(b) Reserves and Local troops	22,800	24,500	24,500	32,980
(a) and (b) Total	158,986	189,224	195,331	214,542

[38] Albedyll to Bismarck, 21 July 1875; Schweinitz to Bülow, Petersburg, 9 March 1876, no. 63 very confid., GFO, IABi 53; 18 April 1876, no. 102, GFO, IABi 57 secretissima. Cf. also further correspondence in that file. Windelband, p. 46; Kessel, p. 647; Langenau to Andrássy, Petersburg, 23 February 1875, no. 16, WS, PA X 67.

[39] Berchem to Bismarck, Vienna, 14 November, no. 465 most confid., GFO, Russland 65 secreta; Moltke to GFO, 2 December, no. 422; Radowitz to Reuss, 15 December, no. 873; Moltke to Bismarck, 2 April 1880, secret, GFO, IABi 57 secretissima; 22 October 1879, no. 405, GFO, Russland 61 secreta; Russell to Salisbury, 28 November, no. 570 secret, FO 64/936; 6 December, private, SP, A/9; Elliot to Salisbury, Vienna, 24 December 1879 & 21 January 1880, nos. 827 confid., and 22 very confid., FO 7/966 and 988; Dufferin to Granville, Petersburg, 5 May 1880, private, PRO 30/29/185; Chanzy to Waddington, Petersburg, 23 December 1879, no. 64, FFM, Russie 259; Radowitz, ii, 108; Taffs, p. 336; Medlicott, *Congress*, p. 397; Schüssler, p. 58; Miliutin, iii, entry for 24 January 1880. Windelband, pp. 118f, writes, erroneously, that the general staff had encouraged Bismarck's fears of the troop dispositions.

Any imminent attack was less disturbing than the possibility of one in the more distant future. Whether Bismarck's policy in the subsequent winter really increased German security is difficult to say. The newspaper campaign was justified to a certain degree by a legitimate concern for preparing public opinion for the new army bill. Since the military budget was designed to last for seven years, this was an important occasion and Bismarck, understandably perhaps, wanted to get what he could out of parliament. But after the conclusion of the Austrian alliance there was less need to press for a reduction in Russian forces. Schweinitz, Haymerle, and Stolberg believed that this only prolonged the mutual mistrust which, in view of the Tsar's otherwise conciliatory attitude, should have been allayed.[40] To a certain extent Bismarck was, again, enthralled by his own bogies. And besides a genuine, but mostly unjustified, concern for the Russian military position, the only other explanation for his continued insistence is that he still hoped to impose his will on Russia. But Miliutin had taken Gorchakov's place as the chief object of his invective.

At the end of October and the beginning of November 1879 it was necessary for Bismarck to find a means of preparing public opinion for the army bill in such a way as to rouse the Russians without antagonizing them, or aggravating Austrian suspicions. So he deemed it advisable to contradict newspaper allegations that the dual alliance was aimed at opposing Russian adventures in the east. The press was inspired to say that the purpose of Austro-German intimacy was solely to preserve peace in the face of direct Russian threats. In support of this contention the necessary indiscretions were made. The German representatives abroad were instructed to take a similar line. In this way the road was left open to a *rapprochement* of the three empires based on a settlement concerning Constantinople; the Austrians were also warned that no support would be forthcoming in the eastern Balkans, or, for that matter, in the Middle East where, it seemed, Austria would have liked to bar the way to Russian expansion. In addition, Bismarck rejected Moltke's suggestion of Austro-German

40 Windelband, p. 119.

general staff talks, fearing that the Russians would get wind of them.[41]

It was probably in line with this policy that Bismarck, in a fit of mental vacuity, betrayed his English alliance feeler to Shuvalov, saying that he had vainly hoped for an offer to blockade the Russian Baltic ports. He must have wanted in this manner to show the Tsar graphically that he was not worried about the Balkans but about a threatened attack on Prussia. The effect in Petersburg was supposed to be sobering; in fact it was stupefying. A few moments of loose talk effectively blotted out the feelings of guilt and remaining illusions about German help which had lingered on amongst the Tsar's advisers.[42]

In mid-January 1880 Schweinitz reported that in accordance with government orders the Russian newspapers had been quiet for some time and had not answered the unfounded accusations of the foreign press of troop concentrations in Poland. He pointed out that amongst the Russian statesmen there were two groups—the larger believed that Germany was trying to goad Russia to war, and the smaller still thought Germany friendly. The latter group was losing ground, however, because of the accusations of the foreign press. The Tsar was upset, but he and his closest advisers affirmed their good-will. The government had recently seen fit to publish an official denial of exaggerated troop concentrations in Poland. Henceforth, the Russian press began to turn against Germany again. The journalists were immediately warned, but with only temporary effect; a second more sharply worded warning followed in three weeks; and a third at the end of February 1880.[43]

[41] H. Bismarck to Limburg-Stirum, Varzin, 30 October; 2 November; H. Bismarck to Stolberg, 4 November; H. Bismarck to GFO, 20 November, GFO, Russland 65 secreta; H. Bismarck to Rantzau, 25 October, FA, B–56; Windelband, pp. 98f, 112f, 119; Miliutin, iii, entry for 12 January 1880; Kessel, p. 671.

[42] Miliutin, iii, entry for 8 December 1879; Valuev, entry for 14 December 1879; Dufferin to Salisbury, Petersburg, 31 December 1879, no. 682 confid., FO 65/1048; Skazkin, p. 132.

[43] Schweinitz to Bismarck, Petersburg, 16 January 1880, no. 19, GFO, IABi 57 secretissima; 17 January, no. 20, GFO, Russland 61; 30 January, no. 34; 27 February, GFO, Russland 69 secreta; 20 February, no. 54; Bucher, 31 January, note, GFO, IABi 60; Schweinitz, ii, 88–93; Plunkett to Salisbury, Petersburg, 8 November 1879, no. 576 confid., FO 65/1048.

The second stage in the campaign against the troop dispositions set in when Saburov returned to Berlin at the end of
January 1880. Bismarck then extended the range of his tactical
offensive while specifying more exactly the objective he wished
to reach. Although, or perhaps because the Russian press
remained fairly restrained, the German papers continued to
attack the fortifications and troop dispositions, especially the
cavalry screen, on the frontier. The exasperation and stubbornness of the Tsar and his army increased steadily. Miliutin
knew how to put the apparent provocation to his own use and
found correspondingly less resistance in satisfying his spiralling
requests for money.[44] As the newspaper agitation progressed,
Bismarck's nervousness increased. Gorchakov was back at the
foreign ministry, Grand Duke Nicholas visited Paris, Gambetta
was reported to be more friendly with Italy and Russia, the
terrain along the Austrian border was allegedly being in-
spected, and the supposedly republican Miliutin was said to
be following a policy in Bulgaria at variance with that of the
Tsar.[45] The chancellor was quite worked up and irritable by
the time Saburov saw him at the beginning of February. He
was in fact in a rather ticklish position. It seems he had expected
Saburov to make more concrete proposals than were forthcoming. The Russian ambassador, now more and not less
sanguine than his government, sought to disguise its readiness
to come to terms in order to prise more concessions from Germany.[46] He still clung to the idea of a Russo-German agreement and Bismarck was forced to leave him in no doubt as to
his preference for a triple understanding; he showed less
irritation only after the third and final conversation when an

[44] Schweinitz to Bismarck, Petersburg, 6 February 1880, no. 38 most confid.;
27 February, GFO, Russland 69 secreta; Széchényi to Haymerle, Berlin, 25
February, no. 11, WS, PA III 120; Chanzy to Freycinet, Petersburg, 10 March,
no. 25 confid., FFM, Russie 260; Miliutin, iii, entry for 29 January; Valuev, entry
for 30 January. For Jomini's explanation of the placement of the cavalry units see
Dufferin to Salisbury, Petersburg, 25 February, no. 99, FO, 65/1078.

[45] Keudell to Bismarck, Rome, 3 February 1880, no. 6 confid., GFO, Italien 70;
—to—Paris, 6 February, copy; Bismarck to Schweinitz, 25 February, no. 93,
GFO, Russland 69 secreta; —to—Paris, 14 February, copy, GFO, Russland 67
secreta; Thielau to Bismarck, Berlin, 22 February, GFO, Bulgarien 1; Wedel to
—Vienna, 1 February, no. 6, GFO, Österreich 70.

[46] See above, p. 220.

agreement *à trois* was drafted which was to form the basis for further negotiations on the *Dreikaiserbund*.[47] It provided for benevolent neutrality should one of the powers go to war; changes to Turkey's European territory were to be approved by all three; Austria's new position in Bosnia was to be recognized; in return Russia demanded explicit acceptance of the principle of the closure of the Straits. Clearly, as far as the Straits were concerned, Russia had no hope that Haymerle's views would be as generous as Bismarck's. In fact, Austria did not concede more in the final treaty signed in June 1881.

These were interesting and concrete proposals, but Bismarck was in no rush because he was hoping for further concessions in the armaments question. This was perhaps the cause of a fit of last minute doubts on Bismarck's part as to the practicability of a triple agreement. A conversation with the Austrian ambassador to Russia, Kálnoky, on 9 February must have shown him once more the extreme difficulty of persuading Austria to reach such an agreement. In addition, the Russians had not yet shown sufficient contrition, he thought, to warrant the necessary effort.

Bismarck believed that if he had spoken more firmly all along the crisis could have been avoided, for he thought it was his show of force culminating in the Austro-German alliance which had persuaded the Russians to be more accommodating. He was determined to increase the pressure not merely to obtain more certain knowledge of Russian intentions, but also to secure a more or less complete acknowledgement of his leadership. Bismarck's diplomatic position was still strong because Russia remained isolated. As if to demonstrate this isolation publicly, he allowed Busch to insert in the press an accurate account of the background, character and intention of the dual alliance.[48] For his own purpose it was desirable to concentrate pressure on the armaments issue so as not to barricade the way to a future understanding with Russia. This

[47] Bismarck to Schweinitz, 6 & 10 February 1880, nos 53 secret and 67; William to [Bismarck], 10 February, GFO, Russland 69 secreta; GP, nos 515–8; Windelband, pp. 116–123; Schüssler, pp. 47ff; Skazkin, pp. 133–5.

[48] Busch, ii, 408–16; cf. Kálnoky to Haymerle, Petersburg, 24 March 1880, no. 18–D secret, WS, PA X 75; Széchényi to Haymerle, Berlin, 20 March 1880, no. 18–C, WS, PA III 120; *DDF*, iii, no. 70.

is the significance of Bismarck's advice to the Austrians to avoid giving Russia the impression of being hemmed in by a coalition, and not to reject feelers for a *rapprochement*. Aside from this, his advice also had the object of probing their willingness to come to terms. But this policy must have appeared somewhat equivocal because in order to talk them into a triple agreement he felt he should first convince them of his own belief in the necessity for the Austro-German alliance. This in turn made Vienna feel justified in expecting closer cooperation with Germany than Bismarck's advocacy of a renewed *Dreikaiserbund* would seem to allow.

In March the Austrians must have become even more puzzled when Bismarck, in what can only be described as a splenetic seizure, hinted about the possibility of joint action to check Miliutin's Bulgarian policy. Haymerle, cautious as ever, asked what Bismarck had in mind. The chancellor professed to be irritated by such patent misunderstanding of his move; what had been intended, he claimed, was to remind Austria of German goodwill: 'we are prepared to follow but not to lead'. He then underlined the danger by arguing that nearer home, in Serbia, Miliutin and the panslavs were also at work.[49] Such moves as this, which undermined Bismarck's own idea of dividing the Balkans into zones of influence, and the sophisticated argumentation for a triple agreement surely made Haymerle additionally cautious when Bismarck tried to hustle him back into the *Dreikaiserbund*.

In the months of February and March several long despatches were sent to Schweinitz stressing the necessity to discover for certain if Alexander's feelings towards Germany were unchanged and if he were in a position to resist the anti-German party. Schweinitz answered both questions in the affirmative, but suggested that Bismarck assist Alexander and the peace party by a policy of *bons procédés*. Bismarck was not inclined, as it were, to purchase sympathy, surely believing this would confirm the belief held by some Russians that Germany would ultimately bow to a policy of force. Not only

[49] Radowitz to Reuss, 8 March 1880, no. 162 confid.; Reuss to Bismarck, Vienna, 12 March, no. 129 confid.; Bismarck to Reuss, 23 March, nos. 203–4, GFO, Bulgarien 1; 30 March, no. 217, GFO, Serbien 1.

did he wish the Russians to renounce any attempts to seek alternatives to German friendship—a line which he himself had not hesitated to follow—but he also hoped to obtain a tangible pledge of goodwill. He desired most urgently the transfer of cavalry units away from the German border as an outward sign of a disavowal of Miliutin, who was largely responsible for the concentration of troops in Poland. For Bismarck policies and personalities were inextricably interwoven; he wanted a personal victory to document his political triumph. Gorchakov had not been dismissed, but his influence was practically nil. At the end of May he went on an extended leave obviously intended as a *de facto* retirement. He told Schweinitz he would spend the coming winter in Paris, and, pathetically, promised 'quant aux journalists, vous pouvez être bien sûr que je ne leur parlerai pas; jamais je ne pardonnerai à Decazes de m'avoir fait perdre ma virginité'. The Tsar spoke of him as an 'enfant terrible', adding that 'it is time for him to retire'. Miliutin replaced him as the Tsar's chief adviser and, therefore, also became Bismarck's bugbear. He was ideally suited for this role. He was thought to be anti-German and was certainly no friend of Bismarck. The chancellor regarded him as the personification of the revolutionary spirit. A moderate liberal, he was also on bad terms with Gorchakov and Shuvalov; he was the last remaining 'reform minister' in Alexander's cabinet and for this reason alone a far more suitable candidate for Bismarck's wrath. Miliutin was vulnerable. At the end of 1880 General Werder argued with customary promptitude that Miliutin's successor would probably be worse yet from the German vantage point.[50] There is no indication that Bismarck had thought of this possibility any earlier.

Throughout the winter Bismarck tried to get the Tsar to disavow Miliutin and his work. The tactics used were the familiar ones. In informal conversation Bismarck associated him with the principle of democracy and revolution, labelled him anti-German and pro-French, and accused him of unreliability and aggressiveness. London and Vienna were kept informed of these apprehensions, the newspapers mobilized,

---

[50] Werder to William, Petersburg, 8 December, no. 34, GFO, Russland 61.

and complaints made to the Tsar about the soundings of Obruchev on the possibility of a link with France,[51] but mainly about the disposition of the Russian troops.

Schweinitz agreed with Bismarck that the cavalry screen was a serious threat to Germany. He felt, however, that the position of the German flank in East Prussia would force the Russians to withdraw behind the Vistula in case of war— therefore the *avant-garde* position was of questionable value. But, partly owing to the inept leadership of the German foreign office itself, the German press continued to refer to increases in the troop dispositions. Tsar Alexander indignantly denied this. Bismarck professed to understand this as a denial of the existence of the disposition, which, of course, it was not. Thus, when the German government began to emphasize especially the placement of cavalry units, the Tsar was in no mood to give way. Alexander surely felt as did Miliutin that even the slightest concession would be humiliating. It was difficult for him to see why the cavalry disposition, in existence since 1875, should all of a sudden be so particularly threatening.[52]

Schweinitz was reluctant to press the Tsar; he had to be repeatedly reminded by Bismarck who could hardly conceal his great agitation. He wished Schweinitz to take a stronger line in Petersburg than he himself had taken with Saburov. But he did, apparently, make one final effort to present his views when Orlov, the Russian ambassador in Paris, passed through Berlin on his way home: he hoped that this might be enough to tip the scales in his favour again as in the previous August.[53]

---

[51] Obruchev, Miliutin's right-hand man, was apparently sent on his authority without the knowledge of the Tsar.

[52] Bismarck to Schweinitz, 6, 10, 18, 25 February 1880, nos. 53 secret, 67, 85, 93; 4 & 16 March 1880, nos. 115 and 142; Schweinitz to Bismarck, Petersburg, 30 January 1880, no. 34; 11 & 12 March 1880, nos. 44 secret and 89, GFO, Russland 69 secreta; 20 February, no. 56 confid., GFO, Russland 67; 29 February, no. 71 very confid.; 24 May 1880, no. 156 confid., GFO, Russland 61; Bismarck to Crown Prince, Friedrichsruh, 17 December 1880, copy, GFO, Russland 61 secreta; Széchényi to Haymerle, Berlin, 28 February 1880, no. 13 confid., WS, PA III 120; Langenau to Foreign Ministry, Petersburg, 12 & 16 January 1880, tel. nos. 7 & 12, WS, PA X 75; Russell to Salisbury, Berlin, 30 March 1880, private, SP, A/9; Dufferin to Salisbury, Petersburg, 18 December 1879, SP, A/14; Miliutin, iii, entries for 28 February & 1 March 1880; Vogüé, entry for 27 February.

[53] See above, p. 191.

Eventually, however, the chancellor saw the futility of it all and under the impression of an anti-Austrian speech by Gladstone on 15 March and surely influenced by an ardent plea from Schweinitz he agreed to let the matter drop.[54] The electoral victory of the English Liberals in April convinced him of the wisdom of abandoning the subject. The swing to the left in Paris and then London made Bismarck reconsider the virtues of conservative solidarity.

In retrospect, Bismarck's campaign against the troop disposition on the German frontier must be considered a failure. The only clearly favourable result for Germany was the passage of the army bill. It is also possible that his pressure on Vienna helped prevent a reduction in the Austrian forces: at any rate, Bismarck successfully stimulated Austria's awareness of a Russian military danger. The abiding concern in Petersburg was for the safety of Constantinople and the containing of Austrian influence in the Balkans. The pro-German turn on the part of the Russians represented a recognition of the facts of life: lofty treatment of Germany did not mix well with fear of English attack and Austrian intrigues. It also was partly due to the conviction that this was the only way to avoid Bismarck's hostility. So the German line had a momentary success, but it was more than outweighed by the negative results of Bismarck's policy. Russo-German relations were strained and the hand of those most suspicious of Germany was strengthened. Miliutin, for instance, was firmly convinced that war was the object of Bismarck's feverish activity.[55] The price paid for an Austro-German united front against Russia in the armaments question was increased, or at least sustained, Austrian suspicion of Germany and her eastern neighbour.

Bismarck had been reluctant to counter the threat emanating

[54] Schweinitz to Bismarck, Petersburg, 23 February 1880, no. 100 secret, GFO, IABi 57 secretissima; Kálnoky to Haymerle, Petersburg, 7 April 1880, private, WS, PA X 74; Széchényi to Haymerle, Berlin, 10 April 1880, no. 22–B confid., WS, PA III 120; Simpson, pp. 103f; but cf. *GP*, no. 515.

[55] Werder to William, Petersburg, 15 April 1880, no. 14, GFO, Russland 67; Valuev, entries for 30 January & 2 June 1880. Compare R. Wittram, 'Bismarcks Russlandpolitik', p. 182 with Medlicott, *Bismarck, Gladstone*, p. 41 and 'Three Emperors' Alliance'. See also Hinsley's review of Medlicott's book, *Cambridge Historical Review*, xiii (1957), 94–6.

from the positioning of the Russian cavalry by shifting military forces to the frontier; he had pointed out the senselessness of adding a weight to one side of the scales only to see another piled on the opposite side. Having failed to press concessions from the Tsar, in April he reversed his policy and persuaded Moltke to re-deploy his troops. It was not German policy to scatter one's forces in an attempt to guarantee the inviolability of the whole frontier, but only the militarily important points. These were strengthened. But a new mobilization plan, reckoning with Austrian troops, committed fewer forces to the east and more to the western front.[56]

In May 1880 Bismarck was willing to comply with a request from the Sultan for the despatch of several high-ranking officers to help re-organize the Turkish army and so strengthen the flank against Russia. But the execution of the plan was postponed until the Porte had complied with the powers' demands concerning Greece and Montenegro, and later because of the conclusion of the Three Emperors' League in June 1881. The officers were finally sent in reaction to the Skobelev affair at the beginning of 1882.[57]

After the formation of the Liberal cabinet in England Gladstone became Bismarck's nightmare; for several months the Russians appeared less reprehensible. Fearing, apparently, that Gladstone could come to terms with Miliutin and the Russian revolutionaries, Bismarck began preaching conservative solidarity. At just this moment Odo Russell, however, wrote home about the 'perfect harmony' which then existed between England and Germany; he thought that Bismarck would 'subordinate' his views to those of England in the remaining questions bound up with the execution of the Treaty.[58] Nothing could have been further from the truth, because Bismarck argued that the results of the English elections indicated the resurgence

[56] Moltke to Bismarck, 23 April 1880, no. 489; 6 & 19 May, nos. 496 and 501 secret; Bismarck to Moltke, 27 April 1880, secret; 16 & 22 May, secret; Bismarck to Kameke, 4 May, secret, GFO, IABi 57 secretissima; Kessel, pp. 672ff.

[57] Correspondence in GFO, Türkei 139; Holborn, *Deutschland und die Türkei*, pp. 10–28; Hohenlohe, ii, 301f.

[58] Russell to Granville, Berlin, 29 April 1880, no. 187 confid., FO 64/959; Knaplund, *Letters*, p. 139.

of Palmerston's anti-monarchical policy except that Palmerston had had to use English and other non-Russian weapons to combat Nicholas I, whereas a revolutionary policy inspired by Gladstone could find allies against the Tsar's throne inside Russia and the countries already united under the panslav banner. To reinforce this argument Bismarck also claimed that a front of panslavs and Latin republicans (such as Gambetta and Crispi) was forming—a further reason for conservative solidarity. Nevertheless his own policy in the simultaneous Hartmann affair, in which France was given moral support, was not guided by such considerations. Bismarck also remained particularly obliging towards France on Greece and Morocco.[59]

Francis Joseph was informed that England's future would be less secure if that essentially conservative country came under the legislative influence of Gladstone and his friends, and if the leadership were assumed—as in all liberal parties—by the most extreme elements (i.e. Dilke and Chamberlain). If legislation aiming at breaking the power of landed property were enacted, events could take a more drastic turn in England than they had in France during the first revolution because of the admixture of socialists whose spiritual ancestors had been defeated in the constituent assembly. The line taken with the pro-English Haymerle had a different slant. He was told that the greatest danger resulting from the ministerial changeover in Britain was that the passionate and undiscriminating Russian chauvinists would misunderstand English policy and be drawn to commit some folly. This was all the more reason to encourage the new conciliatory line of Alexander II and the 'reasonable men' in Russia. Haymerle shared Bismarck's concern, but he had little faith in such 'reasonable men' as Shuvalov whose language had lately been so unguarded. He surely agreed with his ambassador in Russia, Kálnoky, who was convinced that the Russians had merely furled and not burnt the panslav flag.[60]

[59] See above, pp. 230f.
[60] Bismarck to Schweinitz, 7 April, no. 185 secret; Hohenlohe to William, 27 June, GFO, Frankreich 87; Hohenlohe to Reuss, 7 May, no. 326; Bismarck to Reuss, 6 April, no. 233, GFO, Russland 61; 26 March, no. 210, GFO, Italien 70; 23 April, no. 272; Reuss to Bismarck, Vienna, 17 April, no. 180 confid., GFO, England 69; 29 April, no. 203, GFO, Österreich 70; Széchényi to Haymerle,

Obviously, much, although not all, of this was *ad hominem* argumentation: it suited Bismarck's immediate plans to encourage suspicion of England. But the chancellor was also genuinely, although unjustifiably, aroused: if he had regarded Gorchakov as radical, Gladstone was an extremist, and Dilke, if possible, worse yet. Gladstone's policy was 'unacceptable, anti-monarchic, revolutionary, belligerent'. He claimed that since the American war of independence the conduct of English foreign policy had never been in such incompetent hands; the dangers inherent in the unwise, arbitrary and clumsy policy followed by Gladstone and his circle of dilettanti were multiplied by their own doctrinaire feeling of infallibility. Consequently, Bismarck emphasized the principle of conservative solidarity all the more decisively. This was an attitude surely encouraged by his break with the Liberals on the domestic scene, but, in turn, it helped, perhaps intentionally, to make that rupture irrevocable.[61]

In Petersburg close cooperation with Britain was in fact considered for some weeks, and although the decision was taken to follow a more conciliatory line with London, there was no intention of abandoning the attempt to resurrect the Three Emperors' League. When at the end of April the Russian cabinet suggested mutual consultation and close cooperation between the three empires in Constantinople, Bismarck took upon himself the arduous task of persuading the Austrians. Haymerle readily enough accepted the general principle of cooperation (as long as the other powers were not excluded), but, believing that if the Russians were given an inch they would take a mile, he opposed the suggestions for implementation. In this he was supported by Francis Joseph, Kálnoky and the still influential Andrássy. He maintained stubborn resistance

Berlin, 2 May, no. 29 confid., WS, PA III 120; 28 May, private, WS, PA III 121; Kálnoky to Haymerle, Petersburg, 16 April, no. 21–B secret; 19 May, no. 31–B secret, WS, PA X 75; Russell to Granville, Berlin, 17 May, no. 216 most confid.; 2 June, no. 239 most confid., FO 64/960. Reuss still continued to apply the arguments based on *raison d'état*, as in January and February. Haymerle, Vienna, 30 May 1880, memorandum, WS, PA rot 454 Liasse II. Windelband, pp. 138f; Medlicott, *Bismarck, Gladstone*, pp. 53f.

[61] Windelband, pp. 137f, 181f; Medlicott, *Bismarck, Gladstone*, pp. 11, 160f, 178f.

until the autumn, when he began to give way after some persuading and much arm twisting.[62]

May 1880 marked the end of a strange phase of German foreign policy. With the departure of Gorchakov, the abandonment of the attack on Miliutin and the initiation of an assault on Gladstone and his 'Concert of Europe' the 'two chancellors' war' was over. What were the results of this, the essential feature of Bismarck's foreign policy since the Congress of Berlin?

The 'war' was the final phase in the long rivalry between Bismarck and Gorchakov. In the 1860s their personal friendship and the political necessity for cooperation kept the rivalry from becoming severe. From the beginning of the 1870s the necessity for political cooperation was less; the competition between the two statesmen sharpened and their personal friendship dwindled. After the 'war-in-sight' crisis and the revival of the Eastern Question in 1875 the personal and political duel broke into the open. The confrontation of the two chancellors at the Congress marked the beginning of the 'war' in which personal rivalry went far beyond the bounds set by *raison d'état*.

The struggle ended with partial success for both; neither statesman was completely discredited. Russia became more conciliatory and sought a German alliance. This was a victory for Bismarck. But he lost the few friends he had in Russia. The Tsar and his advisers had grown very suspicious; Alexander would no longer spontaneously follow a pro-German policy. This was a victory for Gorchakov. It was characteristic that by the end of 1879 even Shuvalov had turned against Bismarck and inclined towards Gorchakov. He talked to the French of his desire for better relations, but he wanted to avoid an ostensible *rapprochement*. He summed this up quaintly: 'ne nous

[62] Hohenlohe, 24 & 29 April, memoranda; Hohenlohe to Reuss, 27 April, no. 286; 2, 7, 28 May, nos. 306, 326, 397 confid.; Bismarck to Reuss, 18 May, no. 361; Reuss to Bismarck, Vienna, 30 April, no. 210; 4, 21 & 30 May, nos. 216 most confid., 253 and 272, Budapest, 10 May, nos. 231–2, GFO, Russland 69 secreta; Reuss to Bismarck, Vienna, 26 May, no. 265, GFO, IABq 133 i; Haymerle to Széchényi, Vienna, 6 May, secret, WS, PA III 121; Medlicott, *Bismarck, Gladstone*, pp. 53–60; Windelband, pp. 144–9.

faisons pas trop de risettes, mais ne nous tournons pas le dos'. To the British he hinted broadly at the advantages of an alliance. To the Austrians he disclaimed belief in the possibility of reconciliation in the Balkans. There Russia, he argued, had inaugurated a revolutionary policy which offered such great advantages that it could not be changed. Later he complained of Bismarck's failure to comprehend Russia: he wanted to crush everything, but the malady could not be cured merely with soldiers and policemen.[63]

Bismarck and Gorchakov had carried their personal struggle too far. In the end it seriously affected the general complexion of Russo-German relations. Bismarck had been too ready to use massive force in essentially secondary matters: he adopted a more or less permanent measure, the dual alliance, for tactical purposes. As a result, the Russians became more conciliatory, but they did not really accept his leadership; they grew more suspicious of him and Germany. And Bismarck, in turn, lost faith in Russia, not only as an ally but also as a pillar of conservative Europe. It has already been pointed out that Bismarck regarded diplomacy as an endless series of manœuvres.[64] Here one may see with great clarity the limitations of a policy which failed to account for the detrimental long-term effects of purely short-term devices. After the collapse of Shuvalov's candidature Bismarck made no attempt to work for an improvement in the fabric of Russian society; he turned instead to a policy of expedients aimed at preserving tolerably good relations until the ultimate and inevitable disaster in Russia.

Gorchakov's undeniable partial responsibility for the deterioration in Russo-German relations has long been recognized.

---

[63] Széchényi to Haymerle, Berlin, 20 December, no. 50 A–B secret, WS, PA III 119; Trauttenberg to Haymerle, Petersburg, 30 January 1880, no. 7–E confid.; Kálnoky to Haymerle, Petersburg, 17 April 1880, no. 21–C, WS, PA X 75; Schweinitz to Bismarck, Petersburg, 25 March 1880, no. 101 most confid., GFO, Russland 61; Russell to Salisbury, 19 December 1879, no. 613 very confid., FO 64/936; 13 December, private, SP, A/9; Dufferin to Salisbury, Petersburg, 31 December 1879, no. 682 confid., FO 65/1048; St. Vallier to Waddington, 12 December 1879, FFM, Allemagne M & D 166 bis; Valuev, entry for 14 December 1879; Miliutin, iii, entry for 8 December; see also *GP*, no. 515 and Schweinitz, ii, 218f; Skazkin, pp. 129 and 132; Wittram, 'russisch-nationale Tendenzen', p. 327.
[64] Medlicott, 'Three Emperors' Alliance', pp. 82f.

Most historians have accepted in one form or another Bismarck's devastating assessment: 'His vanity, his jealousy of me were greater than his patriotism.'[65] Certainly, there is more than a grain of truth in this criticism, but in the period after the Congress of Berlin Gorchakov was definitely on the defensive. His failing was that his views reflected only too well those of the Tsar, not that he incited his monarch against Bismarck.[66]

After the end of the 'two chancellors' war' really intimate relations between Russia and Germany were virtually impossible—not only because of the bitterness and distrust which the 'war' had left behind. The inherent rivalry between any two neighbouring great powers would have been sufficient to make continuous, close cooperation difficult. But the feud between Gorchakov and Bismarck coincided with and accelerated a period of fundamental change in Russia and, to a lesser extent, Germany. Russia was in a state of great social ferment: the idealistic panslavism of the 1870s was followed by a period of realistic conservative Russian nationalism. In Germany, too, the alliance with Austria and the tariff of 1879 initiated a period of greater national self-confidence. Ironically, perhaps, the gap between the two empires widened when both turned more conservative. Economic and intellectual rivalry replaced cooperation. In the 1880s Russo-German relations were being shaped by forces many of which were beyond the control of Bismarck, Gorchakov, or anyone else. But tolerably good relations were still possible, though more difficult to cultivate than in the past. There was no inevitability in a drastic deterioration in relations between the two empires however likely this may have been.

---

[65] *Gedanken und Erinnerungen*, ii, chapter 12.

[66] Gorchakov later claimed that on returning from the Congress he wrote to the Tsar that the Berlin Treaty was the blackest page of his official career; the Tsar noted in the margin: in mine too. M. Semevskii, p. 179.

Conclusion

This study has attempted to discuss the puzzling reorientation of German foreign policy after the Congress of Berlin when a policy of free hands was abandoned in favour of one of increasing formal commitment. What seems to emerge is that Bismarck's foreign policy from the end of the Congress until the beginning of 1880 can perhaps best be interpreted in terms of a struggle for power with Russia. Both Bismarck and Gorchakov wished to play the leading role in Europe. Therefore, Bismarck did what he could to obtain his rival's dismissal by refusing to support what he regarded as Gorchakov's own policy. At the same time he gave assistance to what he thought was the policy of the moderates, personified by Peter Shuvalov. In both respects Bismarck's policy was largely unsuccessful. He did, of course, force Russia to come to terms with him in a renewed *Dreikaiserbund*, but he neither obtained Gorchakov's dismissal, nor succeeded in furthering the career of Shuvalov, or strengthening the position of the moderates. Contrary to his intentions, his activity did much to poison Russo-German relations. The intensity of his personal struggle with Gorchakov was not without a detrimental influence on the more positive side of his policy towards Russia.

Strained relations with Petersburg made a *rapprochement* with Austria advisable both as an alternative to Russian friendship and as a means of extending his basis of power vis-à-vis Russia. As tension mounted, Bismarck developed cooperation with Austria in order to increase the pressure on Russia. This policy might have been successful, if it had not been complicated by the effects of his attempt to rescue German capital invested in the Rumanian railway. This necessitated a certain amount of cooperation with the western powers and Austria which created the impression that Germany had completely abandoned the Tsar. This impression appeared to be verified by the effects of various minor issues—the German tariff bill, the sanitary measures taken against the plague, and the publication of the revocation of part of article v of the Treaty of Prague—which originally had little or no connection with the Russo-German tension. But Bismarck's attitude towards these issues showed that he no longer felt able to display the same consideration for Russia as in the past. The Russians accordingly became convinced that Germany was a false friend and they therefore did not shy from taking measures which displayed hostility. The army was expanded, and the troop disposition on the German frontier, which had existed before the war, was resumed. There were misleading indications that the panslavs had returned to favour. Bismarck strengthened his *entente* with Austria, and in June 1879 he cooperated demonstratively with her, even in opposition to his eastern neighbour.

Bismarck's aim was to force Russia to adopt a more peaceful policy and come to an agreement with Germany on his own terms. If Russia refused, he was prepared to keep strengthening the *entente* with Austria and, if necessary, to sign an alliance, although he did not like the dependency that close cooperation entailed and was not enthusiastic about an alliance. Russia was completely isolated and the exasperated Tsar made reproaches and hardly veiled threats. This supplied Bismarck with the compelling arguments needed for the Austrian alliance, but until he was sure of Vienna he grew slightly more conciliatory towards Russia. Further evidence of hostility and the assurance that Austria wished to enter an alliance caused Bismarck to become firmer with Russia in September, and it was only after his interview with Saburov at the end of the month which revealed a gradually materializing chance of an understanding that his attitude once more took a conciliatory turn. Relations with England then began to cool. Nevertheless, Russo-German relations did not take a decisive turn for the better until February 1880. Both countries remained extremely suspicious and were prepared rather for a *modus vivendi* than real friendship.

The strained relations were due partly to the changing character of large impersonal forces—the economy and nation-

alism—and the inherent logic of international relations which
defy the control of any statesman. But they were also the
product of personal failings—the poor judgment of the Russians
and Bismarck's own ineptness. He was able to force Russia to
come to terms only after he had started negotiating an alliance
with Austria, which although it ostensibly increased his basis
of power, hindered, but by no means prevented, the restoration
of good relations with Russia. Patience and a willingness to
accept a certain number of affronts were necessary for this, but
these were qualities Bismarck lacked. One of his associates
reports that he once said the Russians should not be treated like
'thinking politicians', but rather like 'bad weather' which
cannot be changed.[1] Clearly, Bismarck realized what policy
was advisable, but did he consistently attempt to carry it out?
Without a doubt the much celebrated dual alliance helped to
consolidate central Europe, but Bismarck's aim in concluding
it was clearly to seize immediate advantages. He appreciated
the support of the nationalists and shared some of their prejudices, but showed little sympathy for their deceptive and
high-flown ideals.

If the central role of Bismarck's Russian policy is accepted,
relations with England appear unproblematical. All the talk
about England as an unreliable partner was not so important
as the consideration that she could neither help nor harm much.
The purpose of the alliance feeler in late 1879 was to see if an
alternative to the Russian *entente* existed in case the Tsar did
not come round. Since Russia was at best an unsteady ally,
Bismarck had to stay on fairly good terms with England, but
he did not want England to be particularly close to any other
power, not even France. Ideally, Bismarck wanted Britain and
France quarrelling, but not fighting, on the fringes of Europe.
He dreamt of a situation in which all the powers *including*
France needed Germany and were kept from opposing coalitions by their relations with one another. In mid-1877 he had
still excluded France from the circle of powers which should
be made dependent on German aid,[2] but since the advent of
Waddington and the accompanying consolidation of the

---

[1] Brauer, p. 127.
[2] *GP*, no. 294.

moderate republic, he thought that French enmity could be blunted, although not eradicated, by drawing her attention to the Mediterranean where other rivals were waiting. The ranks could then easily be closed in case Gambetta and his radical and supposedly aggressive circle came to power.

Historians have often approvingly underscored Bismarck's assertion that the German empire was satiated. Without qualification this statement cannot stand. Bismarck only opposed territorial expansion in Europe; in another dimension, the struggle for ascendency in diplomacy, his line was patently expansionist. Unless we remember the desire to become the indispensable centre of things, his foreign policy must remain inexplicable. The astonishing thing is not that his foreign policy was undeniably expansive, but that it did not square with his recurrent and much exaggerated fears of German vulnerability. In calmer moments, however, he also said that Germany, faced by a Kaunitz coalition (France, Austria and Russia), would be in a precarious but not desperate situation. No other continental statesman at that time could have contemplated an opposing coalition with equal equanimity. We must assume that Bismarck himself was not quite sure whether Germany was the weakest or the strongest European power. The failure to see one's own strength and ambition in constant perspective is not uncommon, but one would have expected more realism from Bismarck.

His academic statements of policy which testify to a genuine understanding of, and a consideration for, the real needs of other states were not always present in his mind when engaged in day-to-day diplomacy. Despite his great mastery of foreign policy and diplomacy he was excessively irritable and acted sometimes contrary to his own better judgment. He was, as Medlicott has suggested, occasionally alarmed by nightmares of his own creation.[3] His long absences from Berlin kept him out of touch with the details for extended periods. This and the difficulties of communication lent a sporadic note to the application of his foreign policy.

Any detailed study of Bismarck's foreign policy must raise the question of an overall evaluation of his practice of diplo-

[3] *Bismarck, Gladstone*, p. 12.

macy. There is, of course, some risk in generalizations based on even the most painstaking analysis of a limited body of material; but the justification of tentative conclusions remains. Keeping this reservation in mind, what clearly emerges from the present study is that the rather common observation, based partly on Holstein's criticism, that Bismarck's later diplomacy progressively deteriorated needs some modification. The limitations to his policy of 'double reinsurance'[4] and the perpetuation of tension between the powers, as well as his tactics of constant shifting, were fairly clear by the end of 1879 and not really suitable for the eighties when he became increasingly concerned with security and his approach to foreign affairs became more institutional. Although Bismarck denied having abandoned a policy of free hands, continuation with the same tactics ran a greater risk of losing his allies and potential allies as well. Yet he was confident enough of his own tactical ability to overcome any difficulties that might arise. His essentially tactical approach to diplomacy was not necessarily fundamentally wrong, but the excessive concentration on the present complicated the safeguarding of essential long-term goals. For states bent on expansion a long-term policy aimed at creating confidence is futile, but for saturated states interested in the preservation of a favourable *status quo*—such as Germany— confidence and mutual trust are a necessity. From the German point of view Bismarck's was a logical, but risky and outmoded approach to diplomacy; and it required a steady hand to direct it. Yet as his tortuous tactics were marred by a certain sporadic application, so was his policy of 'double reinsurance' as well as the preservation of international tension hampered by his overly emotional nature. His rejection of the other powers' alliance feelers during the eastern crisis fits into the picture of the peace-loving chancellor who kept his head when others were losing theirs; but when one considers that in the same period he also took soundings for alliances with Russia, Austria, Italy, and England, which he quickly disavowed, the image of Bismarck looks very different.

One cannot fully understand Bismarck's foreign policy without taking into account the role played by personal rivalry and

---

[4] Holborn, *Bismarcks europäische Politik*, p. 31.

antipathy. This has long been recognized in his domestic policy. Wittram's remark that resentment and hatred may have occasionally influenced his reactions, but not his overall policy is typical, but quite erroneous.[5] He attempted to make up for these short-comings by astonishingly frank declarations of his ideas, by promising more help than he was prepared to give, and by 'aiding' other states to somewhat problematical successes. The post-Congress situation showed clearly enough that such a policy would bear but meagre fruit in periods of crisis. It would have been better if the chancellor had made less abundant use of such methods, especially when he must have realized that they were ineffectual. But he did not, and friends and rivals alike remained suspicious. They constantly looked for ulterior motives, even when there were none.

Langer's now widely accepted view of Bismarck after 1871 as chancellor of the peace battling manfully against cupidity and ignorance does need some modification. For obvious reasons Bismarck did not want war, but his policy and its implementation were not truly pacific; the preservation of peace was more than necessarily dependent on the good sense and moderation of others.[6]

At the other extreme, Bismarck has often been criticized for his use of power politics, or for the immorality implicit in his conflicting promises. Is not such criticism unhistorical for an age in which Gladstone was capable of the bombardment of Alexandria and the occupation of Egypt? Perhaps it might be better to ask whether his policy and methods of diplomacy were well calculated to increase the security and power of his country, that is, the goals he legitimately set out to attain.

In domestic and foreign politics Bismarck attempted to obtain the submission of his rivals by a show of force and a promise of future reward. He usually got his way; but while he was successful in obtaining allies, he won no real friends. He was convinced that friendship in international politics was a will-o'-the-wisp: clashes between the great powers were unavoidable and in these statesmen would invariably consult their own interests. His basically pessimistic approach to diplo-

[5] *Deutsch-Russische Beziehungen*, p. 29.
[6] See the introduction and conclusion of Medlicott's *Bismarck, Gladstone.*

macy which made any combination conceivable did not allow him to value any particular ally very highly; he needed allies, but he was not willing to do much for them. It was simply not Bismarck's way to return 'good for evil', as Odo Russell once wrote.[7] Naturally, he wanted to dominate any alliance, and although he fully understood the difference between bullying and leadership, his temperament prevented him from acting accordingly: allies were expected to dance to his tune. Warnings, threats, hints of a possible change of course, and flirting with opponents were used all too unsparingly. Thus, the belief in the chancellor's unreliability remained.

It has frequently been said that on the domestic scene Bismarck often chose to fight for things that could have been reached more easily by negotiating and making small concessions, and perhaps his country would have been the better for it. Does not the same apply to his foreign policy? This does not mean that power politics were not to a certain extent justified, or even necessary; but, as the success of power politics rests on the premise that opponents have no sensible alternative to submission, it had to be used with discrimination. His Rumanian policy shows that attempts to use political force against a small country could, indirectly, lead to considerable embarrassment; whilst the indiscriminate use of pressure against a great power was obviously an unreliable weapon. Bismarck's campaign against Gorchakov and the Russian troop dispositions shows well enough that he was too willing to use power politics in essentially secondary matters. The result was unnecessary mutual suspicion—not an insuperable difficulty, but certainly an unfortunate circumstance. The struggle for leadership which provided the ultimate justification for the squabbles was, of course, a matter of the utmost political significance, but the German position—as has been pointed out above—emerged from them weakened rather than strengthened.

Foreign policy was surely Bismarck's primary concern and to that extent one can speak of the primacy of foreign policy, but not in the wider and more customary sense that domestic policy was affected by, but without influence on, foreign policy. Politics at home influenced diplomacy as well as foreign policy

[7] See above, p. 131.

in the widest context, but not so much that one can aptly speak of the primacy of domestic politics, as Kehr does. The origin and influence of the 1879 tariff illustrate this point.

The protracted fight with Rumania is the first important example of official support for German capital abroad. Bismarck's growing interest in the protection of German material interests is clearly illustrated; so are, in addition, many of the problems of imperialism. Even at this early stage it was impossible to back the interests of capital without having to pay a political price. It was quite obvious by 1880 that the path to imperialism would be a thorny one to be travelled with the greatest circumspection.

BIBLIOGRAPHY

(list of materials cited in the text)

I. UNPUBLISHED SOURCE MATERIAL

GFO: political files of the German foreign office located in Bonn (Politisches Archiv des Auswärtigen Amtes). See F. G. Stambrook, *A Catalogue of Files and Microfilms of the German Foreign Ministry Archives, 1867–1920* (Oxford, 1959).

DZA: files on economic affairs, etc., of the German foreign office, Reichskanzlei, Reichskanzleramt, and ministry of the interior located in Potsdam (Deutsches Zentralarchiv).

BA: files of the imperial finance office located in Koblenz (Bundesarchiv).

WS: files of the Austro-Hungarian foreign ministry located in Vienna (Wiener Staatsarchiv).

FO: foreign office files located in London (Public Record Office).

FFM: French foreign ministry files (Ministère des Affaires Etrangères, Paris).

The collections of private papers retained in the archives listed above were also examined.

FA: Bismarck's private papers located at Friedrichsruh.

SP: Salisbury papers located in Oxford (Christ Church Library).

II. PRINTED SOURCE MATERIAL (DOCUMENTS)

Otto von Bismarck-Schönhausen, *Die Gesammelten Werke Bismarcks*, 15 vols. (Berlin, 1924–35):
  vol. VI–c *Politische Schriften*, eds. H. von Petersdorff, F. Thimme, W. Frauendienst.
  vol. VIII *Gespräche*, ed. W. Andreas.
  vol. XI–XII *Reden*, ed. W. Schüssler.
  vol. XIV, ii *Briefe*, eds. W. Windelband, W. Frauendienst.
  vol. XV *Erinnerung und Gedanke*, eds. G. Ritter, R. Stadelmann.

Documents Diplomatiques français (1871–1914). First series (1871–1900), vols. ii–iii (Paris, 1930–1), Ministère des Affaires Etrangères, Commission de Publication des Documents relatifs aux Origines de la Guerre de 1914.

Friis, A. & Bagge, P. (eds.), *L'Europe, le Danemark et le Slesvig du Nord. Actes et lettres provenant d'archives étrangères pour servir à l'histoire de la politique extérieure du Danemark après la paix de Vienne 1864–1879*, vols. iii–iv (Copenhagen, 1948, 1959).

Goldschmidt, H., 'Mitarbeiter Bismarcks im aussenpolitischen Kampf', *Preussische Jahrbücher* (1934) ccxxxv, 29–48; ccxxxvi, 27–51, 236–61.

Die grosse Politik der europäischen Kabinette 1871–1914. Sammlung der diplomatischen Akten des Auswärtigen Amtes, vols. ii–iv (Berlin, 1922), eds. J. Lepsius, A. Mendelssohn-Bartholdy, P. Thimme.

Iorga, N., *Correspondance diplomatique roumaine sous le roi Charles Ier (1866–1880)* (Paris, 1923).

Kogalniceanu, V. M., (ed.), *Actes & Documents extraits de la Correspondance diplomatique de Michel Kogalniceanu relatifs à la Guerre de l'Indépendance roumaine (1877–1878)*, 2 vols. (Bucharest, 1893).

Moltke, H., *Die deutschen Aufmarschpläne 1871–1890* (Berlin, 1929), ed. F. von Schmerfeld.

Novotny, A., 'Graf Peter Andrejewitsch Schuwalow. Staatsmann und Kritiker Russlands in den letzten Jahren der Regierung Zar Alexanders II.', *Mitteilungen des Instituts für österreichische Geschichtsforschung*, lviii (1950), 517–33.

Platzhoff, W., K. Rheindorff, J. Tiedje (eds.), *Bismarck und die nordschleswigsche Frage 1864–1879. Die diplomatischen Akten des Auswärtigen Amtes zur Geschichte des Artikels V des Prager Friedens* (Berlin, 1925).

Poschinger, H. von, *Fürst Bismarck als Volkswirt*, vol. i (Berlin, 1889).

—, *Aktenstücke zur Wirtschaftspolitik des Fürsten Bismarck*, vol. i (Berlin, 1890).

Pribram, A. F., *Die politischen Geheimverträge Österreich-Ungarns 1879–1914*, vol. i (Vienna & Leipzig, 1920).

Reichsarchiv, *Der Weltkrieg 1914–1918. Kriegsrüstung und Kriegswirtschaft. Anlagen zum ersten Band* (Berlin, 1930).

Das Staatsarchiv. Sammlung der officiellen Actenstücke zur Geschichte der Gegenwart (Leipzig, 1875, 1878–82, 1885); xxvii, xxxiv–vi eds. H. von Kremer-Auenrode, P. Hirsch; xxxvii, xl ed. H. von Delbrück; xliv ed. E. von Delbrück.

Windelband, W., 'Bismarck über das deutsch-russische Verhältnis 1880' *Deutsche Rundschau*, cclviii (1939), 169–74.

III. LETTERS, DIARIES, MEMOIRS, BIOGRAPHIES, etc.

Aus dem Leben König Karls von Rumänien, 4 vols. (Stuttgart, 1896).

Brauer, A. von, *Im Dienste Bismarcks. Persönliche Erinnerungen* (Berlin, 1936), ed. H. Rogge.

Buckle, G. E., *The Life of Benjamin Disraeli, Earl of Beaconsfield*, vol. vi (London, 1920).

Bülow, B. von, *Denkwürdigkeiten*, vol. iv (Berlin, 1931).

Busch, M., *Bismarck, some secret pages of his history. Being a diary kept by Dr M. Busch*, vol. ii (London, 1898).

Cecil, G., *Life of Robert, Marquis of Salisbury*, vol. ii (London, 1921).

Daudet, E., *La Mission du Comte de Sainte-Vallier (December 1877–December 1881)* (Paris, 1918).

Eyck, E., *Bismarck. Leben und Werk*, vol. iii (Zurich, 1944).

Hatzfeldt, P., *The Hatzfeldt Letters. Letters of Count Paul Hatzfeldt to his wife, written from the Head-Quarters of the King of Prussia, 1870–71* (London, 1905).

Hohenlohe-Schillingsfürst, C. zu, *Denkwürdigkeiten des Fürsten Chlodwig zu Hohenlohe-Schillingsfürst*, vol. ii (Stuttgart & Berlin, 1914) ed. F. Curtius.

Holstein, F. von, *Die Geheimen Papiere Friedrich von Holsteins*, vol. i. *Erinnerungen und politische Denkwürdigkeiten* (Göttingen, Berlin, Frankfurt, 1956) eds. N. Rich & M. H. Fisher; ed. of German edition W. Frauendienst.

—, *Friedrich von Holstein. Lebensbekenntnis in Briefen an eine Frau* (Berlin, 1932) ed. H. Rogge.

Jelavich, C. & B., 'Bismarck's Proposal for the Revival of the *Dreikaiserbund* in October 1878', *JMH* (1957) xxix, 99–101.

—, *Russia in the East, 1876–1880. The Russo-Turkish War and the Kuldja Crisis as seen through the letters of A. G. Jomini to N. K. Giers* (Leiden, 1959).

Kessel, E., *Moltke* (Stuttgart, 1957).

Knaplund, P., *Letters from the Berlin Embassy, 1871–1874; 1880–1885* (Washington, 1944).

—, 'Die Salisbury-Russell Correspondenz', *Die Welt als Geschichte*, (1957) xvii, 119–34.

Krausnick, H., *Neue Bismarck—Gespräche* (Hamburg, 1940).

Lucius von Ballhausen, R., *Bismarck Erinnerungen des Staatsministers Freiherrn Lucius von Ballhausen* (Stuttgart & Berlin, 1920).

Lyall, A., *The Life of the Marquis of Dufferin and Ava*, 2 vols. (London, 1905).

Miliutin, D. A., *Dnevnik D. A. Miliutina*, 4 vols. (Moscow, 1947–50) ed. P. A. Zaionchkovskii.

Newton, Lord, *Lord Lyons*, vol. ii (London, 1913).

Nostitz, H. von, *Bismarcks unbotmässiger Botschafter. Fürst Münster von Derneburg (1820–1902)* (Göttingen, 1968).

Palamenghi-Crispi, T., *The Memoirs of Francesco Crispi*, 3 vols. (London, 1912).

Radowitz, J. M., *Aufzeichnungen und Erinnerungen aus dem Leben des Botschafters Joseph Maria von Radowitz*, 2 vols. (Stuttgart, Berlin, Leipzig, 1925) ed. H. Holborn.

Raschdau, L., *Ein sinkendes Reich: Erlebnisse eines deutschen Diplomaten im Orient 1877–79* (Berlin, 1934).

Reutern, M. von, *Die finanzielle Sanierung Russlands nach der Katastrophe des Krimkrieges 1862 bis 1878* (Berlin, 1914).

Rogge, H., *Holstein und Hohenlohe: neue Beiträge zu Friedrich von Holsteins Tätigkeit als Mitarbeiter Bismarcks und als Ratgeber Hohenlohes. Nach Briefen und Aufzeichnungen aus dem Nachlass des Fürsten Chlodwig zu Hohenlohe-Schillingsfürst 1874–1894* (Stuttgart, 1957).

Schweinitz, H. L. von, *Denkwürdigkeiten des Botschafters General von Schweinitz*, 2 vols. (Berlin, 1927) ed. W. von Schweinitz.

—, *Briefwechsel des Botschafters General von Schweinitz* (Berlin, 1928) ed. W. von Schweinitz.

[Semev]skii, M., 'Kniaz Aleksandr Mikhailovich Gorchakov v ego rasskazakh iz proshlogo', *Russkaia Starina* (1883) xl, 159–80.

Shuvalov, P. A., 'P. A. Shuvalov o Berlinskom Kongresse 1878 g.', *Krasnii Arkhiv* (1933) iv (no. 59) 82–109, ed. V. Khvostov.

Simpson, J. Y. (ed.), *The Saburov Memoirs, or Bismarck and Russia. Being fresh light on the League of the Three Emperors, 1881* (Cambridge, 1929).

Stadelmann, R., *Moltke und der Staat* (Krefeld, 1950).

Taffs, W., *Ambassador to Bismarck, Lord Odo Russell* (London, 1938).

Tatishchev, S. S., *Imperator Aleksandr II. Ego Zhizn i Tsarstvovanie*, vol. ii (Petersburg, 1903).

Valuev, P. A., *Dnevnik 1877–1884* (Petersburg, 1919).

Vogüé, E.-M. de, *Journal du E.-M. de Vogüé. Paris–St. Petersbourg (1877–1883)* (Paris, 1932) ed. E. de Vogüé.

Waldersee, A., *Denkwürdigkeiten des General Feldmarschalls Alfred Grafen von Waldersee*, vol. i (Stuttgart, Berlin, 1922) ed. H. O. Meisner.

Wertheimer, E., *Graf Julius Andrássy. Sein Leben und seine Zeit*, vol. iii (Stuttgart, 1913).

IV. SECONDARY LITERATURE

Ado, V. I., 'Berlinski Kongress 1878 g. i Pomeshchiche-burzhuaznoe Obshchestvennoe Mnenie Rossii', *Istoricheskie Zapiski*, lxix (1961), 101–41.

Ames, E., 'A century of Russian Railroad construction: 1837–1937', *The American Slavic and East European Review*, vi (1947), 57–74.

Bazant, J. von, *Die Handelspolitik Österreich-Ungarns 1875–1892* (Leipzig, 1894).

Becker, O., *Bismarck und die Einkreisung Deutschlands*, vol. i. *Bismarcks Bündnispolitik* (Berlin, 1923).

Benedikt, H., *Die wirtschaftliche Entwicklung der Franz Joseph Zeit* (Vienna & Munich, 1958).

Bergsträsser, L., *Geschichte der politischen Parteien in Deutschland*, 9th edn. (Munich, 1955).

Böhme, H., *Deutschlands Weg zur Grossmacht* (Cologne, Berlin, 1966).

Bussmann, W., *Das Zeitalter Bismarcks* (Constance, 1957).

Carroll, E. M., *Germany and the Great Powers, 1866–1914* (New York, 1938).

Frauendienst, W., 'Bündniserörterungen zwischen Bismarck und Andrássy in März 1878', *Gesamtdeutsche Vergangenheit. Festgabe für H. Ritter von Srbik* (Munich, 1938), 352–62.

Freycinet, C. de, *La Question d'Egypte* (Paris, 1905).

Friis, A., 'Die Aufhebung des Artikels V des Prager Friedens', *HZ*, cxxv (1922), 45–62.

Ganiage, J., *Les Origines du Protectorat Français en Tunisie (1861–81)* (Paris, 1959).

Grüning, I., *Die russische öffentliche Meinung und ihre Stellung zu den Grossmächten 1878–1894* (Berlin, 1929).

Guillen, P., *L'Allemagne et le Maroc* (Paris, 1967).

Haines, G. G., 'Italian Irredentism during the near eastern crisis, 1875–78', *JMH*, ix (1937), 23–47.

Hallgarten, G. W. F., *Imperialismus vor 1914. Die Soziologischen Grundlagen der Aussenpolitik europäischer Grossmächte vor dem ersten Weltkrieg*, vol. i, 2nd edn. (Munich, 1963).

Hardach, K. W., *Die Bedeutung wirtschaftlicher Faktoren bei der Wiedereinführung der Eisen- und Getreidezölle in Deutschland 1879* (Berlin, 1967).

Hatzfeld, K., *Das deutsch-österreichische Bündnis von 1879 in der Beurteilung der politischen Parteien Deutschlands* (Berlin, 1938).

Heller, E., *Das deutsch-österreichisch-ungarische Bündnis in Bismarcks Aussenpolitik* (Berlin, 1925).

Helms, A., *Der Botschafter H. L. von Schweinitz und seine politische Gedankenwelt* (Breslau, 1933).

Hirsch, A., and Sommerbrodt, M., *Mitteilungen über die Pestepidemie im Winter 1878–9 im russischen Gouvernement Astrachan. Nach dem seitens der dorthin entsandten Kommission an die deutsche Reichsregierung erstatteten Berichte* (Berlin, 1880).

Holborn, H., *Bismarcks europäische Politik zu Beginn der siebziger Jahre und die Mission Radowitz* (Berlin, 1925).

—, *Deutschland und die Türkei 1878–1890* (Berlin, 1926).

Jelavich, C., 'The Diary of D. A. Miliutin, 1878–1882', *JMH*, xxvi (1954), 255–59.

Kehr, E., *Der Primat der Innenpolitik* (Berlin, 1965).

Kent, G. O., 'New Notes on H. von Sybel and the "Begründung des deutschen Reiches durch Wilhelm I." ', *Bulletin of the Institute of Historical Research*, xxviii (1955), 89–96.

Kleine, M., *Deutschland und die ägyptische Frage 1878–1890* (Greifswald, 1927).

Krausnick, H., 'Botschafter Graf Hatzfeldt und die Aussenpolitik Bismarcks', *HZ*, clxvii (1943), 566–83.

Lambi, I. N., *Free Trade and Protection in Germany, 1868–1879* (Wiesbaden, 1963).

Langer, W. L., *European Alliances and Alignments, 1871–1890*, 2nd edn. (New York, 1956).

Leven, N., *Cinquante Ans d'Histoire. L'Alliance israélite universelle (1860–1910)*, vol. i (Paris, 1911).

Lhéritier, M., *Histoire diplomatique de la Grèce*, vol. iv (Paris, 1926).

Lotz, W., *Die Ideen der deutschen Handelspolitik von 1860 bis 1891* (Leipzig, 1892).

Maenner, L., *Deutschlands Wirtschaft und Liberalismus in der Krise von 1879* (Berlin, 1928).

Matlekovits, A. von, *Die Zollpolitik der österreichisch-ungarischen Monarchie und des deutschen Reiches seit 1868* (Leipzig, 1891).

Medlicott, W. N., 'Bismarck and Beaconsfield', *Studies in Diplomatic History and Historiography in honour of G. P. Gooch* (London, 1961), ed. A. O. Sarkissian, 225–50.

—, 'Bismarck and the Three Emperors' Alliance, 1881–1887', *Transactions of the Royal Historical Society*, 4th series, xxvii (1945), 61–83.

—, *Bismarck, Gladstone, and the Concert of Europe* (London, 1956).

—, *The Congress of Berlin and After. A diplomatic History of the Near Eastern Settlement, 1878–1880* (London, 1938).

Medlicott, W. N., 'The Recognition of Roumanian Independence, 1878–80', *Slavonic Review*, xi (1933), 354–72, 572–89.

Meisl, J., *Die Durchführung des Artikels 44 des Berliner Vertrages in Rumänien und die europäische Diplomatie* (Berlin, 1925).

Meyer, H. C., 'German economic relations with South-eastern Europe, 1870–1914', *AHR*, lvii (1951–2), 77–90.

Müller, M., *Die Bedeutung der Berliner Kongresses für die deutsch-russischen Beziehungen* (Leipzig, 1927).

Nolde, B., *L'Alliance franco-russe* (Paris, 1936).

Novotny, A., 'Der Berliner Kongress und das Problem einer europäischen Politik', *HZ*, clxxxvi (1958), 285–307.

Oncken, H., *Das deutsche Reich und die Vorgeschichte des Weltkrieges*, vol. i (Leipzig, 1933).

Orloff, N., *Bismarck und die Fürstin Orloff. Ein Idyll in der hohen Politik* (Munich, 1936).

Pfitzer, A., *Prinz Heinrich VII Reuss* (Tübingen, 1931).

Rathmann, L., 'Bismarck und der Übergang Deutschlands zur Schutz-zollpolitik (1873/75–1879)', *Zeitschrift für Geschichtswissenschaft*, iv (1956), 899–949.

Renouvin, P., *Le XIXe Siècle. II. De 1871 à 1914. L'Apogée de l'Europe* (Paris, 1955).

Rosenberg, H., *Grosse Depression und Bismarckzeit* (Berlin, 1967).

Rothfels, H., *Bismarcks englische Bündnispolitik* (Stuttgart, Berlin, Leipzig, 1924).

Sartorius von Waltershausen, A., *Deutsche Wirtschaftsgeschichte 1815–1914*, 2nd edn. (Jena, 1923).

Scharff, A., 'Zur Problematik der Bismarckschen Nordschleswigpolitik', *Die Welt als Geschichte*, xvi (1956), 211–17.

—, 'Bismarck, Andrássy und die Haltung Österreiches zum nordschles-wigschen Vorbehalt', *Zeitschrift der Gesellschaft für schleswig-holsteinische Geschichte*, lxxxvii (1962), 181–256.

Schieder, T., 'Bismarck und Europa', *Begegnungen mit der Geschichte* (Göttingen, 1962), 236–62.

Schulthess, H., *Europäischer Geschichtskalender* (1878–80) xix–xxi (Nördlingen, 1879–81).

Schünemann, K., 'Die Stellung Österreich-Ungarns in Bismarcks Bündnis-politik', *Archiv für Politik und Geschichte*, vi (1926), 549–94.

Schüssler, W., *Deutschland zwischen Russland und England. Studien zur Aussen-politik des Bismarckschen Reiches 1879–1914* (Leipzig, 1940).

Seton-Watson, R. W., *Disraeli, Gladstone and the Eastern Question. A Study in Diplomacy and Party Politics* (London, 1935).

Skazkin, S., *Konets Avstro-russko-germanskogo soiuza* (Moscow, 1928).

Stern, F., 'Gold and Iron: the Collaboration and Friendship of Gerson Bleichroeder and Otto von Bismarck', *AHR*, lxxv (1969), 37–46.

Sumner, B. H., *Russia and the Balkans, 1870–1880* (Oxford, 1937).

Taylor, A. J. P., *The Struggle for Mastery in Europe, 1848–1918* (Oxford, 1954).

Townsend, M. E., *The Rise and Fall of Germany's Colonial Empire, 1884–1918* (New York, 1930).

Waller, B., 'Bismarck and Gorchakov in 1879: "the two chancellors' war" ', *Studies in International History* (London, 1967), eds. K. Bourne & D. C. Watt, 209–35.

Wehler, H. U., *Bismarck und der Imperialismus* (Cologne, 1969).

Winckler, M. B., 'Die Aufhebung des Artikels V des Prager Friedens und Bismarcks Weg zum Zweibund', *HZ*, clxxix (1955), 471–509.

—, 'Bismarcks Rumänienpolitik und die europäischen Grossmächte 1878/9', *Jahrbücher für Geschichte Osteuropas*, N.F. ii (1954), 53–88.

—, *Bismarcks Bündnispolitik und das europäische Gleichgewicht* (Stuttgart, 1964).

—, 'Die Zielsetzung in Bismarcks Nordschleswigpolitik und die schleswigsche Grenzfrage', *Die Welt als Geschichte*, xvi (1956), 40–63; 'Noch einmal: Zur Zielsetzung in Bismarcks Nordschleswigpolitik', ibid., xvii (1957), 203–10.

Windelband, W., *Bismarck und die europäischen Grossmächte 1879–1885. Auf Grund unveröffentlichter Akten*, 2nd edn. (Essen, 1942).

Wittram, R., 'Bismarcks Russlandpolitik nach der Reichsgründung', *Russland, Europa und der deutsche Osten* (Munich, 1960), ed. T. Schieder, 161–84.

—, 'Bismarck und Russland', *Deutsch-russische Beziehungen von Bismarck bis zur Gegenwart* (Stuttgart, 1964), ed. W. Markert, 17–38.

—, 'Die russisch-nationalen Tendenzen der achtziger Jahre im Spiegel der österreichisch-ungarischen diplomatischen Berichte aus St Petersburg', *Schicksalswege deutscher Vergangenheit. Beiträge zur geschichtlichen Deutung der letzten hundertfünfzig Jahre. Festschrift für Siegfried A. Kaehler* (Düsseldorf, 1950), ed. W. Hubatsch, 321–35.

Zuber, C., *La Peste du Gouvernement d'Astrakhan en 1878–9. Rapport présenté à M. Le Ministre de l'Agriculture et du Commerce* (Paris, 1880).

INDEX

(Italicized numbers denote pages with short biographies.)